Global Faith Book Series

Religion and Science in the Globalized World

A Collective Monograph

GLOBAL FAITH BOOK SERIES

Sponsored by Center for Global Philosophy & Religion

FOUNDING EDITOR
Dr. Mikhail Sergeev, University of the Arts, Philadelphia (since 2018).

INTERNATIONAL EDITORIAL BOARD
Necati Alcan, Ph.D., Bamberg University, (*Germany*)
Arthur Dahl, Ph.D., International Environment Forum, (*Switzerland*)
Graham Hassall, Ph.D., independent scholar, (*New Zealand*)
Youli Ioannesian, Ph.D., Institute of Oriental Manuscripts of RAS, (*Russia*)
Moshe Sharon, Ph.D., Hebrew University of Jerusalem (*Israel*)
Peter Smith, Ph.D., independent scholar, (*Thailand*)
Robert Stockman, Th.D., Indiana University South Bend (*USA*)

ADVISORY EDITORIAL COUNCIL
Ian Kluge, poet, playwright, and scholar of philosophy (*Canada*)
Jean-Marc Lepain, scholar of philosophy and Persian studies specializing in philosophy of science (*France*)
Julio Savi, scholar of philosophy with book publications in epistemology, ethics, and philosophy of religion (*Italy*)
Peter Terry, adult educator, author on religious topics, contributor to academic discourse on the Bahá'í Faith (*USA*)

BOOKS PUBLISHED:

Studies in Bahá'í Philosophy: Selected Articles. GFBS Vol. 1, ed. with an Introduction by Mikhail Sergeev. Boston, MA: M·GRAPHICS, 2018, 294 pp., ISBN 978-1940220901

Peter Terry. *Proofs of the Existence of God.* GFBS Vol. 2, Boston, MA: M·GRAPHICS, 2019, 164 pp., ISBN 978-1950319053

Studies in Bahá'í Epistemology: Essays and Commentary. GFBS Vol. 3, ed. with an Introduction by Mikhail Sergeev. Boston, MA: M·GRAPHICS, 2021, 370 pp., ISBN 978-1950319626

Center for Global Philosophy and Religion is a research organization that specializes in the study of philosophy and religion from a global perspective.

Religion and Science in the Globalized World

A Collective Monograph

Edited by Mikhail Sergeev

Boston • 2022

Religion and Science in the Globalized World
A Collective Monograph

(Global Faith Book Series. Vol. 4)

Editor: Mikhail Sergeev, *University of the Arts (Philadelphia)*

> **Disclaimer:**
> The articles appearing in this publication preserve the authors' original texts. The opinions and beliefs expressed in those articles do not necessarily reflect the views of the publisher and the editor, nor are they intended to represent those of any religious or civil organization.

Copyright © 2022 by Authors

All rights reserved. No part of this book may be reproduced, stored in a retrieval system, or transmitted by any means, electronic, mechanical, photocopying, recording, or otherwise, without written permission from the copyright holder(s), except for the brief passages quoted for review.

ISBN 978-1-950319947
Library of Congress Control Number: 2022945585

Cover Image: "Trails of Future Minds" by Andrew Ostrovsky.
Website: https://agsandrew.myportfolio.net/

Published by M·Graphics | Boston, MA
  www.mgraphics-book.com
  mgraphics.books@gmail.com

Printed in the U.S.A.

Contents

From the Editor

MIKHAIL SERGEEV
   *Religion in the Globalized World:
   Philosophical Reflections*   1

Bahá'í Perspectives on Various Aspects of Globalization

GRAHAM HASSALLL
   Global Constitutionalism   21

SOVAIDA MA'ANI EWING
   *Globalization — The Tangible Expression
   of Humanity's Journey Towards Unity*   48

PAUL HANLEY
   *Building a Just and Sustainable
   Global Food System: Some Guiding Principles*   77

HAROLD ROSEN
   *How Can We All Get Along? —
   A Bahá'í Perspective on Globalization*   116

HOOSHMAND BADEE
   Globalization Requires a Bahá'í Foundation   146

Bahá'í Perspectives on Natural and Social Sciences

PETER SMITH
   A Bahá'í View of Human Rights   175

HARRY P. MASSOTH AND MARILU JENO
  *Prophetic Revelation and Sociocultural Evolution:
  Some Scientific Perspectives* — **211**

VAHID RANJBAR
  Plato, Modern Physics, and Bahá'u'lláh — **253**

ANDRES ELVIRA ESPINOZA
  *Iterative Theology: Progressive Revelation
  as the String Theory of Religious Studies* — **269**

MIKHAIL SERGEEV
  *The Issue of Self-Identity in Transhumanism
  and the Bahá'í Writings* — **305**

CHRONOLOGIES

Articles and Books on Globalization and Bahá'í Faith — **325**

Articles and Books on Science and Bahá'í Faith — **335**

ABOUT THE AUTHORS — **345**

FROM THE EDITOR

Religion in the Globalized World: Philosophical Reflections

MIKHAIL SERGEEV

INTRODUCTORY REMARKS

When discussing religion in the globalized world, scholars usually operate under several standard assumptions. First, they proceed from the modern supposition that religion should be separated from the state and, therefore, should not engage in public discourse but rather limit its sphere of influence to personal spirituality and salvation. Second, they usually discuss well-established religious traditions that have been evolving for centuries while paying less attention to new religious movements since their membership is relatively low and so, as they think, is their impact on the global stage. Third, those scholars focus their analysis on the "religious disruptors," i.e., those sects and groups that defy social norms and represent a threat to civilization. As a result, examining Islamic terrorism or various apocalyptic cults often stands at the center of religious studies in the global context.

It is easy to show that all those assumptions largely oversimplify the role religion and religious beliefs play in society, whether on a local, national, or global level. Catholic views on the death penalty and abortion, for instance, are an inalienable part of public discourse on governmental policy in the United States. Modern religious movements, like Mormonism, with its almost two hundred years of existence and now more than sixteen million adherents worldwide,[1] have a growing impact in society's life. An American politician, businessman, and an LDS minister, Mitt Romney was the Republican Party's nominee for President of the United States in the 2012 election. Finally, in our global world, torn apart by cultural divisions and prejudice, religious scholars should undoubtedly pay closer attention to the unifying and value-oriented aspects of spiritual teachings rather than their harmful and militant elements.

There is one more factor that implicitly influences the discussion of religious issues in the contemporary era. It is the collapse of the USSR that took place several decades ago and was entirely unexpected for both the communist bloc countries and their liberal democratic opponents. The whole past century passed under the banner of God's "death," which resulted in the collapse of organized religion and the flourishing of secular culture. Religious scholars of the twenty-first century talk instead about the resurrection of faith and "post-secular age." However, no one seems to propose a plausible explanation for the seventy-five years of the existence of the Soviet Union — the only irreligious empire in the entire human history. Theodore Adorno famously remarked about the Nazi Holocaust's horrors that "to write a poem after Auschwitz is barbaric."[2] Then what about pursuing theological studies after the Gulag? After all, the Soviet atrocities vastly surpassed the crimes of the Nazi regime. Yet, the existential mystery of the atheist outburst in Russia did not receive, in my opinion, adequate and exhaustive explanation both in its native land and the rest of the intellectual world.

RELIGION AFTER THE GULAG

Contemporary Russian philosophers are well aware of this problem since Russia's national identity in the post-Soviet times is

---

[1] The Church of Jesus Christ of Latter-Day Saints: Fact and Statistics, https://newsroom.churchofjesuschrist.org/facts-and-statistics.
[2] Theodore Adorno. "Cultural Criticism and Society." *Prisms*. Trans. Samuel and Shierry Weber. Cambridge, Mass.: MIT Press, 1967, p. 34.

directly related to it. The solutions they proposed are fourfold. Russian communists, who survived the USSR's downfall and reorganized under Marxist-Leninist banners, regard the Soviet period mostly with pride and promote the advantages of the planned socialist economy. On the contrary, Orthodox nationalists view the communist theory and practice as a social disease that Russia contracted from the degrading West, which is rapidly moving toward its own and inevitable decline. In contrast to communists and nationalists, postmodernists in Russia look at the Soviet ideology as the Grand Narratives' last bastion. Their final demise signified the victory of irreducible human diversity and pluralism. Finally, Russian globalists argue that the Soviet experiment, although it ultimately failed, was one of the first practical attempts to create a planetary human society.

All those approaches, in my opinion, vastly underestimate the spiritual dimension of the Soviet period in Russian history, which I explore through the prism of my theory of religious cycles.[3] According to my hypothesis, religion is an organic system that, in the course of its evolution, passes through six typical phases — formative, orthodox, classical, reformist, critical, and post-critical. A particular correlation between any religious system's fundamental components — its sacred scriptures and sacred tradition — characterizes each of those steps or stages. A misbalance between the two elements leads to a structural crisis of religion marked by the doubt in the sacred tradition(s). Such a situation results in novel branches' appearance within the established faith and signals its transition to a new development stage. Unlike the structural problem that transforms the sacred tradition but leaves untouched the holy scriptures, the systemic crisis of re-

---

[3] What follows is a summary of my interpretation of the evolution of religions and the Soviet Union phenomenon. For a detailed exposition of my theory of religious cycles, please see my article "The model of religious cycle: theory and application" in *SENTENTIA. European Journal of Humanities and Social Sciences*, 3(2017), pp. 71–92, URL: http://e-notabene.ru/psen/article_23930.html; or my book *Theory of Religious Cycles: Tradition, Modernity, and the Bahá'í Faith* (Brill, 2015).

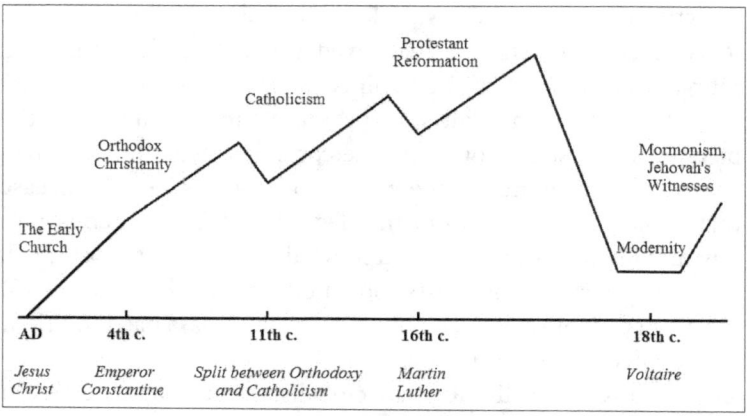

The religious cycle of Christianity

ligion questions the system's very foundation by casting doubt in its scriptural texts. The creation of new religious movements within their mother-faith usually resolves this matter.

Christianity serves as the best illustration of the religious cycles' model. The formative, orthodox, classical, reformist and critical phases are expressed in the Church early, Orthodox, Catholic, Protestant, and modern forms of Christianity accordingly. Let us specifically focus on the European Enlightenment of the seventeenth and the eighteenth centuries, which laid the foundation for the Christian Church's modern period and marked the beginning of the systemic crisis of Christianity. Whether critically-minded theologians, deists, agnostics, or atheists, the Enlightenment thinkers questioned the Bible's absolute authority. For the first time in European history, they conceived an all-embracing worldview that was not of divine but purely human origin.

The rational approach to nature and social reality signaled the dawn of modernity, eventually leading to the establishment of democratic political institutions, the spread of secular culture, and the momentous rise of scientific and technological innovations. The Enlightenment paradigm proved so vital and appealing that it conquered the hearts and minds of people all over the globe in the course of the nineteenth and twentieth centuries.

Regrettably, the modern way of life is at best neutral and at worst suspicious of, if not entirely opposed to, religion. Members of modern societies often regard religious beliefs as old, pre-scientific, and outdated prejudices. As a result, the collapse of traditional moral values and the steady decline of religious affiliation and practices often accompany the advantages of political, social, and cultural modernization.

Not being confined to the Christian confession sphere of influence, its systemic crisis deeply affected other cultures and world religions, most notably Hinduism, Confucianism, Buddhism, and Islam. In the twentieth century, it already became a full-blown crisis of religious consciousness, which led to the Soviet Union's establishment. This atheist empire aimed to exterminate religious beliefs in general and persecuted traditional and modern religious groups and sects. The Soviet system's subsequent collapse significantly changed the political, economic, and social situation in the countries involved and in the whole world. But it did not resolve the spiritual dimension of the crisis that is still deepening and producing religious tensions and threats of a different kind. According to my theory, religion's systemic problems are resolved only with the appearance and maturation of new religious movements capable of regenerating former spiritual traditions. We know from the history of religions that this is a long process, usually up to four centuries. That is why, being at the epicenter of profound religious transformation, we have to consider globalization's spiritual dimension, which is as complicated as its economic, political, or social components.

CULTURE VS. CIVILIZATION

One of the leading contemporary Russian specialists in Global Studies, Alexander Chumakov, in the second of his trilogy of monographs devoted to the subject, *Metaphysics of Globalization*, discussed the philosophical aspects of this worldwide process from the standpoint of two basic categories — "culture" and "civilization." According to Chumakov, "every human being, every community of people, be it a certain group, state, or public association, including global humanity, represents a unique cultural-civilizational system."[4] Those two components, which are always interlaced with and tied to each other, perform, as he argues, quite different functions. Religious beliefs, traditional customs, and standard language usually constitute the foundation of every cultural entity. But it is precisely because of their social nature that cultures are inherently distinctive and varied. As Chumakov puts it,

> all human beings and their communities are special, different from other cultural formations that produce, separate, and make them unique and inimitable. [These] are the natural roots of that cultural diversity and religious pluralism with which we are dealing in reality.[5]

In contrast to various and unique cultures, the civilizational component of human societies, as Chumakov posits, represents a real and effective instrument of achieving a unity of opposing and even conflicting cultural formations. Chumakov's position here is apparently at odds with that of an American political philosopher Samuel Huntington and his assertion of the irreducible diversity not only of cultures but of different civilizations as well. According to Huntington, the Western civilization, with its focus on parliamentary democracy, the rule of law, individual rights, and freedoms, is unique to the West. It cannot, and should not, be exported to other civilizational regions like those of Islam, China, or Russia, for instance. Huntington writes:

> Some Americans have promoted multiculturalism at home; some have promoted universalism abroad, and some have done both. Multiculturalism at home threat-

---

[4] Chumakov, Alexander and Sergeev, Mikhail (2018) "Religion and Globalization: Crossroads and Opportunities," *Occasional Papers on Religion in Eastern Europe*: Vol. 38: Iss. 5, Article 7, p. 112. Available at: https://digitalcommons.georgefox.edu/ree/vol38/iss5/7.
[5] Ibid, p. 111.

ens the United States and the West; universalism abroad threatens the West and the world. Both deny the uniqueness of Western culture. The global monoculturalists want to make the world like America. The domestic multiculturalists want to make America like the world. A multicultural America is impossible because a non-Western America is not American. A multicultural world is unavoidable because global empire is impossible.[6]

Another American political philosopher and Huntington's famous opponent, Francis Fukuyama, argues the opposite in his volume *The End of History* precisely. Fukuyama analyzes the twentieth-century political and military battles and the post-soviet world's prospects in terms of the Hegelian view of history. According to Hegel, universal human history consists of the progress toward a fully realized freedom. In "the universal and homogenous state" of the future, he believed, "the contradiction that existed in the relationship of lordship and bondage [is fully reconciled] by making the former slaves their own masters...each individual, free and cognizant of his own self-worth, [will recognize] every other individual for those same qualities."[7] For Fukuyama, we may as well be living at the peak of this historical process. The closest to the Hegelian idea humanity ever stood is in western republican societies. As he put it, the

> two parallel historical processes, one guided by modern natural science and the logic of desire, the other by the struggle for [equal] recognition...conveniently culminated in the same end point, capitalist liberal democracy.[8]

---

[6] Samuel Huntington, *The Clash of Civilizations and the Remaking of World Order*, New York: Simon & Schuster, 2011, p. 318. Huntington often uses the terms "culture" and "civilization" interchangeably, and when he writes about American or Western cultures, he assumes that civilizational institutions represent an inalienable part of their cultural identity.

[7] Francis Fukuyama, *The End of History and the Last Man*, New York: Free Press, 2006, 1st ed. 1992, p. 300.

[8] Ibid, p. 289.

In his take on cultural and civilizational identities, Alexander Chumakov is much closer to Fukuyama than Huntington. While accepting the unique cultural-civilizational systems in the world, Chumakov argues that they produce "opposition and conflict...due to the discrepancy of cultures" but may reach "agreement and mutual understanding on civilizational grounds." By "civility and civilization," he means, of course, not something abstract but very specific features of modern western societies, which holds universal value in Chumakov's estimation. Namely, "the recognition and respect for human rights, tolerance, separation of powers, the rule of law and the equality of all before the law." As he emphasizes, "the higher the level of civility of the interacting parties and the more of common experience they share, the more effective and fruitful will be mutual understanding and cooperation."[9]

In this ongoing dialogue between the proponents of the uniqueness of western civilization and those who emphasize its universality and applicability to all cultures, the author of this essay would maintain the middle ground's position. I would agree with Huntington that western civilization, like any other civilizational construct, is unique to the West and would face enormous challenges and difficulties when imposed by force on non-western cultures. The outside powers should not compel any governmental system, including democracy, which usually grows from the inside, on other sovereign states. Otherwise, it would seldom take roots on the foreign soil. The latest historical examples that readily come to mind are the results of the American invasion and wars in Iraq and Afghanistan.

At the same time, I would agree with Fukuyama, and Chumakov for that matter, in their assertion of the universal value of western civilization. Capitalist democracy is indeed the most efficient economic and political system humanity was able to develop in several thousand years of its history. The ideology

---

[9] Chumakov, A. and Sergeev, M. (2018) "Religion and Globalization: Crossroads and Opportunities," p. 112.

of the European Enlightenment, which laid the foundation for western liberalism, was formulated as a purely rational enterprise that could successfully be applied to all of humanity in theory.

However, I would also disagree with Chumakov, who argues that it is not culture but civilization that could bring humanity together. Namely, Western civilization, focusing on liberal democratic values, is the surest way to minimize and eventually exterminate social, political, and economic conflicts that tear humanity apart and pose a real threat to its global survival. My argument refers not to Huntington's position about the irreducible plurality of civilizations and the West's uniqueness. It is about the origin of any civilizational construct, which typically does not come out of nothing.

Civilizations grow and flourish by developing from the seeds sowed by the founders and heroes of cultural revolutions. Contemporary western civilization, for instance, is the product of Christian culture. At the same time, it reflects the crisis of Christianity by being based on pure rationality. When this modern civilization penetrates other cultural formations' strata, let alone imposes itself on them, it strongly undermines those cultures by challenging their intrinsic, and especially moral, values.

Fukuyama believes that humanity has two aspirations — the satisfaction of desires and the yearning for equal recognition. But he completely disregards the third one, which is universal, and lies at the center of any cultural organism — the search for divine liberation, enlightenment, or salvation. Modern western civilization cannot offer any meaningful collective response to the spiritual longing because of its empiricist philosophical and rational scientific foundations. Such a civilizational pattern could be extended to all of humanity, but it will still not be able to satisfy its profound spiritual needs and challenges. That is why, I believe, the global society of the future should be built on cultural foundations rather than civilizational grounds, no matter how progressive and unique they may appear.

GLOBALIZATION AND MODERN RELIGIONS

As a case study of a modern religious movement that promotes the global unity of humankind and the building of an "ever-advancing civilization," I take the Bahá'í Faith, a religion that was conceived in Persia (nowadays Iran) in the middle of the nineteenth century with the declaration of the Báb, born Siyyid 'Alí Muḥammad Shírází (1819–1850) whose prophetic mission lasted for six years. After the Báb's assassination in 1850 by the Persian authorities, his religion was continued and renewed by Bahá'u'lláh, born Mírzá Ḥusayn-'Alí Núrí (1817–1892), who proclaimed his divine mission in 1863 in the Najibiyyih gardens of Bagdad.

Since then, the Bahá'í Faith developed into a distinctive and independent religion with millions of adherents worldwide. In 2010, *Encyclopædia Britannica* projected a total of 7.3 million Bahá'ís residing in 221 countries.[10] And in 2020 *The World Religion Database* has assessed a global Bahá'í population at 8.5 million believers.[11]

Every religion holds a critical notion that is associated mainly with its doctrines. Christianity is known for preaching universal love; Buddhism — for promoting selflessness. Bahá'ís focus on the concept of unity or oneness, which occupies the central position in their teachings. The followers of Bahá'u'lláh differentiate between three levels of unity — those of God, religion, and humanity. Since our creator is one and the purpose of progressive revelation is to bring people together on an ever-increasing scale — from clans and tribes to national and international communities — it has finally come a time for humanity to be integrated on a global scale.

The exposition of various principles, doctrines, and strategies, both individual and collective, that aim to unite humankind into a scientifically and technologically advanced while at the same

---

[10] "Religion: Year in Review 2010". *Encyclopædia Britannica*. Encyclopædia Britannica, Inc. 2010.

[11] "Baha'is by Country". *World Religion Database*. Institute on Culture, Religion, and World Affairs. 2020.

time peaceful, moral, and humane planetary community, constitute the nerve of Bahá'u'lláh's message. I want to explore further in this context some of the themes that run throughout his tablets and epistles. The first one concerns the relationship between the Bahá'í teachings and the ideology of the Enlightenment.

In many important ways, the Bahá'í worldview represents a reaffirmation of most of the Enlightenment ideas but in a distinct religious setting, thus adding a spiritual depth to those theories and transforming modern civilizational practices into genuinely held cultural beliefs and norms. Bahá'ís reassert as sacred such principles as the rule of law, the freedom of conscience and expression, the freedom of association, the advancement of human rights, the equality of men and women, and so on. In "Glad Tidings," Bahá'u'lláh proclaims:

> In former religions such ordinances as holy war, destruction of books, the ban on association and companionship with other peoples or on reading certain books had been laid down and affirmed according to the exigencies of the time; however, in this mighty Revelation, in this momentous Announcement, the manifold bestowals and favors of God have overshadowed all men, and from the horizon of the Will of the Ever-Abiding Lord, His infallible decree hath prescribed that which We have set forth above.[12]

In politics, Bahá'u'lláh rejects autocratic and oppressive governments, which he condemns as unjust and unfair to the people. He approves of republican democracies but favors constitutional monarchy as a political system that combines the commoners and aristocrats' interests with the kingship, which represents the divine sanction. In his "Epistle to Queen Victoria" Bahá'u'lláh praises the queen for having

---

[12] Bahá'u'lláh, "Bishárát (Glad-Tidings)," in *Tablets of Bahá'u'lláh*, Bahá'í Reference Library, https://www.bahai.org/library/authoritative-texts/bahaullah/tablets-bahaullah/.

> entrusted the reins of counsel into the hands of the representatives of the people...for thereby the foundations of the edifice of [her] affairs will be strengthened, and the hearts of all that are beneath [her] shadow, whether high or low, will be tranquillized.[13]

And in "Glad Tidings he counsels political scientists:

> Although a republican form of government profiteth all the peoples of the world, yet the majesty of kingship is one of the signs of God. We do not wish that the countries of the world should remain deprived thereof. If the sagacious combine the two forms into one, great will be their reward in the presence of God.[14]

When discussing future global government, Bahá'u'lláh does not provide many specifics about the executive and legislative branches except for the general importance of equity and justice, consultation, collective decision making, and so on. His judicial power proposals are much more detailed — perhaps because the independent and fair court system is the backbone of any stable and long-lasting society. Bahá'u'lláh envisions the establishment of the Supreme Tribunal, whose purpose would be to resolve territorial disputes and international conflicts, thus preventing warfare's brutal practice. As the eldest son of Bahá'u'lláh and the leader of the Bahá'í Faith after his father's passing, 'Abdu'l-Bahá outlined a concrete plan for the world judiciary, which is yet to be fulfilled by the nations. To form such an organization, he said:

> the national assemblies of each country and nation — that is to say parliaments — should elect two or three

---

[13] "Epistle to Queen Victoria," in *The Summons of the Lord of Hosts*, Bahá'í Reference Library, https://www.bahai.org/library/authoritative-texts/bahaullah/summons-lord-hosts/.

[14] Bahá'u'lláh, "Bishárát (Glad-Tidings)," in *Tablets of Bahá'u'lláh*, Bahá'í Reference Library.

persons who are the choicest men of that nation and are well informed concerning international laws and the relations between governments and aware of the essential needs of the world of humanity of this day. The number of these representatives should be in proportion to the number of inhabitants of that country. The election of these souls who are chosen by the national assembly, that is, the parliament, must be confirmed by the upper house, the congress, and the cabinet and also by the president or monarch so these persons may be the elected ones of all the nation and the government. From among these people, the members of the Supreme Tribunal will be elected, and all [hu]mankind will thus have a share therein, for every one of these delegates is fully representative of his nation. When the Supreme Tribunal gives a ruling on any international question, either unanimously or by majority-rule, there will no longer be any pretext for the plaintiff or ground of objection for the defendant. In case any of the governments or nations in the execution of the irrefutable decision of the Supreme Tribunal be negligent or dilatory, the rest of the nations will rise up against it because all the governments and nations of the world are the supporters of this Supreme Tribunal."[15]

Overall, 'Abdu'l-Bahá promoted eleven social principles based on the teachings of Bahá'u'lláh, which should guide humanity toward a sustainable global civilization. For Bahá'ís those precepts serve as a modern equivalent of the Ten Commandments. And like those earlier divine instructions, they can be fulfilled by anyone, no matter religious affiliation or lack thereof.

Most clearly and systematically 'Abdu'l-Bahá discussed those teachings during his European missionary journey when he stayed in Paris from October to December 1911. The eleven prin-

---

[15] 'Abdu'l-Bahá, *Selections from the Writings of Abdu'l-Bahá*, no. 227, Bahá'í Reference Library, https://www.bahai.org/library/authoritative-texts/abdul-baha/selections-writings-abdul-baha/.

ciples that he enunciated during his meeting at the Theosophical Society of Paris are as follows:

1. *The Search for Truth* — "Man must cut himself free from all prejudice and from the result of his own imagination, so that he may be able to search for truth unhindered. Truth is one in all religions, and by means of it the unity of the world can be realized."
2. *The Unity of Humankind* — "All men are the leaves and fruit of one same tree, they are all branches of the tree of Adam, they all have the same origin...Holy Writings tell us: All men are equal before God. He is no respecter of persons."
3. *Religion should be the Cause of Love and Affection* — "Religion should unite all hearts and cause wars and disputes to vanish from the face of the earth...If religion becomes a cause of dislike, hatred and division, it was better to be without it, and to withdraw from such a religion would be a truly religious act."
4. *The Unity of Religion and Science* — "Any religion that contradicts science or that is opposed to it, is only ignorance...Whatever the intelligence of man cannot understand, religion ought not to accept. Religion and science walk hand in hand, and any religion contrary to science is not the truth."
5. *Prejudices of Religion, Race or Sect destroy the foundation of Humanity* — "The whole world must be looked upon as one single country, all the nations as one nation, all men as belonging to one race. Religions, races, and nations are all divisions of man's making only, and are necessary only in his thought."
6. *Equal opportunity of the means of Existence* — "Every human being has the right to live; they have a right to rest, and to a certain amount of well-being...Nobody should die of hunger; everybody should have sufficient clothing; one man should not live in excess while another has no possible means of existence."

7. *The Equality of Men* — equality before the Law — "The Law must reign, and not the individual; thus will the world become a place of beauty and true brotherhood will be realized."
8. *Universal Peace* — "A Supreme Tribunal shall be elected by the peoples and governments of every nation, where members from each country and government shall assemble in unity. All disputes shall be brought before this Court, its mission being to prevent war."
9. *Religion should not concern itself with Political Questions* — "Religion is concerned with things of the spirit, politics with things of the world...It is the work of the clergy to educate the people, to instruct them, to give them good advice and teaching so that they may progress spiritually. With political questions they have nothing to do."
10. *Education and Instruction of Women* — "Women have equal rights with men upon earth; in religion and society they are a very important element. As long as women are prevented from attaining their highest possibilities, so long will men be unable to achieve the greatness which might be theirs."
11. *The Power of the Holy Spirit* — "It is only by the breath of the Holy Spirit that spiritual development can come about...for it is the soul that animates the body; the body alone has no real significance. Deprived of the blessings of the Holy Spirit the material body would be inert."[16]

Now, more than a century from the initial unveiling of these principles in Europe, many of them have become the animating spirit behind social progress and change worldwide and an intrinsic part of the fabric of life in Western societies. Of course, those teachings envision such a profound social transformation

---

[16] 'Abdu'l-Bahá, *Paris Talks: Addresses Given by 'Abdu'l-Bahá in 1911*, Bahá'í Reference Library, p. 40, https://www.bahai.org/library/authoritative-texts/abdul-baha/paris-talks/1#733601770.

that it will require more time and effort to put them all together in practice. Nevertheless, the ideal image of the future they offer to humanity is so spiritual in quality and global in scope that it has no parallel in world history.

REMARKS IN CONCLUSION

In his work, *The End of History*, Francis Fukuyama argues that "liberal democracy may constitute the 'endpoint of [hu]mankind's ideological evolution' and the 'final form of human government,' and as such constituted the 'end of history.'"[17] Fukuyama's position was not based solely on the historical successes of liberal democracy and the collapse of its main rival, the Soviet Union, at the end of the twentieth century. His philosophical inquiry went deeper into the internal worth of a liberal democratic political system coupled with the capitalist free-market economy. Are modern western societies fully satisfying to their citizens, or, maybe, those systems have some hidden defects that will eventually lead to their demise as it had happened with all former cultures? In other words, could Western civilization sustain itself without any external competitors or enemies? Fukuyama answers those questions positively. He writes:

> There is no doubt that contemporary democracies face any number of serious problems, from drugs, homelessness, and crime to environmental damage and the frivolity of consumerism. But these problems are not obviously insoluble on the basis of liberal principles, nor so serious that they would necessarily lead to the collapse of society as a whole, as communism collapsed in the 1980s.[18]

Bahá'í teachings address the same issue implicitly by distinguishing between the so-called Lesser and Most Great Peace.

---

[17] Francis Fukuyama, *The End of History and the Last Man*, p. xi.
[18] Ibid, p. xxi.

The Lesser Peace may come about through political unification of the world. As the Guardian of the Bahá'í Faith and leader of the Bahá'í community from 1922 until 1957, Shoghi Effendi wrote: Some form of a world super-state must needs be evolved, in whose favor all the nations of the world will have willingly ceded every claim to make war, certain rights to impose taxation and all rights to maintain armaments, except for purposes of maintaining internal order within their respective dominions.

This global super-state would most likely be built based on modern ideology, including the election of officials, various branches of power, and the separation between religion and politics. As Shoghi Effendi continues:

> Such a state will have to include within its orbit an international executive adequate to enforce supreme and unchallengeable authority on every recalcitrant member of the commonwealth; a world parliament whose members shall be elected by the people in their respective countries and whose election shall be confirmed by their respective governments; and a supreme tribunal whose judgment will have a binding effect even in such cases where the parties concerned did not voluntarily agree to submit their case to its consideration.[19]

Nevertheless, the cessation of war, however remarkable and progressive it may be, does not equal the establishment of peace among nations, which might still be torn apart by internal strife and conflicts on the ethnic, national, racial, political, social, and religious levels. Hence, the difference between the Lesser and Most Great Peace may be likened to the distinction between external unification and internal unity, a matrimonial arrangement, which is based on convenience or love. In Bahá'í Writings, the Most Great Peace stands as the ideal of spiritual rather than mate-

---

[19] Shoghi Effendi, *The World Order of Bahá'u'lláh. Selected Letters*, Bahá'í Reference Library, pp. 18–19, https://www.bahai.org/library/authoritative-texts/shoghi-effendi/world-order-bahaullah/1#369510938.

rial harmony, a cultural rather than civilizational project. Bahá'ís believe that in those distant times, "Bahá'u'lláh's mission will be fully recognized by the peoples of the earth and its principles consciously accepted and applied by the generality of humankind."[20] The ensuing "ultimate fusion of all races, creeds, classes and nations"[21] will firmly secure the long-term stability and flourishing of global humanity. Shoghi Effendi describes this future civilization as a

> world community in which all economic barriers will have been permanently demolished and the interdependence of Capital and Labor definitely recognized; in which the clamor of religious fanaticism and strife will have been forever stilled; in which the flame of racial animosity will have been finally extinguished; in which a single code of international law — the product of the considered judgment of the world's federated representatives — shall have as its sanction the instant and coercive intervention of the combined forces of the federated units; and finally a world community in which the fury of a capricious and militant nationalism will have been transmuted into an abiding consciousness of world citizenship — such indeed, appears, in its broadest outline, the Order anticipated by Bahá'u'lláh, an Order that shall come to be regarded as the fairest fruit of a slowly maturing age.[22]

Works Cited

'Abdu'l-Bahá, *Selections from the Writings of Abdu'l-Bahá*, Bahá'í Reference Library, https://www.bahai.org/library/authoritative-texts/abdul-baha/selections-writings-abdul-baha/.

---

[20] William S. Hatcher, J. Douglas Martin, *The Bahá'í Faith: The Emerging Global Religion*, Wilmette: Bahá'í Publishing Trust, 1998, p. 144.

[21] Shoghi Effendi, *The Promised Day is Come*, Bahá'í Reference Library, p. 63, https://www.bahai.org/library/authoritative-texts/shoghi-effendi/promised-day-come/1#617979506.

[22] Shoghi Effendi, *The World Order of Bahá'u'lláh*, p. 19.

———. *Paris Talks: Addresses Given by 'Abdu'l-Bahá in 1911*, https://www.bahai.org/library/authoritative-texts/abdul-baha/paris-talks/1#733601770.

Adorno, Theodore. "Cultural Criticism and Society." *Prisms*. Trans. Samuel and Shierry Weber Cambridge, Mass.: MIT Press, 1967.

"Baha'is by Country". *World Religion Database*. Institute on Culture, Religion, and World Affairs. 2020.

Bahá'u'lláh, *Tablets of Bahá'u'lláh revealed after the Kitáb-i-Aqdas*, https://www.bahai.org/library/authoritative-texts/bahaullah/tablets-bahaullah/.

———. *The Summons of the Lord of Hosts*, https://www.bahai.org/library/authoritative-texts/bahaullah/summons-lord-hosts/.

Chumakov, Alexander. *Globalization. Contours of the Integrated World*. Moscow: Prospekt, 2005, 2nd ed., 2009, 3rd ed., 2017.

———. *Metaphysics of Globalization: Cultural and Civilizational Context*. Moscow: "Canon+", 2006, 2nd ed., Moscow: Prospekt, 2017

———. *Global World: Clash of Interests*. Moscow: Prospekt, 2018.

———, and Sergeev, M. (2018) "Religion and Globalization: Crossroads and Opportunities," *Occasional Papers on Religion in Eastern Europe*: Vol. 38: Iss. 5, Article 7. Available at: https://digitalcommons.georgefox.edu/ree/vol38/iss5/7.

Church of Jesus Christ of Latter-Day Saints, The: Fact and Statistics, https://newsroom.churchofjesuschrist.org/facts-and-statistics.

Fukuyama, Francis. *The End of History and the Last Man*, New York: Free Press, 2006, 1st ed. 1992.

Huntington, Samuel. *The Clash of Civilizations and the Remaking of World Order*, New York: Simon & Schuster, 2011, 1st ed. 1996.

Hatcher, William S., Martin, J. Douglas. *The Bahá'í Faith: The Emerging Global Religion*, Wilmette: Bahá'í Publishing Trust, 1998.

"Religion: Year in Review 2010". *Encyclopædia Britannica*. Encyclopædia Britannica, Inc. 2010.

Sergeev, Mikhail. *Theory of Religious Cycles: Tradition, Modernity, and the Bahá'í Faith*, Leiden: Brill, 2015.

———. "The model of religious cycle: theory and application" in *SENTENTIA. European Journal of Humanities and Social Sciences*, 3(2017), pp. 71–92, http://e-notabene.ru/psen/article_23930.html.

Shoghi Effendi. *The World Order of Bahá'u'lláh. Selected Letters*, Bahá'í Reference Library, pp. 18–19, https://www.bahai.org/library/authoritative-texts/shoghi-effendi/world-order-bahaullah/1#369510938.

———. *The Promised Day is Come*, Bahá'í Reference Library, https://www.bahai.org/library/authoritative-texts/shoghi-effendi/promised-day-come/1#617979506.

Bahá'í Perspectives on Various Aspects of Globalization

Global Constitutionalism

GRAHAM HASSALL

INTRODUCTION

This chapter explores a Bahá'í approach to constitutionalism, at global scale. The idea of a "global constitution" germinated for centuries before gaining notable momentum in the twentieth century.[1] It is often characterized as a "normative" project that seeks to identify and articulate the outlines of a rules-based order that transcends the limits of national ideologies, laws, and institutions. There are, on the other hand, immense reservations about transitioning away from nation-state sovereignty toward supranational approaches to global problems. Throughout the twentieth century two tendencies vied for ascendency: one being continued insistence on the autonomy of sovereign nations and the other the rise of trans-national/supra-national political arrangements. There are principles in the Bahá'í Writings and associated texts that can help clarify this conundrum. The chapter examines what

---

[1] Scholars trace ten thousand years of globalization, commencing with "archaic" phase dating back five to ten thousand years, followed by a "pre-modern" phase commencing approx. 1500, a modern phase from 1800 and the newest phase associated with the technological revolution of the twentieth century: Julia Zinkina et al., *A Big History of Globalization: The Emergence of a Global World System*, World-systems evolution and global futures, (Cham: Springer International Publishing AG, 2019). Thomas D. Hall, *Comparing Globalizations: Historical and World-Systems Approaches*, 1st ed. 2018. ed., World-Systems Evolution and Global Futures, (Cham: Springer International Publishing, 2018).

the term "global constitutionalism" could mean and could imply; arguments for and against such a concept; and the contribution that Bahá'í principles can potentially make toward its further articulation and eventual implementation.

THE IDEA OF GLOBAL CONSTITUTIONALISM

Coming to terms with global constitutionalism requires reconceptualizing the relationship between individuals, the communities they build, and the states they construct. It requires, that is, rethinking where sovereignty resides, and what roles should be played by state and non-state actors. The concept of establishing the foundations of a "durable peace" between the nations is not new. It has existed in scriptures for millennia and in the work of jurists and philosophers. Kant, for instance, imagined the conditions necessary for a "perpetual peace".[2] In broad, Kant envisaged a federation of "peaceable states" and his ideas continue to be explored and developed.

In the wake of the first World War the League of Nations was established by more than fifty countries cognizant of the need for collective security and other forms of international cooperation. The League of Nations was the first world-wide organization whose principal mission was to maintain world peace. It was proposed by US President Woodrow Wilson during the Paris Peace Conference of 1919 and was formally established on January 10th, 1920.

Then, following WWII, the United Nations Organisation was established by fifty-one governments on somewhat similar foundations to its predecessor. It had broader socio-economic aspirations and more articulated processes for dialogue, decision-making, and formal agreement than did the League of Nations, but was once again premised on full retention of national sovereignty by member countries.

---

[2] Immanuel Kant, *Perpetual Peace A Philosophical Essay* (London: George Allen & Unwon, 1917).

The expansion of weapons capability since the late nineteenth century has changed countries' calculations of risk, and the most powerful nations — especially after the twentieth century's two world wars — have threatened rather than used force (using doctrines of "deterrence") and shifted their rivalries to "proxy" wars through client states.³ Landmines and small arms have been banned, but chemical weapons and cluster munitions were used against civilians in Syria; acts of Genocide have been committed on at least three continents; the reach of non-conventional warfare now includes cyber-attacks.

The post-world war II security arrangements are no longer respected (particularly the P5 veto power in the UN's security council and lack of effective use of either chapter 6 or chapter 7 of the UN Charter); the lack of progress under the Non-Proliferation Treaty; and the fate of civilian populations, with so many becoming refugees in the care of United Nations humanitarian efforts, all demonstrate the inadequacy of the existing global security architecture during what Bobbitt has termed "the long war" that was the twentieth century.⁴

There is broad agreement that we have reached a "post-international" phase in world affairs, in which the system of International Relations premised on a community of Westphalian nation-states needs to be "re-mapped", reconceptualized, to take into account "...the (re)emergence of novel political entities that straddle conventional boundaries, the sheer velocity of global flows of information and objects and the rise of 'global con-

---

³ By the first decades of the twenty-first century opponents of nuclear weapons based their campaigns on the scientific facts concerning the impact of nuclear explosions on the human world and the physical environment. If detonated in populated areas, millions would die in the explosion, more millions would die of radiation, and yet additional millions would die of hunger and disease in the subsequent months and years. No country is able to prepare for the humanitarian consequences of such a detonation — this is not the scenario of a mere tsunami or hurricane.

⁴ Philip Bobbitt, *The shield of Achilles: war, peace, and the course of history*, 1ˢᵗ Anchor Books ed. ed. (New York: Anchor Books, 2003).

sciousness' and non-territorial communities."[5] Mancini refers to globalization as a "post-Westphalian predicament"[6] because the uncertainties about the boundaries of states and because of political/constitutional and even religious sovereignty that existed in Europe prior to 1648 have re-emerged.[7] At a philosophic level, there is discussion of globalization's impact on concepts of "self" and special expansion of the self's dialogic relations[8], and scholars are articulating a "framework for citizenship in a global age."[9]

Whereas some conceive of global constitutionalism as a set of conditions and relations to be clarified *before* the establishment of world society, others view it as a crowning arrangement to be put in place *after* world society has been established. An intriguing additional possibility is that the world is in the process of constitutionalizing. Atilgan usefully describes global constitutionalism as a 'discourse', by which he means its construction through dialogue between alternative/competing approaches that come from international law, constitutional law, and societal discourses.[10] Similar views are advocated by Teubner and others, who have set out to find the political constitution for a pluralist world.[11] "...There are signs of the emergence of a Global

---

[5] Olaf Corry, "What is a (global) polity?," *Review of International Studies* 36, no. S1 (2010). 157–8.

[6] Susanna Mancini, "Global religion in a post-Westphalia world," in *Handbook on Global Constitutionalism*, ed. Anthony F. Lang and Antje Wiener (Edward Elgar Publishing, 2017). 421.

[7] The religious homogeneity established by the Peace of Westphalia brought a degree of stability, but at the cost of freedom of religion.

[8] Humbert Hermans and Agnieszka Hemans-Konopka, *Dialogical Self Theory: Positioning and Counter Positioning in a Globalizing Society* (Cambridge and New York: Cambridge University Press, 2010).

[9] Theodora Kostakopoulou, *The future governance of citizenship*, Law in context series, (Cambridge, UK: Cambridge University Press, 2008). 47.

[10] Aydin Atilgan, *Global Constitutionalism A Socio-legal Perspective*, 1st ed. 2018. ed., Beiträge zum ausländischen öffentlichen Recht und Völkerrecht, Veröffentlichungen des Max-Planck-Instituts für ausländisches öffentliches Recht und Völkerrecht, 275, (Berlin, Heidelberg: Springer Berlin Heidelberg, 2018).

[11] Jurgen Habermas, "A Political Constitution for the Pluralist World Society," *Journal of Chinese Philosophy* 34, no. 3 (2007).

Constitution" suggests Capaldo[12], in reference to the expanding influence of a global rule of law. "World government has evolved and will evolve through the United Nations as the people are willing for it to evolve," Eichelberger wrote in 1949, "The process has already begun."[13]

The United Nations reform is the focus of those who envisage global constitutionalism as well as those who envisage a better version of global governance that continues premised on the Westphalian state system. The United Nations has four principal aims (maintain international peace and security; develop friendly relations among nations; achieve international cooperation; and "harmonizing the actions of nations") and six principal organs (General Assembly, Security Council, Economic and Social Council, Trusteeship Council, International Court of Justice, and a Secretariat).[14] These principal organs have established a host of additional funds, programs, and specialized agencies, the most well-known being the United Nations Development Program (UNDP), United Nations Environment Program (UNEP), UNICEF, and the World Health Organization (WHO).[15]

At one level the United Nations has made significant progress, but its charter is not a global constitution, even if it contains some of the necessary elements. Yet, for all its progress, the United Nations remains an inter-governmental organization whose members cooperate on issues they agree about, but fail to cooperate when a decision in the collective interest does not suit their indi-

---

[12] Giuliana Ziccardi Capaldo, *The pillars of global law* (Aldershot, England;: Ashgate, 2008). 8.

[13] Clark M. Eichelberger, "World Government via the United Nations," *The Annals of the American Academy of Political and Social Science* 264, no. 1 (1949), 20.

[14] Over time, the UN has come to include 193 nations (on basis of "national sovereignty"). All member countries belong to the General Assembly, but only 15 to the Security Council, 54 to the Economic and Social Council. There are just 15 judges on the International Court of Justice. The Trusteeship Council ceased operations in 1994.

[15] There are a great number of others, and the UN periodically updates a chart at https://www.un.org/en/pdfs/un_system_chart.pdf).

vidual interests: the UN's member-states formed the UN to end the "scourge of war" but have activated few of its Charter provisions designed to achieve this; they "declared" human rights to be universal but have frequently failed to protect them when transgressed; and they closely monitor the world's social and environmental emergencies but are slow to address them. And yet, conventions of international law have steadily emerged, which oblige nations to find agreement where their interests come together, Studies in trans-national governance describe both state and non-state actors incrementally articulating global standards in law, accounting, banking, insurance, pharmaceuticals, commercial arbitration, transport and communications, medicine, among other fields.[16] Yet other strands focus on global justice. Thompson, for instance, seeks a "...well-grounded, universally acceptable conception of international justice."[17] Jimenez argues that it is impossible to establish global justice under current institutional conditions.[18]

Global conceptions of democracy and human rights are well-advanced. Falk, Dryzek, Leinen, Bummel and others, advocate for a "global People's Assembly,"[19] "deliberative global politics,"[20] and a World Parliament.[21] Some scholars and movements propose the establishment of a federal world republic.[22] Habermas

---

[16] Thomas Hale and David Held, eds., *Handbook of Transnational Governance: Institutions and Innovations* (Cambridge & Malden: polity, 2011).

[17] Janna Thompson, *Justice and world order: a philosophical inquiry* (London;: Routledge, 1992). 1.

[18] Ezequiel Jimenez, "Seeking Global Reform: The United Nations Security Council, the International Criminal Court, and Emerging Nations," *The Macalester/Mastricht Essays* 30, no. 10 (2012).

[19] Richard Falk and Andrew Strauss, "On the creation of a Global Peoples Assembly: legitimacy and the power of popular sovereignty," *Stanford journal of international law* 36, no. 2 (2000). 192.

[20] John S. Dryzek, *DELIBERATIVE GLOBAL POLITICS Discourse and Democracy in a Divided World* (Polity Press, 2006).

[21] Jo Leinen and Andreas Bummel, *A World Parliament. Governance and Democracy in the 21st Century* (Berlin: Democracy Without Borders, 2018).

[22] Otfried Hoffe, "A subsidiary and federal world republic: Thoughts on democracy in the age of globalization," in *Global governance and the United*

imagines a political constitution for pluralist world[23] as part of a neo-Kantian "incomplete project of modernity". In the field of international law Sarooshi has described the exercise of sovereign powers as a dialogic contribution toward how sovereignty should best be understood in the context of emergent global institutions.[24] Moshirian has linked the desirability of a world government to the world's banking and finance sectors.[25] A compelling case for global constitutionalism also comes from those seeking global collective security, and a "positive" world peace. The UN has contributed significantly to the progress of global society (notable in human rights, gender and women's rights, development policy, international economic relations, social development, sustainability, peace and human security, and human development).[26]

Global constitutionalism is a collaborative task. It necessarily involves all nations, but at the level of the individual, has room for ordinary citizens as well as experts. Simple contracts between the "citizen" and "the state" are being replaced by "global public policy networks" that link state and non-state actors in a "heteronomous (dis)order of the future," in which "authority will likely be distributed among many foci of political action, organized to address specific issues rather than to exercise a generalized rule over a specific territory,"[27] Initiatives from

---

Nations system, ed. Volker Rittberger (Tokyo, New York, Paris: United Nations University Press, 2001). Otfried Höffe, Democracy in an age of globalisation, Studies in global justice; v. 3, (Dordrecht;: Springer, 2007).

[23] Habermas, "A Political Constitution for the Pluralist World Society."

[24] Dan Sarooshi, International organizations and their exercise of sovereign powers (Oxford: Oxford Univ. Press, 2009). Dan Sarooshi, The United Nations and the Development of Collective Security: The Delegation by the UN Security Council of its Chapter VII Powers, Oxford Monographs in International Law, (Oxford: Oxford University Press, 2000).

[25] Fariborz Moshirian, "The significance of a world government in the process of globalization in the 21st century," Journal of Banking & Finance 32, no. 8 (2008), https://doi.org/10.1016/j.jbankfin.2008.03.004.

[26] Richard Jolly et al., UN Contributions to Development Thinking and Practice (Bloomington and Indianapolis: Indiana University Press, 2004).

[27] Ronnie D. Lipschutz, After Authority: War, Peace, and Global Politics in the 21st Century (Albany: State University of New York Press, 2000).

the Club of Rome's limits to Growth and "World Problematic" to the World Economic Forum's Global Agenda Platforms[28], the International Environment Forum[29], the Centre for United Nations Constitutional Research[30], and the Global Challenges Foundation's Global Governance Forum[31] — in addition to a host of initiatives of the United Nations, the World Bank and other key inter-governmental organizations — demonstrate this new approach to generating "global public goods."[32]

One consequence of the series of global conferences convened by the United Nations has been the emergence of processes for global policy dialogue and summitry which entail the establishment of global norms in a specific field, coupled with procedures for reporting by national governments on implementation and follow-up. The convening of such global conferences, and the ever-increasing inclusion of non-state and civil society actors in UN discourse, has contributed significantly to the expansion of global civil society and precipitated the "unity of thought" ("global public policy" in contemporary parlance) — which 'Abdu'l-Bahá envisaged as one of the "seven candles of unity". Some Bahá'í social teachings have already been broadly embraced — the equal rights of men and women, protection of the rights of children, recognition of the rights of persons with disabilities; the world's peoples whilst continuing to hold strong allegiance to nationality, desire rights to travel the globe for education, employment, tourism, sport and recreation; they value rights to circulate money internationally — such as to make purchases, to send remittances etc. So too, do they desire the protection of such global public goods

---

[28] See: https://www.weforum.org/platforms.
[29] See: https://iefworld.org/.
[30] See: https://cuncr.org/.
[31] See: https://globalchallenges.org/initiatives/partnerships/21st-century/.
[32] Inge Kaul, "The Changing Role of the United Nations: Lessons for Multi-Level Governance," in *Handbook on multi-level governance*, ed. Henrik Enderlein, Sonja Wälti, and Michael Zürn (Cheltenham: Edward Elgar, 2010). Inge Kaul, "Global Public Goods, Commons and Governance: The Current State of Play" (Global Public Goods, Commons and Governance, Victoria University of Wellington, New Zealand, 2014).

as environmental conservation, response to climate change, vigilance against global organized crime, cessation of military conflict, all such values can be said to be part of the emerging global constitution.

The UN has shown how a global campaign — "the world we want" — helped build momentum toward, if not directly shape, the Global Agenda for Development 2015–2030 (The sustainable development goals). Across seventeen thematic areas this first global development plan[33] is constitutionalising global networks comprising non-state as well as state actors: international professional associations, corporations, intergovernmental organizations, civil society organizations, and individuals, as well as nation states.[34]

RESERVATIONS

Notwithstanding the evident shift toward global governance through extensive intergovernmental, supra-national and transnational arrangements and global public policy networks, any shift from the current international order evokes consternation amongst those who cannot yet see the basis of authority beyond the nation-state, or fear of the emergence of a global hegemon.[35] They rightly point to episodes in world history in which one or other ideology or belief system subordinated all others within its jurisdiction.

Late into the nineteenth century, conventional political and legal thought — invariably associated with the notion of national sovereignty that formed the basis of the 1648 Peace of Westphalia — disapproved of the notion of constitutional arrangements beyond the level of the nation-state. Inter-relations and

---

[33] For the first time, all countries are identified as having development needs, not just the "developing" countries of previous plans.

[34] Deborah D. Avant, Martha Finnemore, and Susan K. Sell, "Who Governs the Globe?," in *Who Governs the Globe?*, ed. Deborah D. Avant, Martha Finnemore, and Susan K. Sell (Cambridge University Press, 2010).

[35] Dryzek, *DELIBERATIVE GLOBAL POLITICS Discourse and Democracy in a Divided World*.

UN Global Conferences (selected)

1990
- World Summit on Children – *New York*
- World Conference on Education for all.
- Second UN Conference on the Least Developed Countries.

1992
- United Nations Conference on Environment and Development (UNCED) – *Rio de Janeiro*
- International Conference on Nutrition.

1993
- World Conference on Human Rights – *Vienna*

1994
- International Conference on Population and Development – *Cairo*
- Global Conference on the Sustainable Development of Small Island Development States

1995
- World Summit for Social Development – *Copenhagen*
- 4th World Conference on Women – *Beijing*

1996
- Second UN Conference on Human Settlements (Habitat II) – *Istanbul*
- World Food Summit.

2000
- Millennium Summit: The Role of the UN in the 21st Century – *New York*

2002
- World summit for sustainable development – *Johannesburg*
- International Conference on Financing for Development

2003, 2005 *Tunis & Geneva* – World Summit on the information Society

2009 – *Copenhagen* – Climate Change

2011 – United Nations Conference on Least Developed Countries

2012 – *Doha* – Climate Change

2012 – United Nations Conference on Sustainable Development (Rio+20) – *Rio de Janeiro*

2014
- Third International Conference on Small Island Developing States – *Apia, Samoa*
- World Conference on Indigenous Peoples

2015
- United Nations Summit on Sustainable Development – *New York*
- COP 21

2016
- Summit for Refugees and Migrants – *New York*
- Global Sustainable Transport Conference – *Ashgabat*

2017 – The Ocean Conference – *New York*

commerce were regulated by treaty more than by domestically binding law, and a certain kind of anarchy was preferred over constraints on national sovereignty by any supra-national authority.[36]

This "realist" position has argued that peace at world scale has not been achieved in the past, is impossible to achieve in the future and is therefore an unattainable utopian ideal.[37] The realist argument was ascendant through the nineteenth century, but the catastrophic wars of the twentieth century, in addition to the evident interdependence of nations in the twenty-first century, coupled with the rapid rise of urgent "global public policy" issues such as environmental degradation, pandemics, global supply chain disruption, trans-national crimes in narcotics, and people smuggling, now suggest the need for global cooperation as the stronger "realist" argument. Global "cosmopolitanism" accommodates realists' concerns, by acknowledging globalization yet advancing global cooperation based on continued nation-state sovereignty. The liberal democracy championed by the western world, if adequately promoted in other regions, can be revised to deliver global governance.[38]

BAHÁ'Í CONTRIBUTIONS

To this point the chapter has focused on arguments that support acceptance of a future global constitution and on some reservations. We now turn to consideration of Bahá'í contributions toward its envisioning. There are principles in the Bahá'í Writings and consequent texts that support the idea of global constitutionalism without disregarding the significant benefits and achievements of the hard-won modern world system in which nationally

---

[36] Richard Falk, "Revisiting Westphalia, Discovering Post-Westphalia," *The journal of ethics* 6, no. 4 (2002).

[37] Keith Breen and Shane O'Neill, eds., *After the nation?: critical reflections on nationalism and postnationalism* (Houndsmills, Basingstoke: Palgrave Macmillan, 2010).

[38] Stephen Gill and A. Claire Cutler, eds., *New Constitutionalism and World Order* (New York: Cambridge University Press, 2014).

constituted societies engage with each other in the international community of nations.

First, the Bahá'í view is that the general direction of socio-political change — notwithstanding short-term disruptions — is progressive, toward ever more comprehensive socio-political formations: the question is not whether global integration is inevitable but what form it will take. Second, although socio-politico-technological change is also inevitable, the question as to whether a particular change is desirable depends on the extent to which it contributes to the betterment of the whole of humanity: this standard will assist in determining whether a concept, a technology, institution or law, should be discarded, retained or revised: willingness to innovate and to learn from experience and experimentation are required.[39] Third, whereas the Bahá'í worldview sympathizes with much contemporary critique of religious dogma and institutions, it offers a channel for re-connecting spiritual norms/values with intellectual inquiry.

The Prophetic religions have played important roles in the evolution of world order thus far and will continue to influence future trends. But whereas the major traditions have helped shape politics and constitutionalism up to the level of the nation-state, they are relatively silent about the possibilities for global constitutionalism. Bahá'í Writings, in contrast, anticipate and address governmental arrangements at global scale. The Bahá'í Writings anticipate "far-reaching changes in the governance of human affairs and in the institutions created to carry it out."[40] (Bahá'í International Community 1995a: 14). Bahá'í perspectives have seldom been considered in studies of religion and globalization let alone studies of global constitutionalism.[41]

---

[39] Berger identifies a "fear of failure" that can paralyse an institution's operations: Julia Berger, *Rethinking Religion and Politics in a Plural World: The Bahá'í International Community and the United Nations* (Bloomsbury Academic, 2021). 115.

[40] Bahá'í International Community, *The Prosperity of Humankind: a Statement* (London: Bahá'í Publishing Trust, 1995). 14.

[41] Mark Juergensmeyer, *Religion in global civil society* (Oxford: Oxford University Press, 2005).

In his 1875 treatise *Secret of Divine Civilization* 'Abdu'l-Bahá referred to the necessity of a global security covenant:

> True civilization will unfurl its banner in the midmost heart of the world whenever a certain number of its distinguished and high-minded sovereigns — the shining exemplars of devotion and determination — shall, for the good and happiness of all mankind, arise, with firm resolve and clear vision, to establish the Cause of Universal Peace. They must make the Cause of Peace the object of general consultation and seek by every means in their power to establish a Union of the nations of the world. They must conclude a binding treaty and establish a covenant, the provisions of which shall be sound, inviolable, and definite. They must proclaim it to all the world and obtain for it the sanction of all the human race.[42]

Later in the nineteenth century some of these ideas were discussed among European leaders. Czar Nicolas II of Russia proposed a comprehensive peace conference, which was held at the Hague in 1899 and again in 1907. When 'Abdu'l-Bahá was alerted by Tehran Bahá'ís Ahmad Yazdáni and 'Alí Muhammad 'Ibn-i-Asdaq that the Central Organization for A Durable Peace (established at the Hague in April 1915) had issued an invitation for interested parties to attend a forthcoming peace conference, he wrote — on December 17th, 1919 — his "Tablet to the Central Organization for A Durable Peace"[43] and had Yazdáni and 'Ibn-i-Asdaq personally present it to the organization in Rotterdam. Yazdani and Asdaq accomplished this on May 17th, 1920 but conveyed to 'Abdu'l-Bahá the news that the Organization had disbanded following the establishment of the League of

---

[42] 'Abdu'l-Bahá, *The Secret of Divine Civilization*, trans. Marzieh Gail, 2nd ed. (Wilmette, IL: Bahá'í Publishing Trust, 1970). 64.

[43] See: https://www.bahai.org/library/authoritative-texts/abdul-baha/tablets-hague-abdul-baha/1#188605710.

Nations — which prompted 'Abdu'l-Bahá to pen a second, shorter tablet, on July 1st, 1920.[44]

These two tablets continue[45] themes of global constitutionalism set out in *Secret of Divine Civilization* and in many other of 'Abdu'l-Bahá's letters and talks. The first Tablet included a specific critique of the newly established League of Nations, and set out in considerable detail, Bahá'u'lláh's prescription for a global organization:

> "... although the League of Nations has been brought into existence, yet it is incapable of establishing universal peace. But the Supreme Tribunal which Bahá'u'lláh has described will fulfil this sacred task with the utmost might and power. And His plan is this: that the national assemblies of each country and nation — that is to say parliaments — should elect two or three persons who are the choicest of that nation and are well informed concerning international laws and the relations between governments and aware of the essential needs of the world of humanity in this day. The number of these representatives should be in proportion to the number of inhabitants of that country. The election of these souls who are chosen by the national assembly, that is, the parliament, must be confirmed by the upper house, the congress, and the cabinet and also by the president or monarch so these persons may be the elected ones of all the nation and the government. The Supreme Tribunal will be composed of these people, and all mankind will thus have a share therein, for every one of these delegates is fully representative of his nation. When the Supreme Tribunal gives a ruling on any international question, either unanimously or by majority rule, there will no lon-

---

[44] See: https://www.bahai.org/library/authoritative-texts/abdul-baha/tablets-hague-abdul-baha/2#447425517.

[45] See: https://www.bahai.org/library/authoritative-texts/abdul-baha/tablets-hague-abdul-baha/1#188605710.

ger be any pretext for the plaintiff or ground of objection for the defendant. In case any of the governments or nations, in the execution of the irrefutable decision of the Supreme Tribunal, be negligent or dilatory, the rest of the nations will rise up against it, because all the governments and nations of the world are the supporters of this Supreme Tribunal. Consider what a firm foundation this is! But by a limited and restricted League the purpose will not be realized as it ought and should. This is the truth about the situation, which has been stated."[46]

Despite the reservations expressed, 'Abdu'l-Bahá remained enthusiastic about the League's potential to grow into something more substantial. "I met 'Abdu'l-Bahá lately in his home in Haifa," journalist Marion Weinstein wrote in New York's *Globe and Commercial Advertiser* in July 1919,

> I went to him curious as to his views of the future of Palestine, but he seemed more eager to talk of a matter of world importance — the League of Nations... 'I went to America myself on a mission of universal peace. I proclaimed seven years ago that Europe was an arsenal that needed but a spark to turn it into a volcano. The world leaders, I urged, must prevent this catastrophe. But they did not heed me. Now that they themselves are working for universal peace and we are soon to have a league of nations, there is no need for me to go to America again'.[47]

The League's activities contributed greatly to international coordination in the 1920s and 1930s, but the weaknesses in its collective security provisions were demonstrated through its

---

[46] Abdu'l-Bahá, *Tablets to the Hague*, https://www.bahai.org/library/authoritative-texts/abdul-baha/tablets-hague-abdul-baha/1#188605710.

[47] Marion Weinstein, "Declares Zionists Must Work with Other Races. Leader of Bahaism believes Neutral Government Like British Is Best for Palestine at Present — Says His Father Advocated League Half Century Ago," *Globe and Commercial Advertiser* (New York), 17 July 1919.

inability to halt the world's descent into World War II. Its effectiveness had ceased many years prior to its formal closure on April 20th, 1946 — although its twenty-six years of operation provided many lessons for its successor organization, the United Nations.

Shoghi Effendi's approach to the League of Nations is yet to be fully explored. However, this statement from 1927 summarises his view:

> "...a League so auspiciously welcomed for the ideal that prompted its birth, yet now so utterly inadequate in the actual principles that underlie its present-day structure and working."[48]

At the least, Shoghi Effendi encouraged individuals to participate in League events where possible, and he encouraged the establishment of a "Bahá'í Bureau" in Geneva as a clearing house for literature and a contact point for the League.[49]

Statements offering a Bahá'í perspective on global governance, and particularly on the structure and functioning of the United Nations, have been issued by the Bahá'í International Community since its establishment in 1948 as an UN-accredited Non-Government Organization.[50] These statements indicate strong general support for the work of the United Nations yet are also clear in their criticisms of its structure, processes, programs, and policy choices. In broad terms, this critique suggests the present order is based on rivalry between nations, its institutions lack sufficient executive, legislative, or judicial power, and are not delivering "global public goods" equal to the need: in sum, current conditions do not and cannot deliver global justice.

---

[48] Shoghi, *Bahá'í administration: selected messages, 1922–1932* (Wilmette, Ill.: Bahá'í Pub. Trust, 1974). Letter dated October 18, 1927, p.146.

[49] Shoghi Effendi sought the League's assistance in securing rightful possession of Bahá'u'lláh's house in Baghdad — a campaign that brought the existence of the Bahá'í community to the attention of greater numbers of government officials from many different countries: Shoghi Effendi, *Bahá'í administration*, 5th ed. (Wilmette, Ill.: Bahá'í publishing committee, 1945).

[50] See: https://www.bic.org/.

A statement prepared in 1995 to mark the UN's fiftieth anniversary, *Turning Point for All Nations*[51], focuses on administrative reform, and on improving policy implementation and effectiveness. The General Assembly could be "resuscitated" by (1) raising minimum requirements for membership (to establish consequences for states that violate fundamental principles of human rights); (2) appointing a commission to study state borders and frontiers (to repair the arbitrary construction of many current borders); (3) improving financing (to ensure that the financial contributions of countries are in proportion to their size and ability to pay); (4) committing to a universal auxiliary language and script (to remove the current inefficiencies and lack of unity embedded in the cost of supporting six official languages); and (5) investigating the establishment of a single currency (to better integrate the global economy, curb unproductive speculation and unpredictable market swings, and promote levelling of incomes and prices).

The executive capacity of the UN could be improved by (1) restricting the Security Council by limiting the scope of and gradually eliminating both the veto power and the distinction between permanent and non-permanent members); (2) expanding the concept of "collective security" to "comprehensive security" so as to include such "other problems of the global commons" as drug trafficking, food security, and global pandemics; (3) retaining the independence of agencies that were functioning well (such as ILO, WHO, UPU, ITU, UNICEF); and (4) strengthening the World Court by (1) extending the Court's Jurisdiction (by increase standing to include not just states but other UN organs); and (2) better coordinating the work of thematic courts (notably the International criminal court, and courts of arbitration covering commerce and transportation).

---

[51] Bahá'í International Community, *Turning Point for All Nations: a statement of the Bahá'í International Community on the Occasion of the 50th Anniversary of the United Nations* (New York: Bahá'í International Community, 1995).

Turning Point further suggests that the UN's policy and implementation effectiveness could be improved by measures to release "... the power of the individual" — a deceptively simple phrase that has implications for how economies are organized, how human rights can be protected, how planning can include individual voices, how the gap between rich and poor can be minimized, how women can be admitted to decision-making processes at all levels[52], how education can be oriented to include not just a "narrow body of knowledge or learning" but also "...teach the process for knowledge acquisition, cultivate the powers of intellect and reasoning, and infuse the student with indispensable moral qualities."[53]

Bahá'í principles toward advancing global governance are also being explored in works of scholarship. Lopez-Claros, Dahl and Groff's significant contribution toward re-fashioning global governance, for one, is based on proposals for United Nations reform, together with the creation of additional global institutions.[54] They retain a 'separation of powers' between legislative, executive, and judicial branches, and strengthen their democratic foundations and abilities to ensure compliance. The General Assembly becomes a global parliament, whose members are democratically elected by popular vote in numbers proportional to the population of each nation. The legislature is empowered to make binding legislation on matters of global concern. The size, powers and functions of the global executive are also increased, with membership elected by the General Assembly, and increased oversite of international conflict resolution and security (in this scheme the executive is given security responsibilities that are currently held by the UN Security

---

[52] Bahá'í International Community, *Turning Point for All Nations: a statement of the Baha'i International Community on the Occasion of the 50th Anniversary of the United Nations.* 14–15.

[53] Ibid. 15.

[54] Augusto Lopez-Claros, Arthur Dahl and Maja Groff, *Global Governance and the Emergence of Global Institutions for the 21st Century* (Cambridge: Cambridge University Press, 2020).

Council). The system's third branch, the judiciary, comprises the International Court of Justice, the International Criminal Court, an International Anti-corruption Court, and an office of Attorney-General—all with enforcement capabilities that the current international courts lack. The scheme, as a whole, retains the impressive international governance structure established by the United Nations in the twentieth century, whilst subtly revising its less effective components.

POSSIBILITIES

A constitution at global level needs to be based on a theory of international justice, and this, in turn, must be based on a "universal moral theory."[55] In the Bahá'í view, the "oneness of humankind" provides such a moral foundation, far more inclusive than the assertions of national supremacy that underlays constitutions at nation-state level. Global constitutionalism cannot succeed unless the majority conceive themselves to be members of one human family, all equally entitled.

The global constitution will include institutions establishing and maintaining global collective security, for it is unthinkable that the global system will continue to allow member-states to maintain armaments at levels capable of threatening the well-being of the whole. The principal advance in thinking here is that the entitlement to defend oneself, which is the basis of Just War theory, is replaced by laws outlawing aggression: it is no longer acceptable to invade the territory of others in pursuit of one's own interests. Ewing suggests as elements toward reform (a) a decision by world leaders to agree to establish a genuine global security pact (a "core group" could get the process started); based on (b) agreed principles concerning equality of nations and peoples, justice, equity, reward and punishment, and how best to curtail national sovereignty and implement collective action; leading to (c) necessary institutional and legal reform (security council,

---

[55] Thompson, *Justice and world order: a philosophical inquiry*. 10.

arms treaties; an international boundaries authority, the World Court, and the establishment of an international executive.[56]

Historically, constitutions of nation-states have been written or reformed during "constitutional moments" in the life of a nation, through impetus provided by shared dissatisfaction and unrest, and/or shared vision of possibilities, as in the instance of the American constitution. Such times of revolution or emancipation have included dissolution of empires and decolonization.[57] By analogy, the global constitution awaits such a "constitutional moment" at global scale, which may occur through a pre-emptive act of "consultative will" or, God forbid, following catastrophic events, as was the case prior to the creation of the League of Nations and again prior to the establishment of the United Nations. This is not to say that a global "constitutional moment" must result in a global constitution encapsulated within a single document, having institutional and process characteristics that simply conflate provisions familiar from the constitutions of current nation-states.

The global constitution will build on principles of diversity and subsidiary and will not permit excessive centralization of power. The United Nations charter is not a global constitution, but it does contain some of the necessary elements, even if they require considerable amendment. Nation-states are important components of a federated world. But they are not all-important, and their composition may alter to correct historical injustices, or to match societal preferences and meet the requirements of

---

[56] Sovaida Ma'ani Ewing, "Collective Security: An Indispensable Requisite for a Lasting Peace," in *Lights of 'Irfán: Papers Presented at the 'Irfán Colloquia and Seminars: Book Fourteen*, ed. Iraj Ayman (Evanston, IL: Haj Mehdi Arjmand Memorial Fund, 2013).

[57] Bowen's *Miracle at Philadelphia* shows how delegates seized a "constitutional moment" to draft the constitution of the United States of America: Catherine Drinker Bowen and The Story Of The Constitutional Convention, *Miracle at Philidelphia* (New York, New York: Little, Brown and Co., 1986). For examples from Asia and the Pacific see Graham Hassall and Cheryl Saunders, *Asia Pacific Constitutional Systems* (Melbourne: Cambridge University Press, 2002).

the global era.[58] The existence of approximately 190 member countries in the twenty-first century is merely a reflection of decisions made across the nineteenth and twentieth centuries — often by "foreign" political actors at the helm of now extinct empires and organizations and their expired treaties. Nation-states will continue to exist and provide services.[59]

The "procedural turn" espoused by Habermas and others suggests that legitimacy of outcomes is highly dependent on the fairness of the processes by which those outcomes were derived. Accordingly, the procedures for the transfer of sovereign powers from national to global entities in a constitutionally sound manner is crucial.[60] While the English, French and American traditions that have dominated constitution-building from the eighteenth to twentieth centuries will obviously continue to be influential, the global constitution will not want to limit itself to western experience.

The global constitution will unfold through the reshaping, re-casting of existing institutions and processes, discarding those that are no longer effective, and inventing new institutions where need arises. The institutions of government will include both traditional and novel elements. Traditional elements (at global scale) will include legislative, executive, and judicial branches; potential novel elements include a boundaries authority, a global environmental authority, and a world police force. Global constitutionalism implies the articulation of global law, which will differ from the current system of global governance through treaties.

In the 1930s Shoghi Effendi referred to "an integrative process" toward a "world polity".[61] It cannot be foreseen whether

---

[58] Andreas Pickel, *The Problem of Order in the Global Age: Systems and Mechanisms* (New York: Palgrave Macmillan, 2006).

[59] Timothy William Waters, ""The Momentous Gravity of the State of Things Now Obtaining": Annoying Westphalian Objections to the Idea of Global Governance," *Indiana journal of global legal studies* 16, no. 1 (2009).

[60] Jean-Christophe Merle, "Introduction," in *Spheres of global justice*, ed. Jean-Christophe Merle (Dordrecht: Springer, 2013). 7.

[61] Shoghi Effendi, *The World Order of Bahá'u'lláh: Selected Letters*, (1991). 192.

the process will be gradual or rapid, but either way it will rest on legitimacy and consent. However, realization of these 'far-reaching changes' is predicated on several additional propositions about the source of societal values, the role of the individual, and the purposes for which institutions are created.

CONCLUSION

Because prospects for a future without global agreement are quite bleak, constitutionalism at global scale has become a realist position: it has shifted from an ideal to a necessity. It is no longer a question of "whether" to establish global authorities, but when, and how, through what processes and instruments. This global constitution is already in development rather than being an instrument or condition currently absent but due to emerge later. There are principles in the Bahá'í Writings and associated texts that support the idea of global constitutionalism and that can contribute to this process of articulation. This is evident in the activities and statements of the Bahá'í International Community and in the work of Bahá'í-inspired scholars and organizations, which contribute to the articulation of the future global constitution. This is a new field of inquiry, one to be approached with a learning attitude for, as Berger points out, it seeks a condition that has not yet existed in human history.[62] Two inter-related processes are involved here — the first being the establishment of global institutions with legitimate mandates to deliberate and act in the global interest on matters of global concern, and the second referring to the identification of norms to guide the operation of these institutions. Both processes need to proceed in a manner that provides global governance whilst continuing to value the diversity of preferences at sub-global levels. On the other hand, the global community is in such a preliminary phase of transition to world order and global

---

[62] Berger, *Rethinking Religion and Politics in a Plural World: The Bahá'í International Community and the United Nations.* 113.

constitutionalism that it is not yet possible to identify its precise characteristics.[63]

REFERENCES

'Abdu'l-Bahá. *The Secret of Divine Civilization*. Translated by Marzieh Gail. 2nd ed. Wilmette, IL: Bahá'í Publishing Trust, 1970.

Atilgan, Aydin. *Global Constitutionalism a Socio-Legal Perspective*. Beiträge Zum Ausländischen Öffentlichen Recht Und Völkerrecht, Veröffentlichungen Des Max-Planck-Instituts Für Ausländisches Öffentliches Recht Und Völkerrecht, 275. 1st ed. 2018. Berlin, Heidelberg: Springer Berlin Heidelberg, 2018.

Avant, Deborah D., Martha Finnemore, and Susan K. Sell. "Who Governs the Globe?". In *Who Governs the Globe?*, edited by Deborah D. Avant, Martha Finnemore and Susan K. Sell: Cambridge University Press, 2010.

Bahá'í International Community. *The Prosperity of Humankind: A Statement*. London: Bahá'í Publishing Trust, 1995.

———. *Turning Point for All Nations: A Statement of the Bahá'í International Community on the Occasion of the 50th Anniversary of the United Nations*. New York: Bahá'í International Community, 1995.

Berger, Julia. *Rethinking Religion and Politics in a Plural World: The Bahá'í International Community and the United Nations*. Bloomsbury Academic, 2021.

Bobbitt, Philip. *The Shield of Achilles: War, Peace, and the Course of History*. 1st Anchor Books ed. New York: Anchor Books, 2003.

Bowen, Catherine Drinker, and The Story Of The Constitutional Convention. *Miracle at Philidelphia*. New York, New York: Little, Brown and Co., 1986.

Breen, Keith, and Shane O'Neill, eds. *After the Nation?: Critical Reflections on Nationalism and Postnationalism*. Houndsmills, Basingstoke: Palgrave Macmillan, 2010.

---

[63] Shoghi Effendi, *The Promised Day Is Come*, (1943). 303.

Corry, Olaf. "What Is a (Global) Polity?". *Review of International Studies* 36, no. S1 (2010): 157–80.

Dryzek, John S. *Deliberative Global Politics Discourse and Democracy in a Divided World*. Polity Press, 2006.

Eichelberger, Clark M. "World Government Via the United Nations." *The Annals of the American Academy of Political and Social Science* 264, no. 1 (1949): 20–25.

Ewing, Sovaida Ma'ani. "Collective Security: An Indispensable Requisite for a Lasting Peace." In *Lights of 'Irfán: Papers Presented at the 'Irfán Colloquia and Seminars: Book Fourteen*, edited by Iraj Ayman. Evanston, IL: Haj Mehdi Arjmand Memorial Fund, 2013.

Falk, Richard. "Revisiting Westphalia, Discovering Post-Westphalia." *The journal of ethics* 6, no. 4 (2002): 311–52.

Falk, Richard, and Andrew Strauss. "On the Creation of a Global Peoples Assembly: Legitimacy and the Power of Popular Sovereignty." *Stanford journal of international law* 36, no. 2 (2000): 191.

Gill, Stephen, and A. Claire Cutler, eds. *New Constitutionalism and World Order*. New York: Cambridge University Press, 2014.

Habermas, Jurgen. "A Political Constitution for the Pluralist World Society." *Journal of Chinese Philosophy* 34, no. 3 (2007): 331–43.

Hale, Thomas, and David Held, eds. *Handbook of Transnational Governance: Institutions and Innovations*. Cambridge & Malden: Polity, 2011.

Hall, Thomas D. *Comparing Globalizations: Historical and World-Systems Approaches*. World-Systems Evolution and Global Futures. 1st ed. 2018. Cham: Springer International Publishing, 2018.

Hassall, Graham, and Cheryl Saunders. *Asia Pacific Constitutional Systems*. Melbourne: Cambridge University Press, 2002.

Hermans, Humbert, and Agnieszka Hemans-Konopka. *Dialogical Self Theory: Positioning and Counter Positioning in a Globalizing Society*. Cambridge and New York: Cambridge University Press, 2010.

Hoffe, Otfried. "A Subsidiary and Federal World Republic: Thoughts on Democracy in the Age of Globalization." In *Global Governance and the United Nations System*, edited by Volker Rittberger. Tokyo, New York, Paris: United Nations University Press, 2001.

Höffe, Otfried. *Democracy in an Age of Globalisation*. Studies in Global Justice; V. 3. Dordrecht: Springer, 2007.

Jimenez, Ezequiel. "Seeking Global Reform: The United Nations Security Council, the International Criminal Court, and Emerging Nations." *The Macalester/Mastricht Essays* 30, no. 10 (2012): 84–109.

Jolly, Richard, Louis Emmerij, Dharam Ghai, and Frederic Lapeyre. *UN Contributions to Development Thinking and Practice*. Bloomington and Indianapolis: Indiana University Press, 2004.

Juergensmeyer, Mark. *Religion in Global Civil Society*. Oxford: Oxford University Press, 2005.

Kant, Immanuel. *Perpetual Peace. A Philosophical Essay*. London: George Allen & Unwon, 1917.

Kaul, Inge. "The Changing Role of the United Nations: Lessons for Multi-Level Governance." In *Handbook on Multi-Level Governance*, edited by Henrik Enderlein, Sonja Wälti and Michael Zürn. Cheltenham: Edward Elgar, 2010.

———. "Global Public Goods, Commons and Governance: The Current State of Play." Global Public Goods, Commons and Governance, New Zealand: Victoria University of Wellington, 2014.

Kostakopoulou, Theodora. *The Future Governance of Citizenship*. Law in Context Series. Cambridge, UK: Cambridge University Press, 2008.

Leinen, Jo, and Andreas Bummel. *A World Parliament. Governance and Democracy in the 21st Century*. Berlin: Democracy Without Borders, 2018.

Lipschutz, Ronnie D. *After Authority: War, Peace, and Global Politics in the 21st Century*. Albany: State University of New York Press, 2000.

Lopez-Claros, Augusto, Arthur Dahl and Maja Groff. *Global Governance and the Emergence of Global Institutions for the 21st Century*. Cambridge: Cambridge University Press, 2020.

Mancini, Susanna. "Global Religion in a Post-Westphalia World." In *Handbook on Global Constitutionalism*, edited by Anthony F. Lang and Antje Wiener, 421–32: Edward Elgar Publishing, 2017.

Merle, Jean-Christophe. "Introduction." In *Spheres of Global Justice*, edited by Jean-Christophe Merle. Dordrecht: Springer, 2013.

Moshirian, Fariborz. "The Significance of a World Government in the Process of Globalization in the 21st Century." *Journal of Banking & Finance* 32, no. 8 (2008): 1432–39. https://doi.org/10.1016/j.jbankfin.2008.03.004.

Pickel, Andreas. *The Problem of Order in the Global Age: Systems and Mechanisms*. New York: Palgrave Macmillan, 2006.

Sarooshi, Dan. *International Organizations and Their Exercise of Sovereign Powers*. Oxford: Oxford Univ. Press, 2009.

———. *The United Nations and the Development of Collective Security: The Delegation by the UN Security Council of Its Chapter VII Powers*. Oxford Monographs in International Law. Oxford: Oxford University Press, 2000.

Shoghi Effendi. *Bahá'í Administration: Selected Messages, 1922–1932*. Wilmette, Ill.: Bahá'í Pub. Trust, 1974.

———. *Bahá'í Administration*. 5th ed. Wilmette, Ill.: Bahá'í publishing committee, 1945.

———. *The Promised Day Is Come*. (1943): 136 p.

———. *The World Order of Bahá'u'lláh: Selected Letters*. (1991): xii, 234 p.

Thompson, Janna. *Justice and World Order: A Philosophical Inquiry*. London: Routledge, 1992.

Waters, Timothy William. ""The Momentous Gravity of the State of Things Now Obtaining": Annoying Westphalian Objections to the Idea of Global Governance." *Indiana journal of global legal studies* 16, no. 1 (2009): 25–58. https://doi.org/10.2979/GLS.2009.16.1.25.

Weinstein, Marion. "Declares Zionists Must Work with Other Races. Leader of Bahaism Believes Neutral Government Like British Is Best for Palestine at Present — Says His Father Advocated League Half Century Ago." *Globe and Commercial Advertiser* (New York), 17 July 1919.

Ziccardi Capaldo, Giuliana. *The Pillars of Global Law*. Aldershot, England: Ashgate, 2008.

Zinkina, Julia, David Christian, Leonid Grinin, Ilya Ilyin, Alexey Andreev, Ivan Aleshkovski, Sergey Shulgin, and Andrey Korotayev. *A Big History of Globalization: The Emergence of a Global World System*. World-Systems Evolution and Global Futures. Cham: Springer International Publishing AG, 2019.

Globalization — The Tangible Expression of Humanity's Journey Towards Unity

SOVAIDA MA'ANI EWING

The term "globalization" tends to evoke extremely strong reactions in those who hear it. Before we delve into the nature of and reason for these typical reactions, I want to begin by clarifying precisely what I mean when I use this word for purposes of this essay. It is important to do this especially because, in addition to the strong reactions it elicits, there is also broad disagreement about what "globalization" means.

DEFINITION OF GLOBALIZATION

My definition of "globalization" is the process of increasing human interdependence across long distances resulting in increased global integration. It is essentially a meld of two definitions offered by two leading thinkers of our time: Professor Jeffrey Sachs of Columbia University and Professor Ian Goldin of Oxford University. Sachs defines globalization as the fact of humanity's interdependence across large distances.[1] Goldin defines it as the process of increasing global integration and cross-border flows of people, goods, services, and ideas across an ever-widening set of countries.[2]

Globalization has yielded incredibly positive benefits to humanity while also exposing it to great risks. The manner in which a person reacts to the term "globalization" depends largely on

---

[1] Andy Fitch, "Expanding Interdependence: Talking to Jeffrey D. Sachs," *Los Angeles Review of Books*, August 14, 2020, https://blog.lareviewofbooks.org/interviews/expanding-interdependence-talking-jeffrey-d-sachs/.

[2] Ian Goldin, Mike Mariathasan, *The Butterfly Defect*. Princeton University Press, 2016, p. xiii.

which of these two impacts of globalization they choose to train their focus.

BENEFITS OF GLOBALIZATION

One of the greatest benefits resulting from globalization is that it has created opportunities for economic growth and rising incomes, lifting millions out of poverty especially in emerging economies. It has also created tremendous opportunities for the wide dissemination of knowledge and learning through the spread of advanced technologies such as mobile telephones and the internet, both of which have been powerful drivers in human progress. It has also raised awareness about the benefits of diversity and different forms of political organization. Goldin goes so far as to claim that it "has been the most powerful driver of human progress in the history of humanity."[3]

DOWNSIDES OF GLOBALIZATION

While the benefits of globalization are tremendous, there is also a dark side to it. The very fact that globalization has made humanity more interconnected, integrated, and interdependent means that it has also made humanity susceptible to threats and risks of a systemic nature, some of which have resulted in actual damage. These risks include the risk of contagion in different spheres of human activity. For example, even as transportation and travel have become easier and tourism has flourished, pathogens have traveled around more easily and at lightening speed. Humanity's current experience with the spread of the Covid-19 virus is a perfect example of the high risk and damaging effects of contagion caused by globalization. It is instructive to compare the risk of disease contagion today to that which existed during the Black Death: While historians estimate that the Black Death traveled from China to Italy over the course of sixteen years, the

---

[3] Ibid., p. 3.

coronavirus arrived from China to Italy in what is estimated to have been a mere sixteen hours.[4]

Another example of a major contagion risk and the damage it can bring in its wake is in the environmental sphere as manifested in one of the biggest global challenges of our day: climate change. The rise in the export and import of fossil fuels has increased their availability worldwide and contributed to a vast increase in the release of carbon dioxide and other greenhouse gases into the environment. This behavior has had an impact far beyond the borders of nations responsible for trading in these fuels and of those responsible for burning them. It has resulted in the warming of our planet and increasingly catastrophic events arising from more frequent and extreme heat waves, droughts, flooding, forest fires, the melting of glaciers, the destruction of coastlines as well as the loss of biodiversity on an unimaginable scale.

Terrorism is another threat that results from globalization. The ease with which terrorists can move from one country to another, coupled with the ease with which they can both gain knowledge about destructive technologies such as dirty bombs and get their hands on the weapons and other material necessary to wreak havoc, has exposed the lives of humans in every part of the world to heightened dangers.

While many have benefited from globalization, there are also many who have stood to lose from it. Among this number workers in wealthy countries stand out, large number of whom have lost their jobs or seen a sharp decline in their wages. Moreover, there is no doubt that globalization has facilitated the sharp rise in extremes of wealth and poverty around the world.

Another downside of globalization is the enhanced risk of war that is both more geographically widespread and more lethal. Indeed, thanks to modern communication and trade, two large contributors of globalization, the facility with which nations can

---

[4] Jeffrey Sachs, "Will covid-19 reverse globalization?" *The Economist Asks* podcast, June 11, 2020; https://www.economist.com/podcasts/2020/06/11/will-covid-19-reverse-globalisation.

gain access to both conventional and nuclear technologies and materials has put humanity in the position of dramatically increasing the risk that it will destroy itself.

Humanity's interconnection through the internet has also made it extremely vulnerable to the threat of cyberattacks which can hold individuals and businesses hostage and make critical infrastructure ranging from the electrical grid to nuclear installations to hospital systems, electoral systems, and governmental agencies vulnerable to failure.

We have also witnessed the extent to which the unprecedented interdependence of the global financial system has made the world susceptible to banking crises that start in one region of the world and end up spreading like wildfire to the rest of the globe. The banking crisis of 2008 which started as a housing price bubble in the United States eventually triggered a global financial crisis from which the world has never fully recovered and is a stark example of a key risk brought on by globalization.

KNEE-JERK REACTION TO THE THREATS OF GLOBALIZATION

The tendency of human beings when the going gets tough is to either repeat the same behavior that led to the problem in the first place, or to take a few steps back, undoing some of the progress that they have made. It is not surprising then, given the extent of the potential threats resulting from globalization, that the instinctive reaction of many is to slow down globalization or better still reverse it. This reaction to globalization is so ubiquitous that it has been referred to as "slowbalization" — a term coined in 2015 by Adjiedj Bakas, a Dutchman who was regarded as global trend-watcher.

However comforting and natural such a reaction may seem at first blush, it should be resisted at all costs. There are two main reasons for this. Firstly, as Goldin points out, globalization is a process that has been with us for a very long time, indeed, ever since modern humans first migrated from Africa 70,000 years ago and started trading, exchanging ideas, communicating with each other, exchanging diseases, and engaging in conflict and war. So, while we tend to think of it as something relatively recent, we are mistaken in this belief. Secondly, it follows that this process of deepening interdependence and integration over ever-widening geographical areas has so woven and bound the destiny of all humans with each other, that it is impossible to undo it, even if we wanted to. It's like scrambling an egg. Once it's done, it is impossible to unscramble it! Thirdly, as Sachs points out, previous attempts in human history to reverse the course of globalization have always had disastrous consequences and ultimately failed to stem the overarching tide of growing interdependence. It follows that as a practical matter we will not succeed in stopping the forces of integration and globalization. Now that we are interconnected, we will remain so.[5]

It is worth spending some time considering what happens when we attempt to arrest and reverse the inexorable march of globalization. We can do this by considering some historical examples. One clear example can be found in the story of the Luddites in nineteenth-century Britain and their reaction to the industrial revolution. The Luddites were originally British weavers and textile workers who feared the impact of the industrial revolution on their jobs and livelihood. They were particularly worried that the increased use of knitting frames and mechanized looms would strip them of their jobs and make them redundant. They feared that having invested so much time learning their craft and honing their artisanal skills, unskilled machine operators would usurp their means of living. As a consequence, they resorted to breaking into textile factories and smashing the machines in a futile attempt to arrest the process. Another example can be seen in the after-effects of the fall of the Roman Empire: There was a serious reversal in long-distance communication and trade with a renewed focus on small village life resulting in what we have come to consider the "Dark Ages."

---

[5] Ibid.

A more recent example can be seen in Europe's experience in the aftermath of World War l. The Treaty of Versailles, far from ensuring peace, exacerbated the economic and political malaise in Europe. International trade collapsed and finance fell into disarray. The combination of all these factors ultimately contributed vastly to the Great Depression. The economic collapse that ensued contributed in turn to the rise of the Nazi regime in Germany and Hitler's reign of terror, all of which led to the Second World War. It is not surprising that Sachs posits his view that every time humanity has attempted to reverse the process of globalization the result has been negative resulting in chaos, or what are considered the dark ages, or militarism.[6]

Moreover, we should be cognizant that any attempt to deglobalize or slowbalize would inevitably lead to a decline in growth worldwide. It would also lead to higher unemployment and destabilize the markets including the all-important market for food. Consequently, it would decimate the global economy, lead to conflict, and have a disproportionately impact on the most vulnerable amongst us, namely the poor worldwide.

A PROCESS TO BE MANAGED, NOT A PROBLEM TO BE SOLVED

If we accept that humanity's increasing interdependence and move towards deeper integration has always been part of our history and is a feature of our societal existence that is here to stay and if we also accept that attempts to slow it down or reverse it will prove detrimental to humanity's well-being as they have in the past and should therefore be avoided, the next question is what should we or ought we to do? Should we just accept the tremendous risks that are endemic to globalization? Surely the answer is to accept that globalization while conferring tremendous benefits upon the well-being of humans also brings in its wake systemic risks and that we can and ought to set about mitigating the effects

---

[6] Ibid.

of such risks as opposed to ignoring them or wishing them away, which currently seems to be our preferred course of action. The result of our denial is that the risks and threats fester and proliferate, subjecting us to enormous global challenges that include nuclear proliferation, run-away climate change, global financial crises, global pandemics, and terrorism to name but a few.

DANGERS OF FAILURE TO MANAGE AND MITIGATE SYSTEMIC RISKS

Failure to manage and mitigate the costs of these risks will lead to cascading global crises and will inevitably cause the public to associate globalization solely with negative and undesirable effects, entirely forgetting all the benefits. When we couple such negative associations with our intrinsic discomfort with, and fear and suspicion of, interdependence, we exacerbate fears that we are losing national autonomy and becoming reliant on other states. We understandably feel that our national independence is being eroded and we are losing control thereby making us weaker. Therefore, we try to get back the power we've given away—namely our national sovereignty—and instinctively move to more insular practices all in the name of regaining control.

This backlash of insular practices appears to take a variety of forms including xenophobia, protectionism, isolationism, and nationalism. It is interesting to observe that these maladaptive habits tend to appear in clusters very much like autoimmune diseases that occur when the immune system is under strain in a sustained manner for long periods of time. Just as developing one such disease significantly increases the chances of developing one or more others, clinging to one of the above-mentioned insular habits is usually accompanied by other sister habits that are each corrosive in their own right.

It is no wonder that in this era of unprecedented interdependence and interconnectedness, in which the inevitable systemic risks associated with globalization have been left to run rampant without adequate attempts to identify and manage them or mitigate their costs, we are understandably witnessing the rise of the dysfunctional and destructive reactions mentioned here. The severe backlash against the tsunami of migration from the Middle East and Africa to Europe which gave rise to xenophobia, strengthened the far-right in Europe and resulted in efforts to keep the migrants at bay, is one example. So severe was this backlash that it contributed in no small part to a cleavage in the unity of the European Union as demonstrated by Britain's departure from the European Union. A similar backlash has been experienced in the United States which has continued to have a restrictive immigration policy and has seen a rise in xenophobic acts within its borders.

Nationalism has also reared its ugly head in many parts of the world with various nations resorting to a doctrine of "our country first," heedless of the fact that in an interconnected world we sink or swim and rise or fall together. The absence of logic in taking this stance has been starkly on display with the appearance of what has been coined "vaccine nationalism" during the coronavirus pandemic. Even though the scientists have repeatedly warned us that we are only as safe as our weakest link and that failure to vaccinate people will result in the rampant spread of the virus inevitably leading to mutations that will likely evade the vaccines we have, we have been insistent on focusing on the well-being of our own nations even if it is at the expense of the well-being of our fellow human-beings elsewhere and despite the boomerang effects of such behavior. Consequently, the world is faced with the Omicron variant that is said to be more transmissible than the Delta variant and better able to evade our immune and vaccine defenses.

The tariff trade wars between China and the United States are also emblematic of this cluster of social autoimmune diseases. They arise from an outworn assumption that human relationships are intrinsically competitive as opposed to cooperative. Such assumptions and dysfunctional beliefs give rise to protectionism — another form of nationalism whereby a nation places its economic interests over and above the interests of other nations.

REGIONALIZATION IS NOT THE ANSWER

In some quarters people believe that the time may be ripe for a shift from a global system to a regional one with the United States, China, and Europe forming three dominant regional centers. However, one of the key problems with resorting to a regional approach is that so many of our existential challenges are global in nature and require global solutions. A world that is centered around regional systems would be hard-pressed to solve these global challenges including climate change, pandemics, nuclear proliferation, and cybercrime. Humanity has arrived at the next inevitable stage in its collective growth which requires that it finds an effective and viable way to organize and manage its affairs at a global level.

WE SHOULD ACT SMARTER BY COOPERATING

If reversing the course of globalization by slowing it down or undoing it are not viable solutions, and if resorting to the insular practices of xenophobia, nationalism, isolationism, and protectionism is destructive to our well-being, how then should we set about mitigating the costs of the systemic risks brought about by globalization?

The answer, according to Sachs is to act smarter. What that means in practice, is a couple of things. Firstly, given that humanity has become so interdependent and susceptible to systemic risks which are, by definition, collective, it follows that we must find ways of reaching collective solutions based on extensive collective consultation. To do this, we have to ramp up our ability to cooperate and collaborate effectively in tackling global challenges and crises. One of the gifts of the coronavirus pandemic is that it has definitively proven that this is something we are capable of doing. Scientists have led the way in role modeling how this can be done. Before the Covid-19 pandemic, it would take scientists an average of 12–14 years to find and produce a vaccine that was effective. Yet, during this global pandemic, scientists have been able to discover and produce not just one, but several viable vaccines in the course of a mere eleven months — a feat that is nothing short of miraculous. The reason they were able to do this is that their first loyalty was to ensure the collective well-being of humanity. They subsumed their egos for this higher cause. Whereas in the past, many were driven by a desire for recognition and pursued their scientific explorations in great secrecy, and in an intense spirit of competition, hoping to be the first to be credited with important breakthrough discoveries, during the pandemic they put these old ways aside. Instead, scientists from around the world used the new technological platforms available to them — such as twitter and slack — and as soon as they made a finding they would post it, allowing their peers to speedily test their findings and provide valuable feedback. In this way, the process of weeding out unworkable ideas and finding what worked became a lot more efficient and speedy redounding to the benefit of humanity. Imagine what the world would look like if we could bring that same kind of focused cooperative energy to bear on solving other global challenges like climate change and nuclear proliferation. There is no challenge we humans would be incapable of tackling.

Fortunately, globalization and the interdependence it has brought about give us an inbuilt advantage given the massive strides we have made in the fields of communication and technology, it is easier than it has ever been for human beings to communicate and collaborate on projects. If there was ever a time in which we have all the tools we need at our disposal to facilitate global cooperation and collaboration especially in those areas in which systemic risks transcend national boundaries, it is now. Again, the stellar example set by our scientists world-wide in creating life-saving vaccines for humanity, is one that demonstrates this reality and one we should emulate with alacrity.

A compelling reason to pursue the path of active cooperation and collaboration is that we now live in a world where it is not only ineffective for one nation to take actions to tackle global challenges, but it often redounds to the detriment of humanity as a whole. A stark example of this can be seen in the attempts made by various governments during the global financial crisis of 2008 to require their banks to take certain measures to protect their own country's economy. They soon discovered that while a set of decisions made at the national level to protect the national economy was theoretically effective, as a practical matter it could severely harm the well-being and recovery of other nations, and given the interconnectedness of all, those decisions would eventually come to haunt the entire global community.

In the end, just as we fault the Luddites for their failure to recognize that in lieu of smashing the modern looms they were better off embracing the new-fangled machinery and focusing their energy on creating a social system in which income would be redistributed to those who stood to lose their jobs so they would not be unfairly disadvantaged, so too, it behooves us to accept that international trade with all its benefits, also leads to inequalities in income distribution. Therefore, in lieu of focusing our energies on dismantling globalization or slowing it down, both of which would cause inordinate harm to people everywhere, with a disproportionate burden falling on the poor of the world, we should create social systems in which income is equitably redistributed to ensure that all benefit from the positive effects of globalization.

A RADICALLY NEW PERSPECTIVE ON GLOBALIZATION

If we are to make the transition from a knee-jerk reaction to globalization to a mindful crafting of mechanisms to manage the systemic risks and threats it brings with it, we need to motivate ourselves to make the change. Such motivation begins with a reframing of our conception of globalization. To this end we need to let go of our old limiting beliefs and assumptions that globalization is inherently bad for us and that we therefore need to quash or reverse it and instead recognize and embrace it for all the benefits it has brought us, while understanding that we need to develop smarter and effective strategies for managing its downsides.

The teachings of the Bahá'í Faith are extremely relevant and helpful in this respect. To start with, they offer a radically new perspective of the history of humanity. The Universal House of Justice, the governing body of the Bahá'í community states that the Bahá'í perspective includes "a particular conception of history, its course and direction."[7] They expound on this statement with the following words:

> Humanity, it is the firm conviction of every follower of Bahá'u'lláh, is approaching today the crowning stage in a millennia-long process which has brought it from its collective infancy to the threshold of maturity — a stage that will witness the unification of the human race.[8]

This idea that humanity has been on a collective journey taking it from its infancy towards maturity is a recurring theme in the Bahá'í Writings. This evolution towards maturity unfolds in successive developmental stages each of which is characterized by a widening circle of integration and unity. Humanity has grown through various stages in which it has owed its primary loyalty to the family, the tribe, the city-state, and the nation. The Bahá'í Writings affirm that the next inevitable stage in its evolution is global integration and unity:

> Unification of the whole of mankind is the hallmark of the stage which human society is now approaching. Unity of family, of tribe, of city-state, and nation have been successively attempted and fully established. World unity is the goal towards which a harassed humanity is striving.[9]

The Bahá'í Writings attribute much of the turmoil that humanity is currently experiencing, including our global challeng-

---

[7] The Universal House of Justice. Letter to the Bahá'ís of Iran, March 2, 2013.
[8] Ibid.
[9] Shoghi Effendi, *World Order of Bahá'u'lláh*. Wilmette, IL: Bahá'í Publishing Trust, 1991, p. 202.

es, to "... the commotions invariably associated with the most turbulent stage of its evolution, the stage of adolescence." This perspective equips us with an understanding of why our collective lives today are so filled with commotion, turbulence, and chaos and infuses us with hope that this stage of turbulent adolescence will pass and give way to a collective maturity in which "the impetuosity of youth" will gradually be "superseded by the calmness, the wisdom, and the maturity that characterize the stage of manhood."[10] Such a perspective also enables us to recognize that the historical phase through which we are passing represents a distortion of our spirit and does not reflect the essence of who we are. Such an understanding enables us in turn to muster the compassion we deserve to give our poor selves the patience to persevere and make the requisite efforts to get us to the next stage in which the human race will "reach that stature of ripeness which will enable it to acquire all the powers and capacities upon which its ultimate development must depend."[11]

As the Universal House of Justice so clearly states, the process of humanity's maturation entails that the following will occur: "Widely accepted practices and conventions, cherished attitudes and habits, are one by one being rendered obsolete, as the imperatives of maturity begin to assert themselves."[12] These imperatives include the abandonment of old fetishes such as unfettered nationalism which may have been appropriate for humanity during its earlier, immature stages of growth but which now form an impediment to the next stage of its collective development which requires global integration and unity. These old fetishes must then be replaced through the acquisition of "all the powers and capacities upon which its [humanity's] ultimate development must depend"[13] — powers and capacities that meet humanity's needs as it evolves into maturity.

---

[10] Ibid., p. 202.
[11] Ibid.
[12] The Universal House of Justice. Letter to the Bahá'ís of Iran, March 2, 2013.
[13] Shoghi Effendi, *World Order of Bahá'u'lláh*, p. 202.

The central theme of the Bahá'í Revelation is the assertion that humanity's interdependence is a reality which we cannot deny:

> The world is, in truth, moving on towards its destiny. The interdependence of the peoples and nations of the earth, whatever the leaders of the divisive forces of the world may say or do, is already an accomplished fact.[14]

HUMANITY IS A SINGLE ORGANISM

Indeed, the Bahá'í teachings tell us that humanity has become so interdependent and interconnected that it essentially functions as a single organism. Bahá'u'lláh, the prophet-founder of the Bahá'í Faith compared the world to the human body: "Regard the world as the human body which, though at its creation whole and perfect, hath been afflicted, through various causes, with grave disorders and maladies."[15] He says that the "sovereign remedy and mightiest instrument" for healing these illnesses "is the union of all its peoples in one universal Cause, one common Faith" and that this can only be achieved "through the power of a skilled, an all-powerful and inspired Physician."[16]

If we reflect on this analogy of humanity as a single organism in the context of our discussion on globalization, we come to realize that if we were to accept the definition of globalization proposed in this essay as a process of increasing interdependence and integration of humanity over vast distances, then it must follow that, from a Bahá'í perspective, globalization can be viewed as an expression of humanity's evolution towards its collective maturity. We also recognize that the hallmark of that collective maturity will be the unification of the peoples of the

---

[14] Shoghi Effendi. *Promised Day Is Come*. Wilmette, IL: Bahá'í Publishing Trust, 1996, p. 200.
[15] Bahá'u'lláh. *Gleanings From the Writings of Bahá'u'lláh*. Wilmette, IL: Bahá'í Publishing Trust, 1976, CXX, pages 254–255.
[16] Ibid., p. 255.

world. Consequently, we also must admit that our typical reactions to this inexorable march of increasing global integration as manifested in the destructive habits of nationalism, xenophobia, isolationism, and protectionism, simply reflect our immaturity. While understandable, we must take care not to unnecessarily prolong this period of immaturity as it will only lead to increased suffering. Indeed, prolongation of our immaturity will only hinder us from tackling the gravest systemic challenges of our time, including climate change, and nuclear proliferation. It therefore behooves us to resolutely put aside our childish behavior and develop the requisite capacities and tools by which we can manage our systemic risks more intelligently and constructively.

THE ROLE OF SUFFERING

A word must be said about the role of suffering in humanity's process of maturation. The Bahá'í teachings tell us that suffering can and does play an important catalytic role in shifting our mindset and raising awareness of our spiritual reality and collective destiny, which is the ultimate unification of the human race. In this regard, Shoghi Effendi says: "That the forces of a world catastrophe can alone precipitate such a new phase of human thought is, alas, becoming increasingly apparent."[17] The Bahá'í Writings also posit that calamities including the ones caused by the systemic risks associated with globalization and increasing interdependence will serve to "stir the conscience of the world, disillusion the masses, precipitate a radical change in the very conception of society" finally resulting in a coalescing of the "disjointed, the bleeding limbs of mankind into one body, single, organically united, and indivisible."[18] Shoghi Effendi, the Guardian of the Bahá'í Faith and the second authorized interpreter of Baha'u'llah's teachings says that it is unlikely that humanity will heed the lessons of our oneness and achieve global

---

[17] Shoghi Effendi, *World Order of Bahá'u'lláh*, p. 46.
[18] Shoghi Effendi. *Promised Day Is Come*, p. 201.

unity without "intense mental as well as physical agony"[19] He further asserts

> That nothing short of the fire of a severe ordeal, unparalleled in its intensity, can fuse and weld the discordant entities that constitute the elements of present-day civilization, into the integral components of the world commonwealth of the future...[20]

He points to the "violence and vicissitudes" and the consequent fires of suffering occasioned by the Civil War in America that forged its disparate and discordant parts into a single, indivisible nation as an example of the way humanity has typically achieved new milestones in its development.

The Bahá'í Writings also point to further reasons for, and positive by-products of, intense suffering. One of these is that such suffering will instill the kind of responsibility which leaders of the age of humanity's maturity must possess. In the following unequivocal statement, Shoghi Effendi asserts:

> Nothing but a fiery ordeal out of which humanity will emerge, chastened and prepared can succeed in implanting that sense of responsibility which the leaders of a new-born age must arise to shoulder.[21]

Another reason for its suffering, is humanity's refusal to heed to the call of God for today. Consequently, "much suffering will still be required" in order to "engrave in the soul of an unheeding generation those truths and principles that it has disdained to recognize and follow."[22] Moreover, as the following words indicate, this suffering will serve the dual purpose of punishing humanity for this failure while also purifying and preparing it to achieve its collective glorious destiny: "It is at once a visitation

---

[19] Shoghi Effendi, *World Order of Bahá'u'lláh*, p. 45.
[20] Ibid., p. 46.
[21] Ibid.
[22] Ibid., p. 193.

from God and a cleansing process for all mankind"; through it humanity is "being simultaneously called upon to give account of its past actions, and is being purged and prepared for its future mission."[23]

It is interesting to note that while the Bahá'í Revelation introduced these ideas into the world at the time of its birth in the nineteenth century, today, over a hundred and seventy years later, experts in globalization, like Sachs and Goldin, also acknowledge the role of the systemic threats brought about by increasing interdependence and globalization in bringing about shifts in collective growth. In this regard, Sachs expounds upon the role of diseases caused by globalization in shaping societies, economies, and global politics.[24] Goldin on his part talks about the role of suffering and disaster in bringing about the next level of change. He points to the fact that it was the Great Depression of the 1930s that spurred nations to adopt the gold standard thereby coordinating monetary policy. He also cites the shifts that were brought about in the world in the aftermath of World War II, such as the establishment of the United Nations and the Bretton Woods institutions comprising the International Monetary Fund and the World Bank.[25]

PRINCIPLE OF THE ONENESS OF HUMANITY

At the very heart and core of the Bahá'í teachings lies the principle of the oneness of humanity. The Writings themselves view it as "the pivot round which all the teachings of Bahá'u'lláh revolve."[26] The principle of oneness is akin to a law that governs our social existence very much like the law of gravity governs our physical existence. While we can choose to deny or ignore its existence, we do so at our peril. While most of us accept that

---

[23] Shoghi Effendi. *Promised Day Is Come*, p. 6.
[24] Sachs, Jeffrey D. *The Ages of Globalization*. New York: Columbia University Press, 2020, p.x.
[25] Ian Goldin, Mike Mariathasan. *The Butterfly Defect*, pages 202–203.
[26] Shoghi Effendi, *World Order of Bahá'u'lláh*, p. 42.

we would be foolish to attempt building an airplane without taking gravity into account and that we would suffer great harm if we did so, we have been content to blind ourselves to the reality that ignoring the law of oneness in building our political, environmental, economic, and religious institutions, will inevitably lead them to collapse of their own weight. It is no surprise that our social systems are spectacularly crashing about our ears, for we have failed to heed the truth that the principle of the oneness of humanity "implies an organic change in the structure of present-day society, a change such as the world has not yet experienced."[27]

The key to grasping the reality of this principle of oneness requires that we all arrive at "a vision of [our] shared identity and common purpose" without which we "fall into competing ideologies and power struggles" and succumb to "countless permutations of "us" and "them" that fragment us into increasingly narrow group identities and consequently rend the cohesion of our social fabric asunder."[28] The ultimate truth we must come to recognize and embrace is "that humanity is on a common journey in which all are protagonists."[29]

THREE NEW BEHAVIORS

Having armed us with a new set of assumptions grounded in reality and with constructive new beliefs about the experiences that humanity is going through, their reason, purpose, and direction, the Bahá'í Writings also offer a comprehensive blueprint of steps our globalized, interdependent society must take to develop the capacities, powers, and tools that can serve us as we move towards our collective maturity which is marked by deepening integration and the unification of the globe.

---

[27] Ibid., p. 43.
[28] The Universal House of Justice. Letter to the Bahá'ís of the world, January 18, 2019.
[29] Ibid.

NEW GLOBAL INSTITUTIONS

The first step involves the creation of collective decision-making and enforcement institutions fit to meet both the needs and the challenges of humanity in an era of unprecedented interconnectedness. In a world as interdependent as ours, buffeted on every side by a growing number of systemic risks that are global in nature and each of which is increasing in intensity and frequency, it stands to reason that the solutions must also be collective. Yet, we lack the very mechanisms we need, in the form of collective decision-making and enforcement institutions, to meet these challenges effectively. As Goldin points out, our biggest challenge is that "our capacity to manage global issues has not kept pace with the growth in their complexity and danger."[30] He also points out that "Global institutions which may have had some success in the twentieth century are now unfit for purpose."[31]

Another enlightened thinker, Prof. Kishore Mahbubani, offers the following analogy to describe the conundrum in which humanity finds itself. He says that whereas in the past humanity consisted of 193 boats bobbing on the sea of international life, each a self-contained unit intent on not colliding with another, times have changed. Our increased interdependence has made of us a ship consisting of 193 cabins. The problem is that while the affairs of each cabin are served by stewards in charge of that cabin, the ship, as a whole, lacks both captain and crew. It follows that when turbulent storms arise, the ship that is our world is at risk of sinking. When we consider that our global community lacks democratically legitimate global institutions that have the authority to consult, then take swift, effective, and binding decisions to counter the global dangers we face, supported by a global system of enforcement, we understand how susceptible humanity is to systemic global threats and how ill-equipped it currently is for this stage in its journey towards collective maturity.

---

[30] Ian Goldin, *Divided Nations*. Oxford University Press, 2013, p. 2.
[31] Ibid.

The Bahá'í teachings categorically state that the world will eventually need to create "a world government."³² This government will initially come about when

> the majority of the world's nation-states formally commit themselves to a global order comprising institutions and laws and equipped with the means by which collective decisions can be enforced.³³

Then, as humanity continues to evolve and progress, the Baha'i Writings envision the creation of a world federation that will be the ultimate expression of a unified world in a globalized era and will represent the final consummation in society's social evolution. Such a federation must be comprised of certain key institutions.

The first of these is "a world parliament whose members shall be elected by the people in their respective countries and whose election shall be confirmed by their respective governments."³⁴ The members of this world legislature will act "as trustees of the whole of mankind" and will

> ultimately control the entire resources of all the component nations and will enact such laws as shall be required to regulate the life, satisfy the needs and adjust the relationships of all races and peoples.³⁵

In addition, the parliament will have limited rights of taxation. In this way funds will be available to address global challenges. One can imagine that such funds could be used to alleviate the plight of refugees caused by climate change, to assist countries in adapting to climate change, to fund research and development

---

³² Shoghi Effendi. *Citadel of Faith*. Wilmette, IL: Bahá'í Publishing Trust, 1999, p. 33.
³³ The Universal House of Justice. Letter and Memorandum to an individual about Unity of Nations and the Lesser Peace, April 19, 2001.
³⁴ Shoghi Effendi, *World Order of Bahá'u'lláh*, pages 40–41.
³⁵ Ibid., p. 203.

into alternative renewable sources of clean energy, to help governments who need financial bail-outs, and to maintain an international police force. In addition, the Bahá'í vision is that nations will cede all rights they currently have to make war to the parliament, which will be supported by "an international executive adequate to enforce supreme and unchallengeable authority on every recalcitrant member of the commonwealth."[36] This world executive

> backed by an international Force, will carry out the decisions arrived at, and apply the laws enacted by, this world legislature, and will safeguard the organic unity of the whole commonwealth." In addition, "a world tribunal will adjudicate and deliver its compulsory and final verdict in all and any disputes that may arise between the various elements constituting this universal system.[37]

The need for such a world federal government has been apparent for many years. Interestingly, almost a hundred and ten years ago, during 'Abdu'l-Bahá's extensive travels throughout North America, a high official in the U.S. government asked Him how he could best serve his countrymen. 'Abdu'l-Bahá's response was as follows:

> You can best serve your country if you strive, in your capacity as a citizen of the world, to assist in the eventual application of the principle of federalism, underlying the government of your own country, to the relationships now existing between the peoples and nations of the world.[38]

What few realize is that almost a century later, in 2011, in the midst of the global financial crisis, an official of a European cen-

---

[36] Ibid.
[37] Ibid.
[38] Shoghi Effendi. *Advent of Divine Justice*. Wilmette, IL: Bahá'í Publishing Trust, 2006, p. 133.

tral bank came to America to meet with financial officials seeking advice on how to address the financial crisis in Europe. The response was an unusual one: the American officials handed the European a copy of the 1781 Articles of Confederation along with a copy of the 1789 U.S. constitution and advised him to take these home and study them carefully. They observed that the United States had been in a similar quandary when it was a confederation, with grave fiscal difficulties and similar debt problems. In the end, it had concluded that the only way out of the crisis was to forge a stronger and deeper union, moving from a loose association of 13 colonies to a federation with a strong central government possessing certain rights to act in the collective interest of all its federated units.[39]

A SET OF SHARED GLOBAL ETHICS

A careful reading of the Bahá'í Writings seems to indicate that building a global institutional infrastructure to govern the planet is not in itself sufficient. There is another process that must happen in tandem. Leaders of nations must identify and agree upon a set of universal values or shared global ethics and having done so, must mindfully weave them into the very fabric of the new global institutions they establish to meet the needs and challenges of our interdependent world. These foundational principles must also be applied methodically and without compromise to solving any and every global challenge that we encounter. The Universal House of Justice articulated this idea in its message "Promise of World Peace" addressed to the peoples of the world in 1985: "Leaders of governments and all in authority would be well served in their efforts to solve problems if they would first seek to identify the principles involved and then be guided by them."[40] Since then, other progressive and influential think-

---

[39] Story, Louise, and Matthew Saltmarsh. "Europeans Talk of Sharp Change in Fiscal Affairs." *New York Times*, September 5, 2011.

[40] The Universal House of Justice. *The Promise of World Peace*. Wilmette, IL: Bahá'í Publishing Trust, 1985, Part II, p. 28.

ers have echoed this call. One of these was the former foreign minister of Australia and head of the International Crisis group, Gareth Evans, who asserted that after years in governance at the national and international levels he had concluded that the only viable and effective way to solve problems was to identify and agree upon the principles involved first and then apply them to the problem at hand.

Kishore Mahbubani whose analogy of humanity as a ship consisting of 193 cabins was discussed earlier in this essay, points to the weakness inherent in the fact that the affairs of each cabin are governed by the cabin's own unique set of rules. The problem with this approach is that the internal rules of some of the cabins can be harmful to other cabins and can also endanger the ship as a whole. He therefore argues for the need of a shared set of global ethics. Others such as Goldin also argue that it is necessary to make ethics the central concern in our discussions on the future of global governance.[41] In this regard, Sachs says we need to agree upon a model of understanding and ethics on the basis of which we can build a global peace. He refers to this as the challenge of identifying a set of universal values.[42]

In studying the Bahá'í Writings, we can glean certain principles that ought to be included as part of these universal values or shared ethics that underpin and lace the fabric of the institutions comprising the world government envisioned in those Writings. The most important of these is the principle of the oneness of people and nations which the Writings repeatedly highlight — a principle I have already dwelled on at some length. Shoghi Effendi clearly asserts that

> the intermittent crises that convulse present-day society [are] due primarily to the lamentable inability of the world's recognized leaders to read aright the signs of the times ... and to reshape the machinery of their respective governments according to those standards

---

[41] Ian Goldin, *Divided Nations*, p. 167.
[42] Jeffrey D. Sachs, *The Ages of Globalization*, p. 31.

that are implicit in Bahá'u'lláh's supreme declaration of the Oneness of Mankind...[43]

Elsewhere he describes as "pathetic" the efforts of leaders of human institutions who are striving to adjust national processes suited to humankind's days of immaturity when nations were self-contained "to an age which must either achieve the unity of the world... or perish."[44] He further asserts that the principle of the Oneness of Humankind "... represents the consummation of human evolution."[45] Ultimately, he says that the oneness of all nations must be made "the ruling principles of international life."[46]

A corollary principle that flows from this principle of oneness and that is also clearly articulated in the Bahá'í Writings, is that we must "not hesitate to subordinate every particular interest, be it personal, regional or national, to the over-riding interests of the generality of mankind" because we know full well that

> in a world of interdependent peoples and nations the advantage of the part is best to be reached by the advantage of the whole and that no lasting result can be achieved by any of the component parts if the general interests of the entity itself are neglected...[47]

Another related and key principle articulated in the Bahá'í Writings that we would do well to agree upon is the necessity of curtailing "unfettered national sovereignty."[48] Shoghi Effendi says that

> the anarchy inherent in state sovereignty is moving towards a climax. A world, growing to maturity, must abandon this fetish, recognize the oneness and wholeness of human relationships, and establish once for all

---

[43] Shoghi Effendi, *World Order of Bahá'u'lláh*, p. 36.
[44] Ibid.
[45] Ibid., p. 43.
[46] Ibid., p. 193.
[47] Shoghi Effendi, *Promised Day Is Come*, p. viii.
[48] Shoghi Effendi, *World Order of Bahá'u'lláh*, p. 40.

the machinery that can best incarnate this fundamental principle of its life.[49]

The Universal House of Justice unpacks this idea further by saying that "Unbridled nationalism, as distinguished from a sane and legitimate patriotism, must give way to a wider loyalty, to the love of humanity."[50]

The principle of collective security set forth in the Bahá'í Writings is a cornerstone principle that leaders would do well to agree upon and apply. During His life, Bahá'u'lláh called on the kings to be united saying "should any one among you take up arms against another, rise ye all against him, for this is naught but manifest justice."[51] The Bahá'í Writings envision that a number of "[d]istinguished and high-minded sovereigns" will arise to establish Universal Peace. To this end, they must conclude a binding treaty. The treaty should, amongst other things, limit the quantity of armaments each government can possess to what is needed to preserve internal order within its borders. Most crucially, the Treaty should provide that if any government violates any of its provisions, all the governments will "arise to reduce it to utter submission."[52]

Another key foundational principle is that force is to be used solely in service of justice. The Bahá'í Writings envision that although humanity will reach the degree of maturity in which nations will no longer resort to force as an instrument of international relations, the world government that is established to ensure the peace, security, and collective well-being of humanity will have an international force at its disposal that "will safeguard the organic unity" of the world.[53] 'Abdu'l-Bahá goes so far as to say there are occasions when the use of force is appropriate:

---

[49] Ibid., p. 202.
[50] The Universal House of Justice, *The Promise of World Peace*, p. 25.
[51] Bahá'u'lláh. *Gleanings*, CXIX, p. 254.
[52] 'Abdu'l-Bahá, *Secret of Divine Civilization*. Wilmette, IL: Bahá'í Publishing Trust, 2015, p. 76.
[53] Shoghi Effendi, *World Order of Bahá'u'lláh*, p. 203.

"there are times when war becomes the powerful basis of peace, and ruin the very means of reconstruction."[54]

RESPONDING TO SKEPTICS

There will undoubtedly be those who are skeptical that it is possible to get all nations to agree upon a shared set of global ethics. Fortunately, humanity's relatively recent experience in identifying and agreeing upon a principle, known as "the Responsibility to Protect," demonstrates that such a feat is indeed achievable. Moreover, it is encouraging to note that it only took five years for this principle to go from initial conceptualization in 2001 to endorsement by representatives of all nations gathered at the World Summit in New York in 2005. Fortunately, we can now use the process followed in arriving at this success as a roadmap to follow in agreeing upon other principles that can form part of a new set of global ethics that will meet humanity's needs as it moves inexorably towards unity and its collective maturity.

ELECTING FIT LEADERS

Our treatment of a Bahá'í-inspired response to the systemic risks brought on by the process of globalization and increasing interdependence would be incomplete without considering a third category of action to be layered in with the first two categories of building a world government and achieving consensus around a set of shared first principles. This third category involves training ourselves to elect leaders who have the requisite qualities and motivations that render them fit to meet humanity's needs as it stands on the threshold of maturity for, as 'Abdu'l-Bahá astutely observes,

> any agency whatever, though it be the instrument of mankind's greatest good, is capable of misuse. Its proper

---

[54] 'Abdu'l-Bahá, *Secret of Divine Civilization*, p. 82–83.

use or abuse depends on the varying degrees of enlightenment, capacity, faith, honesty, devotion, and high-mindedness of the leaders of public opinion.[55]

The Bahá'í Writings highlight some of the key qualities our leaders must possess; they include honesty, lack of prejudice, a spirit of service, selflessness, competence, wisdom, compassion, and the all-important quality of working for the collective interests of humanity. In this regard, Bahá'u'lláh addressing the elected representatives of the people in every land says: "Take ye counsel together, and let your concern be only for that which profiteth mankind and bettereth the condition thereof..."[56]

The Bahá'í Writings suggest that if we are to be successful in electing leaders fit for purpose, we must first change our concept of power and let go of outworn assumptions that power is "a means of domination."[57] Instead, we should come to associate the concept of power with "words such as "release", "encourage", "channel," "Guide" and "enable"" and we should come to understand that "Power is not a finite entity which is to be "seized" and "jealously guarded"" but rather that "it constitutes a limitless capacity to transform that resides in the human race as a body."[58] Current thinkers like Goldin also highlight the importance of having a visionary leadership that can comprehend and manage our looming global challenges.[59]

CONCLUSION

If we begin from the premise that globalization can be understood as the growing interdependence and integration of human society across vast distances, it seems reasonable to conclude

---

[55] Ibid., p. 16.
[56] Bahá'u'lláh. *Gleanings*, CXX, p. 254.
[57] The Universal House of Justice. Letter to the Bahá'ís of Iran, March 2, 2013, p. 4.
[58] Ibid.
[59] Ian Goldin, *Divided Nations*, p. 46.

that within the framework of the Bahá'í Writings, we can construe globalization as the tangible expression of humanity's progress towards its collective maturity. Furthermore, we can further conclude that the systemic risks to which this increasing interdependence has made us susceptible can and ought to be managed and contained by doing three things: firstly, establishing a world government comprising of collective decision-making and enforcement institutions along the lines discussed in this essay; secondly, identifying and achieving consensus around a set of global ethics that will be woven into the fabric of this new institutional infrastructure and also applied methodically and without compromise to tackling global challenges; and thirdly, reframing our concept of the role of power and those in authority and insisting that our leaders possess certain key qualities of character and selfless motivation.

Imagine how different our world would look if we were to follow this roadmap. We would finally have a world in which critical natural resources including food, water, and energy are equitably managed and distributed, in which the quantity of arms possessed by each nation is strictly restricted to what is necessary to maintain internal order thereby liberating humanity from the fear and suspicion that lead to ever-escalating arms races and consequently from the scourge of both conventional and nuclear wars. It would mean that our current fears of a potential war between the United States and China over Taiwan or between the United States and Russia over Ukraine, and our fears of uncontrolled nuclear proliferation would finally be put to rest. It would also mean that we would finally have the mechanisms to manage and mitigate the existential global challenge that is climate change in an effective manner and to manage our financial and economic affairs in a coordinated fashion that protects us from recurring and destabilizing financial crises. Last, but not least, we would have the tools to tackle global pandemics swiftly, fairly, and effectively without falling into the old traps of nationalistic, competitive, and self-destructive behaviors. In sum, we would live in a world that is at peace and secure in which we would finally have the opportunity to fulfill our highest potential both as individuals and as a global community. Surely this is a goal worth striving for!

REFERENCES AND CITATIONS

'Abdu'l-Bahá. *Secret of Divine Civilization.* Wilmette, IL: Bahá'í Publishing Trust, 2015.

Bahá'u'lláh. *Gleanings From the Writings of Bahá'u'lláh.* Wilmette, IL: Bahá'í Publishing Trust, 1976.

Goldin, Ian. *Divided Nations.* Oxford University Press, 2013.

Goldin, Ian; Mariathasan, Mike. *The Butterfly Defect.* Princeton University Press, 2016.

Sachs, Jeffrey D. *The Ages of Globalization.* New York: Columbia University Press, 2020.

Shoghi Effendi. *World Order of Bahá'u'lláh.* Wilmette, IL: Bahá'í Publishing Trust, 1991.

Shoghi Effendi. *Promised Day Is Come.* Wilmette, IL: Bahá'í Publishing Trust, 1996.

Shoghi Effendi. *Citadel of Faith.* Wilmette, IL: Bahá'í Publishing Trust, 1999.

Shoghi Effendi. *Advent of Divine Justice.* Wilmette, IL: Bahá'í Publishing Trust, 2006.

Story, Louise, and Matthew Saltmarsh. "Europeans Talk of Sharp Change in Fiscal Affairs." *New York Times*, September 5, 2011.

The Universal House of Justice. Letter to the Bahá'ís of Iran, March 2, 2013.

The Universal House of Justice. Letter to the Bahá'ís of the world, January 18, 2019.

The Universal House of Justice. Letter and Memorandum to an individual about Unity of Nations and the Lesser Peace, April 19, 2001.

The Universal House of Justice. *The Promise of World Peace.* Wilmette, IL: Bahá'í Publishing Trust, 1985.

Building a Just and Sustainable Global Food System: Some Guiding Principles

PAUL HANLEY

In late March 2020, I went to a major supermarket in my hometown, Saskatoon, to buy flour. There was none to be had. In fact, the entire baking section, usually stocked to overflowing, was empty. Why had the basic staple of the Western diet, wheat, disappeared from the shelves? After all, Saskatoon is in Saskatchewan, where farmers produce 15 million tonnes of wheat every year, about 15 tonnes (540 bushels) per resident.

The problem was, of course, triggered by the arrival of Covid-19. But, surely, supplies had not run out so quickly? No, the issue was demand: when normal life routines shut down due to the pandemic, people decided to stock up on food items in the event of shortages and also to devote some of their spare time to making their own baked goods. There was no shortage of wheat in storage, but supply chains couldn't react quickly enough to fill the explosive demand, especially with many workers staying home to prevent the spread of a frightening and potentially fatal new disease.

While it wasn't long before this particular supply issue was sorted, the pandemic exposed weaknesses in the food system. If local supply chains could falter, what could we expect from the long supply chains that characterize a global food system?

While for middle-class Canadians, supply issues were a short-term inconvenience, the pandemic had dire consequences for many segments of the global population. According the World Food Program, an estimated 270 million people faced potentially life-threatening food shortages in 2021, compared to 150 million before the pandemic. The number of people on the brink of famine, the most severe phase of a hunger crisis, jumped to 41 million from 34 million in the previous year.¹ Overall, more than 2.3 billion people (or 30 percent of the global population) lacked year-round access to adequate food: this indicator — known as the prevalence of moderate or severe food insecurity — leapt in one year as much in as the preceding five combined.²

Supply interruptions due to restricted trade flows in food systems highly dependent on imports was one factor, but the pandemic's impact on food and agriculture was multifaceted. Restrictions on the movement of farm labourers, for instance, impacted supply but also incomes, as job losses reduced purchasing power and interrupted the flow of remittances to the families of agricultural workers. School meal program cancelations impacted the poorest segments of the population, even in higher income countries. And, of course, the illness itself killed millions and sickened tens of millions.

As the pandemic drags on, how will the food system manage? Will there be future variants — and future pandemics — to contend with? And, more ominous, how will climate change impact our food supply?

The last question gained new urgency in the summer of 2021. Across Canada, summer temperature records were shattered, with temperatures reaching unheard of highs of 50C under a "heat dome". Widespread wildfires filled the air with smoke. Crop reports for the Canadian Prairies³ anticipated low yields due to drought and heat. The problem was by no means confined to Canada. Five heat domes formed over landmasses in the Northern Hemisphere.⁴ Heat and fire were so widespread that a historian specializing in the history of wildfire published a book titled,

---

[1] Christina Goldbaum, No work, no food: Coronavirus pandemic deepens global hunger, *New York Times*, August 6, 2021.

[2] UN report: Pandemic year marked by spike in world hunger, accessed at www.fao.org/news/story/en/item/1415595/icode/

[3] Saskatchewan Ministry of Agriculture, Crop Report for the Period July 27 to August 2, 2021, August 5, 2021.

[4] Jason Samenow, The Northern Hemisphere has a punishing heat wave infestation, *The Washington Post*, posted July 20, 2021.

The Pyrocene: How We Created an Age of Fire, and What Happens Next.[5] As we witnessed the "pyric pandemic" unfold, we were forced to accept that the consequences of a changing climate were arriving sooner than climate scientists had anticipated.

With similar conditions unfolding across multiple regions, the near and longer term outlooks for agroecosystems are troubling, to say the least. Equally troubling are the impacts of a warming climate on natural ecosystems, including marine systems. The high heat events of 2021, for example, killed billions of marine creatures, like mussels, clams, and oysters, in the Pacific Northwest. "In changing our planet's climate," writes environmental journalist Stephen Leahy, in an article titled "If the Hardest Species are Boiled Alive, What Happens to Humans,"[6] "we're permanently altering the natural world that is our life-support system. And we're seeing this happen in real time." He continues:

> As the marine biologist and National Geographic explorer in residence Enric Sala told me, 'Every morsel of food, every sip of water, the air we breathe is the result of work done by other species. Nature gives us everything we need to survive. Without them, there is no us.

Climate change "threatens our ability to ensure global food security, eradicate poverty, and achieve sustainable development," reports the UN Food and Agriculture Organization (FAO).[7]

> Climate change has both direct and indirect effects on agricultural productivity including changing rainfall patterns, drought, flooding, and the geographical redistribution of pests and diseases. Those most threatened

---

[5] Stephen J. Pyne, *The Pyrocene: How We Created an Age of Fire, and What Happens Next*, University of California Press, September 2021.
[6] Stephen Leahy, If the Hardest Species Are Boiled Alive, What Happens to Humans? *The Atlantic*, posted July 31, 2021, www.theatlantic.com/ideas/archive/2021/07/billions-victims-heat-dome/619604/.
[7] FAO, Climate Change and your food: Ten Facts, www.fao.org/news/story/en/item/356770/icode/

are the 75% of the world's poor and food insecure people who rely on agriculture and natural resources for their livelihoods.

While the FAO estimates that world food production must rise 60% to keep pace with population growth, the Intergovernmental Panel on Climate Change (IPCC) predicts crop yield declines of 10–25% may be widespread by 2050. Meanwhile, rising temperatures are predicted to reduce catches of the world's main fish species by 40%.

We are facing an existential crisis. In an article in the *Guardian* titled "The IPCC report is clear: nothing short of transforming society will avert catastrophe,"[8] the United Kingdom's chief scientific adviser, Patrick Vallance, states,

> The climate crisis is as much a rural problem as an urban one. It is both economic and human, domestic and international. This means transformation is required at every level of society: individuals, employers, institutions, and international partners will need to work together to understand the trade-offs, agree on compromises and seize opportunities. And just as scientists are pooling insights from diverse fields of expertise, policymakers will need to work in new ways, sharing ideas across disciplines to plot a clear path from here to net zero. This is a whole systems challenge. Tackling it will require a systemic approach.

A call for transformative change is even more emphatic considering that a variety of threats to stability—environmental, social, financial, and political—are mounting at the same time, raising the possibility of what the political scientist Thomas Homer-Dixon calls synchronous failure, where breakdowns in one system cascade across other systems. This may already be happening with respect to the global food system.

---

[8] Patrick Vallance, *The Guardian*, August 9, 2021, www.theguardian.com/commentisfree/2021/aug/09/ipcc-report-transforming-society-avert-catastrophe-net-zero.

"I have never seen it as bad globally as it is right now," Amer Daoudi, senior director of operations of the World Food Program. "Usually you have two, three, four crises—like conflicts, famine—at one time. But now we're talking about quite a number of significant crises happening simultaneously across the globe."[9]

It is increasingly evident the foundations of human progress—including the agriculture and food system—are threatened.

Diagnosing the Disease

In the 19th century, Bahá'u'lláh, Founder of the Bahá'í Faith, foresaw the threats to civilization and identified their root cause:

> The civilization, so often vaunted by the learned exponents of arts and sciences, will, if allowed to overleap the bounds of moderation, bring great evil upon men. Thus warneth you He Who is the All-Knowing. If carried to excess, civilization will prove as prolific a source of evil as it had been of goodness when kept within the restraints of moderation... The day is approaching when its flame will devour the cities...[10]
>
> If a thing is carried to excess, it will prove a source of evil. Consider the civilization of the West, how it hath agitated and alarmed the peoples of the world...[11]

He goes on to state, in a possible allusion to the environmental crises of today, that, "Strange and astonishing things exist in the earth... These things are capable of changing the whole atmosphere of the earth and their contamination would prove lethal."[12] In discussing these and similar warnings, the Guardian of the Bahá'í Faith, Shoghi Effendi, zeroed in on the root problem iden-

---

[9] Christina Goldbaum, No work, no food: Coronavirus pandemic deepens global hunger, *New York Times,* August 6, 2021.
[10] Bahá'u'lláh, *Gleanings from the Writings of Bahá'u'lláh,* CLXIV.
[11] Bahá'u'lláh, *Tablets of Bahá'u'lláh revealed after the Kitáb-i-Aqdas,* 69.
[12] ibid.

tified by Bahá'u'lláh and further elaborated its consequences. After speaking of a moral crisis affecting the world, the Guardian stated:

> Parallel with this, and pervading all departments of life…is the crass materialism, which lays excessive and ever-increasing emphasis on material well being, forgetful of those things of the spirit on which alone a sure and stable foundation can be laid for human society. It is this same cancerous materialism, born originally in Europe, carried to excess in the North American continent, contaminating the Asiatic peoples and nations, spreading its ominous tentacles to the borders of Africa, and now invading its very heart, which Bahá'u'lláh in unequivocal and emphatic language denounced in His Writings, comparing it to a devouring flame and regarding it as the chief factor in precipitating the dire ordeals and world-shaking crises that must necessarily involve the burning of cities and the spread of terror and consternation in the hearts of men.[13]

These statements align with our understanding of the roots of the environmental crisis, including climate change. The core problem is humanity's excessive ecological footprint resulting from the excessive consumption of resources, especially energy, and the consequent release of wastes and emissions, including greenhouse gases. Evidence shows that the human ecological footprint, already exceeding Earth's carrying capacity by more that 60%, it on track to exceed Earth's capacity by as much as 500% by century's end, as it rises in lockstep with Gross World Product.[14]

Rather than moving decisively to address such issues, real human progress is stymied by a near anarchy in global governance, the rise of extreme political partisanship, the rejection of reason, the cynical manipulation of public opinion, and the entrench-

---

[13] Shoghi Effendi, *Citadel of Faith*, 125.
[14] See Paul Hanley, *Eleven*, Friesen Press, 2014, 50–52.

ment of economic self-interest as an operating principle for society.

In the 19th century, as the Industrial Revolution intensified, Bahá'u'lláh had warned the peoples of the world that, "The signs of impending convulsions and chaos can now be discerned, inasmuch as the prevailing Order appeareth to be lamentably defective."[15] This will have consequences, He continued: "an unforeseen calamity is following them and that grievous retribution awaiteth them," and furthermore, that "there is no place to flee to, no refuge that any one can seek..." Wealth and position will not protect us, as we now see the catastrophic impacts of climate change in the wealthiest and most privileged locales on Earth.

Grave dangers face humanity as result of its excesses, yet the Guardian further explains[16] that, given humanity's intransigence, the impending crises are a necessary step to the achievement of a new world order built around the pivotal principle of the unity of humankind. He anticipates a:

> ...transformation of unparalleled majesty and scope which humanity is in this age bound to undergo. That the forces of a world catastrophe can alone precipitate such a new phase of human thought is, alas, becoming increasingly apparent. That nothing short of the fire of a severe ordeal, unparalleled in its intensity, can fuse and weld the discordant entities, that constitute the elements of present-day civilization, into the integral components of the world Commonwealth of the future is a truth which future events will increasingly demonstrate... Nothing but a fiery ordeal, out of which humanity will emerge, chastened and prepared, can succeed in implanting that sense of responsibility which the leaders of a new-born age must arise to shoulder.

---

[15] Shoghi Effendi, *The World Order of Bahá'u'lláh*, 161–163.
[16] Ibid. 33–48.

The Guardian argues that conventional or human-devised solutions will never be sufficient to solve this dilemma, because they would fail to address the root cause.

> Nor would any general scheme of mere organized international co-operation, in whatever sphere of human activity, however ingenious in conception or extensive in scope, succeed in removing the root cause of the evil that has so rudely upset the equilibrium of present day society. Not even, I venture to assert, would the very act of devising the machinery required for the political and economic unification of the world — a principle that has been increasingly advocated in recent times — provide in itself the antidote against the poison that is steadily undermining the vigour of organized peoples and nations.
>
> What else, might we not confidently affirm, but the unreserved acceptance of the Divine Programme enunciated, with such simplicity and force...by Bahá'u'lláh, embodying in its essentials God's divinely-appointed scheme for the unification of humankind in this age, coupled with an indomitable conviction in the unfailing efficacy of each and all of its provisions, is eventually capable of withstanding the forces of internal disintegration which, if unchecked, must needs continue to eat into the vitals of a despairing society. It is towards this goal — the goal of a new World Order, Divine in origin, all-embracing in scope, equitable in principle, challenging in its features — that a harassed humanity must strive.

Prescribing the Remedy

"The All-Knowing Physician hath His finger on the pulse of mankind," explains Bahá'u'lláh. "He perceiveth the disease, and prescribeth, in His unerring wisdom, the remedy."[17] Bahá'u'lláh

---

[17] Bahá'u'lláh, *The Tabernacle of Unity*, 18.

did not stop with a diagnosis of the underlying "disease". He also prescribed the remedy: a new world order built on spiritual principles derived from the Word of God.

> The purging of such deeply rooted and overwhelming corruptions cannot be effected unless the peoples of the world unite in pursuit of one common aim and embrace one universal faith.[18]
> That which the Lord hath ordained as the sovereign remedy and mightiest instrument for the healing of all the world is the union of all its peoples in one universal Cause, one common Faith. This can in no wise be achieved except through the power of a skilled, an all-powerful and inspired Physician.[19]

Building and sustaining civilization is, He clearly states, the purpose of our creation: "All men have been created to carry forward an ever-advancing civilization."[20] The Divine ordinances revealed by Bahá'u'lláh are the means of preserving civilization and the ecosphere on which it is founded and sustained.

> O people of Bahá! Each one of the ordinances We have revealed is a mighty stronghold for the preservation of the world of being. Verily, this Wronged One desireth naught but your security and elevation. ."[21]
> ...the precepts laid down by God constitute the highest means for the maintenance of order in the world and the security of its peoples. He that turneth away from them is accounted among the abject and foolish. We, verily, have commanded you to refuse the dictates of your evil passions and corrupt desires, and not to trans-

---

[18] Bahá'u'lláh, *Tablets of Bahá'u'lláh revealed after the Kitáb-i-Aqdas*, 69.
[19] Bahá'u'lláh, *Gleanings from the Writings of Bahá'u'lláh*, 254–255.
[20] Bahá'u'lláh, *Gleanings from the Writings of Bahá'u'lláh*, 215.
[21] Bahá'u'lláh, *Tablets of Bahá'u'lláh revealed after the Kitáb-i-Aqdas*, 69.

gress the bounds which the Pen of the Most High hath fixed, for these are the breath of life unto all created things."[22]

The Bahá'í Writings contain a wealth of concepts and principles to guide the development of the new world order. Although the Bahá'í revelation emerged in the modern, industrial era, Bahá'u'lláh identified agriculture as foremost among the fundamental principles for organizing human affairs.

Agriculture in the World Order of Bahá'u'lláh

In the Tablet of the World[23], revealed in 1891, Bahá'u'lláh outlined "that which is conducive to the advancement of mankind and to the reconstruction of the world." He identified several principles that would contribute to achieving social order, including international cooperation and disarmament; a new ethos of universal fellowship, epitomized by the adoption of a common auxiliary language; the training and education of children; and agricultural development. Bahá'u'lláh stated that "special regard must be paid to agriculture," as "unquestionably" it preceded the other principles in importance.

A survey of the Bahá'í writings indicates more than 100 concepts, principles, or laws relevant to agriculture and food. Together, they provide a vision and guide for people, now and in future, to design a global food system. Importantly, this discourse is not overly prescriptive; a key point is that effective systems, although inspired by the Writings, will be co-designed collaboratively by three protagonists involved in civilization building, individuals, institutions, and communities, based on their assessment of conditions and using a process of planning, action, reflection, and adjustment.

In the World Order of Bahá'u'lláh[24], Shoghi Effendi wrote that

---

[22] Bahá'u'lláh, *Gleanings from the Writings of Bahá'u'lláh*, 331.
[23] Bahá'u'lláh, *Tablets of Bahá'u'lláh revealed after the Kitáb-i-Aqdas*, 89–90
[24] Shoghi Effendi, *World Order of Bahá'u'lláh*, 19.

> ...(Bahá'u'lláh) as well as 'Abdu'l-Bahá after Him, has, unlike the Dispensations of the past, clearly and specifically laid down a set of Laws, established definite institutions, and provided for the essentials of a Divine Economy.

However, these do not take the form of detailed teachings on technical economics; instead, principles are provided to guide the Universal House of Justice and future economists. These teachings typically apply at the international, national, and local levels, and many are relevant to food and agricultural systems.

Although closely linked, for the purposed of exposition, the Bahá'í teachings on this topic might be divided into four areas: building unified and prosperous communities; building individual capacity for service; building a just and equitable world order; and sustaining an ever-advancing civilization. Three of these areas correspond, in general, to the activities of the three protagonists. The fourth involves the relationship of the protagonists with the ecosphere and the myriad species with which we cohabit.

A simple diagram showing the four key elements of the model suggested in the Writings is shown below.

Several major themes emerge in this exploration: the centrality of agriculture in the world order of Bahá'u'lláh; agriculture's role in achieving universal, equitable prosperity; our responsibility to ensure the sustainability of natural systems; and the importance of building capacity in individuals, communities, and institutions to achieve these objectives.

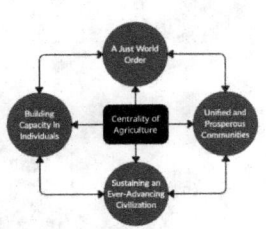

BUILDING UNIFIED AND PROSPEROUS COMMUNITIES

The Bahá'í teachings with regard to the social and economic development of communities are extensive, including many Writings related to rural communities and their agricultural endeavours. Abdu'l-Bahá said that the development process "begins with the village, and when the village is reconstructed, then the cities will be also."[25] Thus, the global food system is built up from local and regional communities that have achieved a high degree of food security and sovereignty. The teachings provide a number of guidelines for building unified and prosperous communities, as summarized in the following diagram.

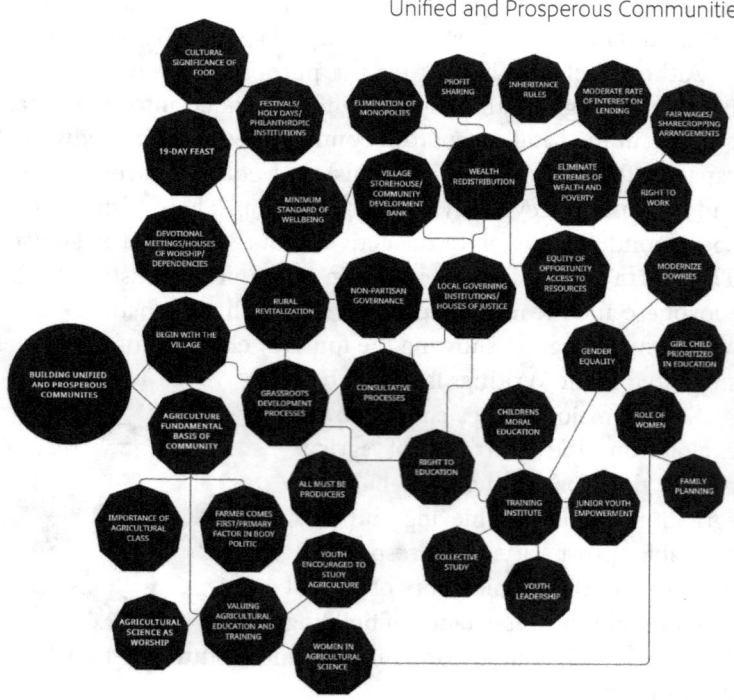

Elements of a Bahá'í Approach to Building Unified and Prosperous Communities

RECOGNIZING THE STATION OF FARMERS

'Abdu'l-Bahá asserted that the transformation of economic systems as envisaged by the Bahá'í teachings

---

[25] qtd. in Bahá'í World, Vol. 4, 450–451.

must commence with the farmer and then be extended to the other classes inasmuch as the number of farmers is greater than all other classes, many, many times greater. Therefore, it is fitting that the economic problem be first solved with the farmer, for the farmer is the first active agent in the body politic.[26]

While demographics have shifted since 'Abdu'l-Bahá's time, farmers and other agricultural workers remain the largest occupational group.

GRASSROOTS AND CONSULTATIVE PROCESSES

"Stirrings as the grassroots" are the beginning of the development process, as members of local communities themselves read their reality and identify ways to improve it.

Progress in the development field will largely depend on natural stirrings at the grassroots, and it should receive its driving force from those sources rather than from an imposition of plans and programs from the top.[27]

Thus, perfecting the practice of consultation is an essential element of the development process. In fact, Bahá'u'lláh has stated,

No welfare and no well-being can be attained except through consultation.[28] ...should the people of a village consult one another about their affairs," 'Abdu'l-Bahá said, "the right solution will certainly be revealed. In

---

[26] The Redistribution of Wealth — Some Specific Measures. Extracts from the Bahá'í Writings and from Letters written by or on behalf of Shoghi Effendi and the Universal House of Justice. Comp. The Research Department of the Universal House of Justice, May 1 1997, 4.

[27] From a letter from the Universal House of Justice to the Baha'is of the World, 20 October 1983.

[28] Consultation: A Compilation. Extracts from the Writings and Utterances of Bahá'u'lláh, 'Abdu'l-Bahá, Shoghi Effendi, and The Universal House of Justice. Comp. Research Department of the Universal House of Justice, Wilmette, Ill.: National Spiritual Assembly of the Bahá'ís of the United States, 1980, 3.

like manner, the members of each profession, such as in industry, should consult..."[29]

A Non-Partisan Governance Model

Local Spiritual Assemblies, the Bahá'í community's governing institutions, are consultative bodies elected through a unique, non-partisan voting system. They are charged with administering the affairs of the community and operate in close communication with the community members, through means such as the consultative portion of the 19-Day Feast, a regular community gathering with a spiritual, administrative, and social function.

Among many functions, local Assemblies have the responsibility "to lend their support to agricultural and industrial development, to consolidate the foundations of mutual assistance and co-operation..."[30]

> The Local Spiritual Assemblies...must gradually widen the scope of their activities, not only to develop every aspect of the spiritual life of the believers within their jurisdiction, but also, through Bahá'í consultation, and through such Bahá'í principles as harmony between science and religion, the importance of education, and work as a form of worship, to promote the standards of agriculture and other skills in the life of the people.[31]

In addition to their unifying, community-building function, feasts, as well as observances of holy days, are seen as opportunities to initiate projects.

---

[29] Ibid. 176

[30] Shoghi Effendi, gtd. In Trustworthiness. A compilation of extracts from the Bahá'í Writings. Comp. Research Department of the Universal House of Justice. London: The Bahá'í Publishing Trust, 1987, 21.

[31] From a letter written on behalf of the Universal House of Justice to an individual believer dated 27 July 1976, Agriculture and Rural Life — Additional Extracts. Comp. The Research Department of the Universal House of Justice, 1995, 3.

During such blessed days, institutions should be founded that may be of permanent benefit and value to the people...Therefore, the intelligent must...investigate reality to find out what important affair, what philanthropic institutions are most needed and what foundations should be laid for the community... If, however, the community is in need of widening the circle of commerce or industry or agriculture they should start the means so that the desired aim may be attained...[32]

The Mashriqu'l-Adhkár

The institution of the Mashriqu'l-Adhkár, i.e. the House of Worship and its dependencies, are focal centres of development. Bahá'u'lláh has stated that Houses of Worship, open to everyone, will form

> the spiritual centre of every Bahá'í community round which must flourish dependencies dedicated to the social, humanitarian, educational and scientific advancement of mankind...[33] The first part to be built is the central edifice which is the spiritual heart of the community. Then, gradually, as the outward expression of this spiritual heart, the various dependencies, those 'institutions of social service as shall afford relief to the suffering, sustenance to the poor...and education to the ignorant' are erected and function.[34]

The Mashriqu'l-Adhkár will foster scientific research and development, including agricultural science, described in the Writings as a "noble science."[35]

---

[32] 'Abdu'l-Bahá, *Lights of Guidance*, 304–305.
[33] From a letter from the Universal House of Justice to the Baha'is of the World, 20 October 1983.
[34] Agriculture and Rural Life — Additional Extracts. Comp. The Research Department of the Universal House of Justice, May 1, 1997, 3.
[35] 'Abdu'l-Bahá, from a Tablet translated from the Persian, qtd. In Conservation of the Earth's Resources, https://www.bahai.org/documents/com-

Gender Equity

The Bahá'í teachings place great importance on gender equity. Women play a significant but often undervalued role in agricultural production. Through measures such as the promotion of gender equality in all areas, the prioritization of the girl child in education, reform of dowry laws, freedom to choose one's own marriage partner, and the emphasis on women's engagement in agricultural science, women take on a full and equal role in rural development. The advancement of women is a proven key to reducing the population growth rate.

The Village Storehouse

'Abdu'l-Bahá provides a model for village development, commonly called "The Village Storehouse" or the "House of Finance." The model is site specific; driven by the community itself; involves a general plan for development, including education, health care and social welfare; serves to ameliorate vagaries of climate which can lead to economic instability; provides measures for obtaining credit and for income stabilization; and seeks to broaden the bases of development by exploiting non-agricultural as well as agricultural opportunities. Several of the salient points of this model are taken from the writings of 'Abdu'l-Bahá.

The village storehouse is an institution created to administer the economic activities of the village. It serves as a "community development bank" which takes in, manages and redistributes revenues. "In every village there must be established a general storehouse which will have a number of revenues."[36] It is administered by an elected board and financed by various revenues, including a progressive income tax.

> Each person in the community whose income is equal to his individual producing capacity shall be exempt from

---

piled-research-department-universal-house-of-justice/conservation-earths-resources.

[36] 'Abdu'l-Bahá, *Foundations of World Unity*. 2d ed. Wilmette, Ill.: Bahá'í Publishing Trust, 1972, 39–41.

taxation. But if his income is greater than his needs he must pay a tax until an adjustment is effected. That is to say, a man's capacity for production and his needs will be equalized and reconciled through taxation.[37]

Revenues are redistributed in several ways. If for example a village member's "necessities exceed his production he shall receive an amount sufficient to equalize or adjust. Therefore taxation will be proportionate to capacity and production and there will be no poor in the community."[38] The storehouse will stabilize incomes, provide social services, and support community development measures.

'Abdu'l-Bahá's said that His ideas were intended as a model rather than a prescription:

> What hath been stated is only an example and this doth not mean that it should be enforced exactly in this manner... These are only the preliminary principles; the House of Justice will arrange and widen them in accordance with time and place.[39]

BUILDING INDIVIDUAL CAPACITY

A system can't be so good that people within it do not have to be good. No matter how well designed and organized, for the system to function well, the individuals within it must buy in to it, support it, and cooperate with and within it. In the context of a systems approach, achieving an effective and resilient food and agriculture system will be dependent on the values, qualities, and capacities of its participants, the whole population.

---

[37] Ibid., 37.
[38] Ibid., 37.
[39] From a Tablet dated 25 July 1919 to an individual believer, provisional translation from the Persian, in Extracts from the Bahá'í Writings on the Subject of Economics, Agriculture and Related Subjects. Comp. The Research Department of the Universal House of Justice, 2000. https://bahai-library.com/compilation_economics_agriculture.

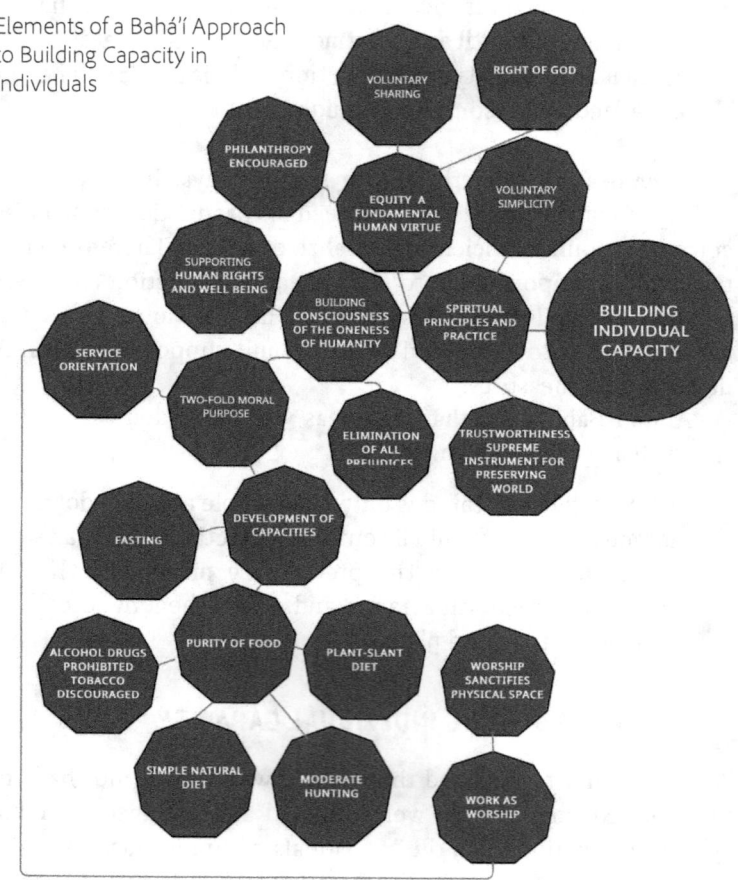

Elements of a Bahá'í Approach to Building Capacity in Individuals

While space does not permit a full discussion of the function of individuals in the food system, it is important at minimum to state that the Bahá'í teachings offer a comprehensive approach to the development of the capacities of individuals to assume a two-fold moral purpose, to develop their material and spiritual capabilities, skills, and talents and to offer these in service to their communities. Briefly, this process is facilitated initially in one's family and is augmented through the activities of a training institute, which engages children, youth, and adults in moral education and acts of service. The educational process encourages the development of socially constructive qualities, particularly trustworthiness, freedom from prejudice, and equity. The Bahá'í teachings also support voluntary simplicity and sharing, a healthy lifestyle, and an understanding that work done in a spirit of service is a form of worship. Personal development is reinforced through participation in practices such as daily prayer and meditation and study of the Bahá'í writings. As indicated in the diagram, building individual capacity is integral to the Bahá'í vision.

Individuals are encouraged to engage in productive activities. Wealth is praiseworthy, but only under certain conditions.

> Wealth is praiseworthy in the highest degree, if it is acquired by an individual's own efforts and the grace of God, in commerce, agriculture, art and industry, and if it be expended for philanthropic purposes. Above all, if a judicious and resourceful individual should initiate measures which would universally enrich the masses of the people, there could be no undertaking greater than this, and it would rank in the sight of God as the supreme achievement, for such a benefactor would supply the needs and insure the comfort and well-being of a great multitude.[40]

It is understood that such contributions to the Cause of God will be compensated through divine bestowals:

> O Friends of God! Be ye assured that in place of these contributions, your agriculture, your industry, and your commerce will be blessed by manifold increases, with goodly gifts and bestowals. He who cometh with one goodly deed will receive a tenfold reward. There is no doubt that the living Lord will abundantly confirm those who expend their wealth in His path.[41]

---

[40] Secret of Divine Civilization, 24–25
[41] 'Abdu'l-Bahá, Bahá'í Prayers, 84.

For the individual, moderation and generosity are qualities to be fostered and are conducive to spiritual attainment. Bahá'u'lláh stated that, "[The true seeker] should be content with little, and be freed from all inordinate desire... He should succour the dispossessed, and never withhold his favour from the destitute."[42] Voluntary simplicity and sharing contribute to a smaller ecological footprint for the food system. While legal measures are needed to ensure equity, voluntary sharing is an important spiritual principle.

> Man reacheth perfection through good deeds, voluntarily performed, not through good deeds the doing of which was forced upon him. And sharing is a personally chosen righteous act: that is, the rich should extend assistance to the poor, they should expend their substance for the poor, but of their own free will, and not because the poor have gained this end by force.[43]

Individual moral development is particularly important in those who take leadership roles. Elected leaders, at whatever level of society, are responsible to ensure the honesty of their governments, to prevent corruption, and to minister to the poor.

BUILDING A JUST AND EQUITABLE WORLD ORDER

The Bahá'í teachings propose a realignment of international governance such that a reasonable measure of national sovereignty is guaranteed while providing a form of democratic global governance appropriate to an interdependent and highly connected planet. Such as system will operate at a level capable of fairly and equitably managing the global food system, including the flow of trade, finance, labour, and resources. Truly international institutions, acting on behalf of humanity as a whole, would counterbalance the power of any particular nation or bloc.

---

[42] Bahá'u'lláh, The Kitáb-i-Íqán, 193–194.
[43] 'Abdu'l-Bahá, Selections from the Writings of 'Abdu'l-Bahá. Comp. Research Dept. Bahá'í World Centre. Trans. Marzieh Gail et al. (Haifa: Bahá'í World Centre, 1978, 115.

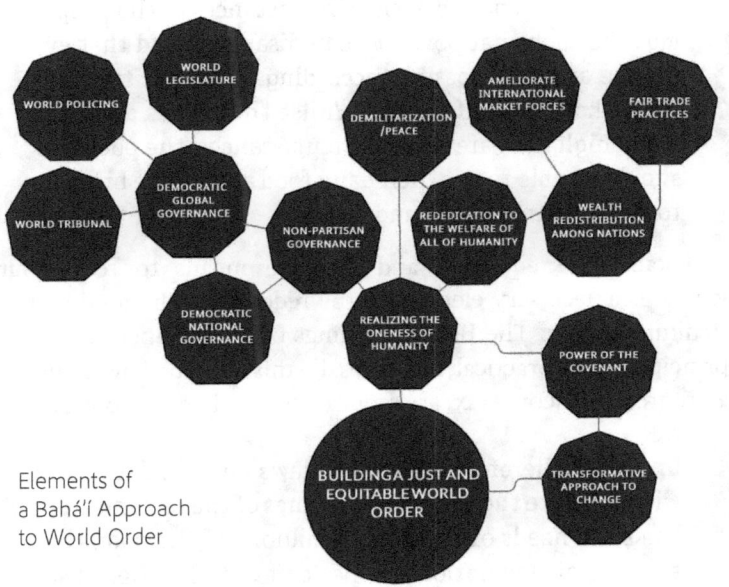

Elements of a Bahá'í Approach to World Order

These would include a world legislature, a world executive, an international police force, and a world tribunal to adjudicate disputes.[44] The global vision, however, "repudiates excessive centralization...and disclaims all attempts at uniformity... Its watchword is unity in diversity."[45]

The world order envisioned by Bahá'u'lláh is a prosperous one. "Wealth is most commendable," said 'Abdu'l-Bahá, "provided the entire population is wealthy."[46] The principle of oneness implies that a minimum standard of well being is an inalienable human right.

> Every human being has the right to live; they have a right to rest, and to a certain amount of well being.[47]

---

[44] Shoghi Effendi, *World Order of Baha'u'llah*, 203–204.
[45] Ibid. 42
[46] 'Abdu'l-Bahá, *Secret of Divine Civilization*, Trans. Marzieh Gail. 2d.ed. Wilmette, Ill.: Bahá'í Publishing Trust, 1970, 24–25.
[47] 'Abdu'l-Bahá Paris Talks, London: Bahá'í Publishing Trust, 1995, 134.

> The arrangements of the circumstances of the people must be such that poverty shall disappear, and that everyone as far as possible, according to his position and rank, shall be comfortable. Whilst the nobles and others in high rank are in easy circumstances, the poor also should be able to get their daily food and not be brought to the extremities of hunger.[48]

Establishing equitable and effective means to redistribute wealth is a necessary element in the redesign of the food and agriculture system. The Bahá'í teachings offer a number of spiritual principles and practical measures in this regard. Laws, such as a progressive income tax, are required to regulate economic status.

> One must therefore enact such laws and regulations as will moderate the excessive fortunes of the few and meet the basic needs of the myriad millions of the poor, that a degree of moderation may be achieved. However, absolute equality is just as untenable, for complete equality in wealth, power, commerce, agriculture, and industry would result in chaos and disorder, disrupt livelihoods, provoke universal discontent, and undermine the orderly conduct of the affairs of the community.[49]

> The degrees of society must be preserved. The farmer will continue to till the soil, the artist to pursue his art, the banker to finance the nations... But in this Bahá'í plan there is no class hatred. Each is to be protected and each individual member of the body politic is to live in the greatest comfort and happiness. Work is to be provided for all and there will be no needy ones seen in the streets.[50]

---

[48] 'Abdu'l-Bahá, 'Abdu'l-Bahá in London, 29.
[49] 'Abdu'l-Bahá, Some Answered Questions. Trans. Laura Clifford Barney Wilmette: Bahá'í Publishing Trust, 2014, 402.
[50] 'Abdu'l-Bahá, Economics, Agriculture and Related Subjects. Comp. The Research Department of the Universal House of Justice, May 1 1997, 6.

One of the chief means of redistributing wealth is Huqúqu'lláh or Right of God. While this theme is associated with individual responsibility, the institution has far reaching implications for the advancement of a global food system. Bahá'u'lláh said that 19 percent of net wealth belongs to God, and should be paid by the Bahá'ís to the House of Justice for various purposes, including the "relief of the poor." Although this amount is "owed to God", it is not permissible to solicit payment; it must be given willingly. As the size of the Bahá'í community grows, this institution will become a massive resource for uplifting the status of the poor. Bahá'u'lláh said, "This ordinance is binding upon everyone, and by observing it one will be raised to honour inasmuch as it will serve to purify one's possessions and will impart blessing, and added prosperity".[51] So significant is this law, that "If the offering be but a single grain it is regarded as the crowning glory of all the harvests of the world."[52]

Other means of wealth distribution are the guarantee of fair wages to workers and their sharing in the profits of the enterprise, including agricultural properties and enterprises.

> ...the owners of properties, mines and factories should share their incomes with their employees and give a fairly certain percentage of their products to their workingmen in order that the employees may receive, beside their wages, some of the general income of the factory so that the employee may strive with his soul in the work.[53]

Monopolistic enterprises designed to eliminate competition are not permitted according to Bahá'í principles: "No more trusts will remain in the future. The question of the trusts will be wiped

---

[51] Huqúqu'lláh — The Right of God. A Compilation prepared by the Research Department of The Universal House of Justice. Huqúqu'lláh — The Right of God. A Compilation prepared by the Research Department of The Universal House of Justice. https://www.bahai.org/library/authoritative-texts/compilations/huququllah-right-god/ 9.

[52] Ibid., 7.

[53] 'Abdu'l-Bahá 'Abdu'l-Bahá, *Foundations of World Unity*. 2d ed. Wilmette, Ill.: Bahá'í Publishing Trust, 1972, 43–44.

away entirely."⁵⁴ How this principle would apply in practice is not clear, but its spirit would seem to favour small and medium sized enterprises over those larger enterprises which result in the control of agricultural resources in the hands of a few. Similarly, arrangements that favour the accumulation of wealth in the richest and most advantaged industrial nations would be contrary to Bahá'í principle. The world order envisioned by Bahá'u'lláh is designed to ameliorate international market forces, which tend to shortchange low-income nations and ignore negative impacts on the rural poor. The Bahá'í model recommends trade instruments designed to foster genuine human progress.[55,56]

Land tenure and property ownership is a central concern for farmers. On this subject, the Bahá'í writings are clear in their endorsement of the right of ownership. According to Shoghi Effendi,

> the Cause neither accepts the theories of the Capitalistic economics in full, nor can it agree with the Marxists and Communists in their repudiation of the principle of private ownership and of this vital sacred right of the individual.[57]

However, while the Writings explicitly uphold the institution of private ownership, they also stress the necessity of introducing fundamental changes in its methods and features.[58] An example of these changes would be profit sharing, which could be applied to agricultural workers on large estates and plantations or corporate farms.

---

[54] ibid.
[55] 'Abdu'l-Bahá. *Selections from the Writings of 'Abdu'l-Bahá*, p. 301.
[56] See for example Hooshmand Badee, *Bahá'í Teachings on Economics and Their Implications for the Bahá'í Community and the Wider Society*, The University of Leeds, August 2015, 256.
[57] Economics, Agriculture and Related Subjects. Comp. The Research Department of the Universal House of Justice, 2000. https://bahai-library.com/compilation_economics_agriculture https://bahai-library.com/compilation_economics_agriculture
[58] Shoghi Effendi, *Directives from the Guardian*. New Delhi: Bahá'í Publishing Trust, 1973, 19.

Support for the right of private ownership should not be taken to mean that other forms of ownership or tenure such as cooperative enterprises or the communal ownership found in many Indigenous communities is not acceptable. It may also be that novel forms of tenure will be devised or adopted according to local requirements. Shoghi Effendi states that the Bahá'í principles are meant to apply under widely different conditions; he said, for example, "where the countries are rarely industrial and mostly agricultural, we should have to apply different laws from the West..."[59]

Intellectual property is an important issue in agriculture today, whether in enterprises involving biotechnology or for Indigenous people with a unique knowledge of their local flora. A statement relevant to this topic is found in the letters of Shoghi Effendi: "Those whose brains have contributed to the creation and improvement of the means of production must be fairly rewarded, though these means may be owned and controlled by others."[60] Further to this issue, the principle that the benefits of civilization should be shared equitably would be important in determining the benefits that derive from scientific discoveries or Indigenous knowledge.

Lending and interest is another key issue for farmers. Bahá'u'lláh abrogated the Islamic law against charging interest but recommended a moderate rate of interest:

> this is a matter that should be practiced with moderation and fairness... We exhort the loved ones of God to observe justice and fairness, and to do that which would prompt the friends of God to evince tender mercy and compassion towards each other."[61] He further stated "the conduct of these affairs hath been entrusted to the men of the

---

[59] Economics, Agriculture and Related Subjects. Comp. The Research Department of the Universal House of Justice, 2000. https://bahai-library.com/compilation_economics_agriculture

[60] Ibid., 10.

[61] Bahá'u'lláh, Tablets of Bahá'u'lláh revealed after the Kitáb-i-Aqdas, 134.

House of Justice that they may enforce them according to the exigencies of the time and the dictates of wisdom.[62]

THE SUSTAINABILITY OF AGRICULTURE

Bahá'u'lláh stated, "All men have been created to carry forward an ever-advancing civilization."[63] Logically, to fulfill the purpose of our creation, the processes of civilization building must be sustainable; our relationship to nature must be informed by the fact that civilization ultimately depends on the viability of natural systems. Bahá'u'lláh's statement raises the sustainable development of civilization to the status of a spiritual principle, one that is central to the purpose of our existence.

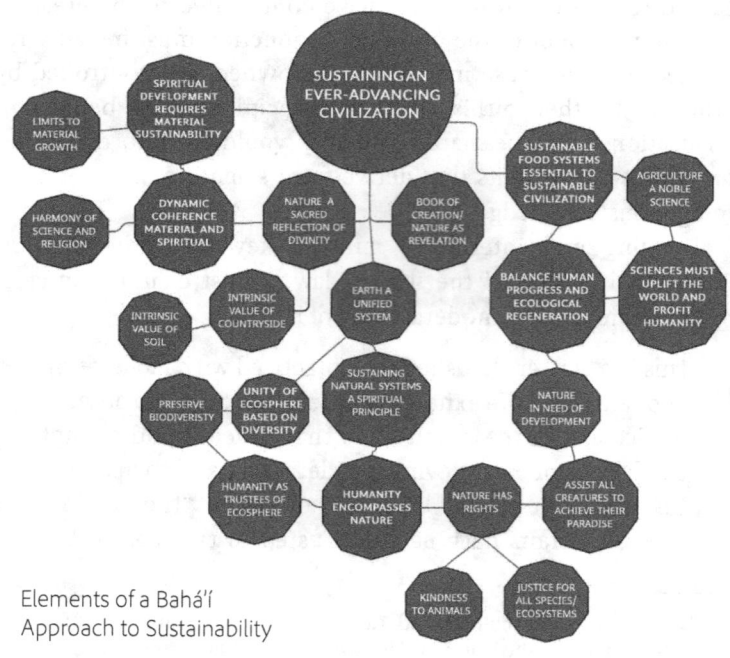

Elements of a Bahá'í Approach to Sustainability

---

[62] Ibid.
[63] Bahá'u'lláh, *Gleanings from the Writings of Bahá'u'lláh*, 215.

The Bahá'í International Community elaborated on this point in a concept paper on development:

> Bahá'í Scriptures describe nature as a reflection of the sacred. They teach that nature should be valued and respected, but not worshipped; rather, it should serve humanity's efforts to carry forward an ever-advancing civilization. However, in light of the interdependence of all parts of nature, and the importance of evolution and diversity "to the beauty, efficiency and perfection of the whole," every effort should be made to preserve as much as possible the earth's bio-diversity and natural order.
>
> As trustees, or stewards, of the planet's vast resources and biological diversity, humanity must learn to make use of the earth's natural resources, both renewable and non-renewable, in a manner that ensures sustainability and equity into the distant reaches of time. This attitude of stewardship will require full consideration of the potential environmental consequences of all development activities. It will compel humanity to temper its actions with moderation and humility, realizing that the true value of nature cannot be expressed in economic terms. It will also require a deep understanding of the natural world and its role in humanity's collective development both material and spiritual. Therefore, sustainable environmental management must come to be seen not as a discretionary commitment mankind can weigh against other competing interests, but rather as a fundamental responsibility that must be shouldered, a pre-requisite for spiritual development as well as the individual's physical survival.[64]

---

[64] Bahá'í International Community. *Valuing Spirituality in Development: Initial Considerations Regarding the Creation of Spiritually Based Indicators for Development*. A concept paper written for the World Faiths and Development Dialogue, Lambeth Palace, London, 18–19 February 1998. London: Bahá'í Publishing Trust, 1998.

Since agriculture is fundamental to civilization, a sustainable food and agriculture system is intrinsic to the world order prescribed by Bahá'u'lláh. The following points outline many of the ideas underlying a Bahá'í perspective on the sustainability of agriculture. Together, these ideas give substance to a new environmental ethos appropriate to a world civilization.

The Bahá'í teachings emphatically encourage the processes of building civilization, including the development of sciences and technologies, which "uplift the world of being, and are conducive to its elevation."[65] In fact, the capacity for science and technical innovation in a sense defines what it means to be human, and our scientific ability is seen as a means to reveal the hidden qualities of nature, fulfilling its God-given potential.[66] This same capacity is, however, potentially dangerous, as is clearly evident when we consider current environmental conditions.

To ensure that science and technology are beneficial, the Bahá'í teachings prescribe various measures. As previously noted, civilization must be kept within the restraints of moderation. Only those sciences "as can profit the peoples of the earth" should be pursued.[67] The teachings of Bahá'u'lláh are meant to restrain, moderate and balance science and technology, and thereby protect society and preserve nature. In fact, Bahá'u'lláh said, "Each one of the ordinances We have revealed is a mighty stronghold for the preservation of the world of being. Verily, this Wronged One desireth naught but your security and elevation."[68] Religion is meant to moderate the influence of science by ensuring that its motivation is pure and that its goal is beneficial. 'Abdu'l-Bahá remarked that "Every kind of knowledge, every science, is as a tree: if the fruit of it be the love of God, then is it a blessed tree..." However, he warned that if the love of God is

---

[65] Bahá'u'lláh, *Epistle to the Son of the Wolf*, 26.
[66] Matt Weinberg, *Technology, Values, and the Shaping of Social Reality*, The Bahá'í World, 2019.
[67] Bahá'u'lláh, Tablets of Bahá'u'lláh revealed after the Kitáb-i-Aqdas, 51–52.
[68] Ibid. 69.

not intrinsic to the pursuit of science, "that tree is but dried-up wood, and shall only feed the fire."[69]

In innumerable passages in the Bahá'í texts, both human progress and world regeneration are advanced as goals of God's revelation.

> That which is conducive to the regeneration of the world and the salvation of the peoples and kindreds of the earth hath been sent down from the heaven of the utterance of Him Who is the Desire of the world.[70]
>
> ...the counsels which the Pen of the Wronged One hath revealed constitute the supreme animating power for the advancement of the world and the exaltation of its peoples. Arise, O people, and by the power of God's might, resolve to gain the victory over your own selves, that haply the whole earth might be freed and sanctified from its servitude to the gods of its idle fancies...[71]
>
> The Call of God, when raised, breathed a new life into the body of mankind, and infused a new spirit into the whole creation. It is for this reason that the world hath been moved to its depths, and the hearts and consciences of men been quickened. Erelong the evidences of this regeneration will be revealed, and the fast asleep will be awakened.[72]
>
> Great is the station of man. Great must also be his endeavours for the rehabilitation of the world and the well-being of nations.[73]

Agroecosystems are derived from and remain dependent on natural systems. The Bahá'í discourse contains many significant

---

[69] Selections from the Writings of 'Abdu'l-Bahá. Comp. Research Dept. Bahá'í World Centre. Trans. Marzieh Gail et al., Haifa: Bahá'í World Centre, 1978, 181.
[70] Bahá'u'lláh, Tablets of Bahá'u'lláh revealed after the Kitáb-i-Aqdas, 223.
[71] ibid. 86.
[72] 'Abdu'l-Bahá qtd. in Shoghi Effendi, *World Order of Baha'u'llah*, 169.
[73] Bahá'u'lláh, Tablets of Bahá'u'lláh revealed after the Kitáb-i-Aqdas, 174.

ideas about nature, its functions, purpose and value that will influence our understanding and practice of agriculture. A number of these points follow.

- Nature is sacred in the sense that it is an expression of the divine.[74]
- Nature's hidden capacities and potentials are educed by God's revelation. *"The moment the word expressing My attribute 'the Omniscient' issueth forth from My mouth, every created thing will, according to its capacities and limitations, be invested with the power to unfold the knowledge of the most marvelous sciences, and will be empowered to manifest them in the course of time..."*[75] *"Consider, for instance, the revelation of the light of the Name of God, the Educator. Behold, how in all things the evidences of such a revelation are manifest, how the betterment of all beings dependeth upon it... Its influence pervadeth all things and sustaineth them."*[76]
- Physical space is made sacred through worship. *"Blessed is the spot, and the house, and the place, and the city, and the heart, and the mountain, and the refuge, and the cave, and the valley, and the land, and the sea, and the island, and the meadow where mention of God hath been made, and His praise glorified."*[77]
- Nature is a "Book" of revelation. *"The Book of Creation is in accord with the written Book...the Book of creation is the command of God and the repository of Divine mysteries. In it there are great signs, universal images, perfect words, exalted symbols and secrets of all things, whether of the past or of the future...when thou gazest at the Book of Creation thou will observe the signs, symbols, realities and reflections*

---

[74] Ibid. 142.
[75] Bahá'u'lláh, Gleanings from the Writings of Bahá'u'lláh, 142.
[76] ibid. 189–190.
[77] Bahá'u'lláh, Bahá'í Prayers, Baha'i Publishing Trust, 2002, frontispiece.

of the hidden mysteries of the bounties of His Holiness the Incomparable One."[78]
- That nature is the source of human prosperity should humble humanity. *"Every man of discernment, while walking upon the earth, feeleth indeed abashed, inasmuch as he is fully aware that the thing which is the source of his prosperity, his wealth, his might, his exaltation, his advancement and power is, as ordained by God, the very earth which is trodden beneath the feet of all men."*[79]

The Bahá'í writings contain many passages that demonstrate a profound appreciation and understanding of ecology and provide insights into the operation of agroecosystems.

- The unity of nature is derived from its diversity. 'Abdu'l-Bahá said, *"Were one to observe with an eye that discovereth the realities of all things, it would become clear that the greatest relationship that bindeth the world of being together lieth in the range of created things themselves..."*[80] He further said that an indwelling spirit of cooperation is a fundamental property of nature: *"...all beings are linked together like a chain; and mutual aid, assistance, and interaction are among their intrinsic properties and are the cause of their formation, development, and growth."*[81]
- An example of the cooperative nature of relationship is the complementary functions of plants and animals: *"Each of these two maketh use of certain elements in the air on which its own life dependeth, while each increaseth the*

---

[78] 'Abdu'l-Bahá, 'Abdu'l-Bahá. *Min Makátíb-i-'Abdu'l-Bahá.* (From the Collected Letters). Vol. 1. Rio de Janeiro, Brazil: Editora Bahá'í Brasil, 1982. qtd. in Nakhjavani, Bahiyyih. Response. Oxford: George Ronald, 1981, 13.

[79] Bahá'u'lláh, *Epistle to the Son of the Wolf*, 44.

[80] The Redistribution of Wealth—Some Specific Measures. Extracts from the Bahá'í Writings and from Letters written by or on behalf of Shoghi Effendi and the Universal House of Justice. Comp. The Research Department of the Universal House of Justice, May 1 1997, 17.

[81] 'Abdu'l-Bahá, *Some Answered Questions*, 262.

quantity of such elements as are essential for the life of the other." 'Abdu'l-Bahá then extends this idea to all relationships: *"Of like kind are the relationships that exist among all created things. Hence it was stated that co-operation and reciprocity are essential properties which are inherent in the unified system of the world of existence, and without which the entire creation would be reduced to nothingness."*[82]

- Limiting ourselves to the boundaries of the physical undermines the purpose of nature, which is to provide a place for faith to become manifest. Sole identification with the physical, with nature, is dangerous to humankind, and ultimately makes our presence dangerous to the physical realm itself. We are told to, *"Walk thou high above the world of being through the power of the Most Great name, that thou mayest become aware of the immemorial mysteries and be acquainted with that wherewith no one is acquainted."*[83] At the same time, we understand that the human being, detached from nature, becomes a source of education and of life to the natural world. In the same passage, Bahá'u'lláh continues, *"Be thou as a throbbing artery, pulsating in the body of the entire creation, that through the heat generated by this motion there may appear that which will quicken the hearts of those who hesitate."*

- The Bahá'í teachings give human beings the responsibility to conserve the ecological balance of nature. *"Great is the station of man,"* says Bahá'u'lláh. *"Great must also be his endeavours for the rehabilitation of the world and the well-being of nations.*[84] *Be ye the embodiments of justice and fairness amidst all creation.*[85] *Truly, We desire to behold you*

---

[82] Huqúqu'lláh. Extracts from the Writings of Bahá'u'lláh, 'Abdu'l-Bahá, Shoghi Effendi and The Universal House of Justice. Comp. Research Department of The Universal House of Justice. Thornhill, ON: National Spiritual Assembly of the Bahá'ís of Canada, 1989, 21.
[83] (Bahá'u'lláh, Tablets of Bahá'u'lláh revealed after the Kitáb-i-Aqdas 142–43).
[84] Ibid. 174.
[85] Bahá'u'lláh, The Kitáb-i-Aqdas, 87.

as manifestations of paradise on earth..."[86] Consequently, 'Abdu'l-Bahá said, *"Let your ambition be the achievement on earth of a heavenly civilization! I ask for you the supreme blessing, that you may be so filled with the vitality of the heavenly spirit that you may be the cause of life to the world."*[87]

Future agricultural systems will benefit from this profound understanding of the responsibilities of our species for the sustainability and development of nature.

ADASIYYAH: 'ABDU'L-BAHÁ'S MODEL VILLAGE

The Central Figures of the Bahá'í Faith were directly involved in agricultural activities and rural development. Bahá'u'lláh, for example, managed His father's farming operations for a period of time preceding His exile. As a child, 'Abdu'l-Bahá accompanied His father in these activities and throughout His life maintained a keen interest in farming. In fact, 'Abdu'l-Bahá's activities in the field of rural reconstruction offer an extraordinary example of the application of Bahá'í principles to rural development.

Among His innumerable labours as head of an emerging world religion, 'Abdu'l-Bahá found time to put into practice many of the Bahá'í principles of rural development in the village of 'Adasiyyah, about 100 kilometers from his home in Haifa.[88] It is instructive, then, to consider, at least briefly, how he applied these concepts and principles.

In 1901, 'Abdu'l-Bahá purchased the lands of 'Adasiyyah, situated southeast of the Sea of Galilee, as a whole village estate. The 690 hectares estate was developed in several phases. With the

---

[86] (ibid. 57–58)
[87] 'Abdu'l-Bahá, The Reality of Man, Wilmette: Bahá'í Publishing Trust, 1969, 15.
[88] The description of the 'Adasiyyah project is a summary based on Iraj Poostchi, 'Adasiyyah: A Study in Agriculture and Rural Development, Bahá'í Studies Review 16, 2010, 61–105 doi: 10.1386/bsr.16 61/7.

encouragement of 'Abdu'l-Bahá, the community of 'Adassiyah overcame extraordinary obstacles to restore degraded, eroded, and deforested land, improve soil quality, improve water use efficiency, and increase crop diversity, including the use of perennial tree crops and forages. Today, this approach, which requires minimal external inputs, might be described as regenerative farming or agroecology, an effort to farm in a manner that mimics the functions of natural ecosystem.

Along with the gradually improving farming operations, 'Abdu'l-Bahá encouraged spiritual and social aspects of village life. He emphasized the application of moral and spiritual values in day-to-day life and farm work. These values had a significant influence on the production and marketing systems of the farmers, improving their fortunes. Furthermore, he strongly recommended that they establish warm bonds of friendship with the people they met or had business dealings with, and conduct all their affairs with high rectitude of conduct.

During the lifetimes of both 'Abdu'l-Bahá and Shoghi Effendi, these efforts to foster agricultural and rural development attracted the attention of many people near and far. 'Adasiyyah soon became an agricultural showplace for the whole of Jordan. If the government wished to show how advanced it was in agricultural production and farming techniques it would bring foreign guests and dignitaries to 'Adasiyyah, a brilliant star in an otherwise semi-arid scrubland. Even members of the royal family visited the village.

The principles and practices of village life and farming initiated by 'Abdu'l-Bahá in 'Adassiyah still offer a relevant example of just, productive, and sustainable rural development applicable to one third of humanity, the smallholder farmers who produce much of the world's food. In fact, the development principles followed by 'Abdu'l-Bahá addressed a range of social and ecological concerns that have since intensified. The redevelopment of 'Adassiyah accomplished three things which if replicated would be essential to the development of rural areas and the global community:

ECOLOGICAL AND CLIMATE SERVICES — With the encouragement of 'Abdu'l-Bahá, the community of 'Adassiyah restored degraded lands. Applying low input farming methods to an estimated 3.5 billion hectares of degraded land around the world could provide opportunities for rural people, especially rural youth, to restore ecosystem services, increase biodiversity, mitigate climate change, and increase the food supply.[89]

SOCIAL-ECONOMIC DEVELOPMENT — The initial capital investment by 'Abdu'l-Bahá was the catalyst that allowed families in 'Adassiyah to prosper. They were able to transform scrubland into a productive farm that eventually supported hundreds of residents, and contributed to the local and regional economy. The farm provided high quality food for the village and urban areas. The generous sharecropping arrangement and profit sharing improved the standard of living of residents and non-resident farm labourers.

MORAL CAPACITY — Material self-reliance brings a sense of dignity. 'Abdu'l-Bahá went further, encouraging the residents of 'Adassiyah to pay equal attention to their moral development. This was achieved through education, both material and spiritual, for the children, youth, and adults, and through regular devotional meetings. Education supported a dual moral purpose, to develop the potentialities

---

[89] The distinguished soil scientist Rattan Lal has estimated that the technical potential of a range of measures to increase carbon sequestration in croplands, forests, and grasslands — similar to those adopted in Adassiyah — is greater than the net annual increase in atmospheric CO_2. If smallholder farmers were paid for their climate and ecological services, this would be a low cost approach to climate change mitigation. It would also increase food production and raise the living standard of farmers. The potential of this approach is large. Lal estimates that 3.5 billion hectares, close to one quarter of Earth's land surface, are degraded and desertified lands. Small investments in smallholder farms and villages could eliminate extreme poverty while improving productivity, assuring a sustainable food supply for a burgeoning world population. Rattan Lal estimates that green investments of as little as US$25 per smallholder farm would facilitate the adoption of sustainable methods.

of the individual and to enhance capacity to be of service. Building this capacity helped community members to live harmoniously. A democratic institution was elected to administer to the material and spiritual needs of the community. In this way, the moral capacity of the individual, the community, and its institutions increased.

CONCLUSION

In summary, agricultural development is a "fundamental principle" for the advancement of humankind. For this reason we are instructed to give "special regard" to agricultural development, more specifically to a form of development shaped by and serving the cause of justice, equity, and sustainability. The task of building a new social and economic order is associated with the redesign of agriculture to ensure economic viability for producers and the equitable development of nations. The global food system envisioned in the Writings will be built on a foundation of food secure local communities, favour small and medium size agricultural and food enterprises, require a high level of moral rectitude among individuals and institutions, and ensure the every person enjoys a moderate level of prosperity.

The Bahá'í teachings invite us to elevate our agricultural work to a form of worship and to conduct our lives individually and collectively in such fashion as to ensure a sustainable society by balancing technical and spiritual development. We are given a vision of our relatedness to the earth but called to an inspired station where we are empowered to take full responsibility in carrying forward an ever-advancing civilization. In this view, the practice of agriculture is elevated from mere commerce to a spiritual practice.

The task of agricultural development cannot be carried out in isolation from the process of spiritual development recognizing, as 'Abdu'l-Bahá said, "when the love of God is established, everything else will be realized."[90] Great disparities entrench hunger

---

[90] 'Abdu'l-Bahá, The Promulgation of Universal Peace, 239.

and poverty, rural communities are stagnant and destabilized, and the agricultural environment is threatened, but the transformative power of the Word of God is available to help humanity in its herculean task, to transform the world.

In this regard, 'Abdu'l-Bahá offered these words of hope:

> ...thanks to the unfailing grace of God, the loving-kindness of His favored ones, the unrivaled endeavors of wise and capable souls, and the thoughts and ideas of the peerless leaders of this age, nothing whatsoever can be regarded as unattainable.[91]

WORKS CITED

'Abdu'l-Bahá, *'Abdu'l-Bahá in London*. London: Bahá'í Publishing Trust, 1982.
'Abdu'l-Bahá, *Foundations of World Unity*. 2d ed. Wilmette, Ill.: Bahá'í Publishing Trust, 1972.
'Abdu'l-Bahá, *Paris Talks*, London: Bahá'í Publishing Trust, 1995.
'Abdu'l-Bahá, *The Promulgation of Universal Peace*. Wilmette: Bahá'í Publishing Trust, 1982.
'Abdu'l-Bahá, *The Reality of Man*, Wilmette: Bahá'í Publishing Trust, 1969.
'Abdu'l-Bahá, *Secret of Divine Civilization*, Trans. Marzieh Gail. 2nd. ed. Wilmette, Ill.: Bahá'í Publishing Trust, 1970.
'Abdu'l-Bahá, *Selections from the Writings of 'Abdu'l-Bahá*. Comp. Research Dept. Bahá'í World Centre. Trans. Marzieh Gail et al. Haifa: Bahá'í World Centre, 1978.
'Abdu'l-Bahá, *Some Answered Questions*. Trans. Laura Clifford Barney, Wilmette: Bahá'í Publishing Trust, 2014.
Agriculture and Rural Life — Additional Extracts. Comp. The Research Department of the Universal House of Justice, May 1, 1997. https://bahai-library.com/compilation_agriculture_rural_life.

---

[91] 'Abdu'l-Bahá, qtd. in Shoghi Effendi, World Order of Bahá'u'lláh, 38.

Badee, Hooshmand, *Bahá'í Teachings on Economics and Their Implications for the Bahá'í Community and the Wider Society*, The University of Leeds, August 2015.

"Bahá'í International Community. Valuing Spirituality in Development: Initial Considerations Regarding the Creation of Spiritually Based Indicators for Development. A concept paper written for the World Faiths and Development Dialogue," Lambeth Palace, London, 18–19 February 1998. London: Bahá'í Publishing Trust, 1998.

Bahá'í World, Vol. 4. New York: Bahá'í Publishing Committee, 1932

Bahá'u'lláh, *Epistle to the Son of the Wolf*. Wilmette: Bahá'í Publishing Trust, 1979.

Bahá'u'lláh, *Gleanings from the Writings of Bahá'u'lláh*. Wilmette: Bahá'í Publishing Trust, 1988.

Bahá'u'lláh, *Tablets of Bahá'u'lláh revealed after the Kitáb-i-Aqdas*. Wilmette: Bahá'í Publishing Trust, 1988.

Bahá'u'lláh, *The Kitáb-i-Aqdas*. Haifa: Bahá'í World Centre, 1992

Bahá'u'lláh, *The Kitáb-i-Iqán*. Wilmette: Bahá'í Publishing Trust, 1974.

Bahá'u'lláh, *The Tabernacle of Unity*. Haifa, Israel: Bahá'í World Centre, 2006.

Bahá'u'lláh, The Báb, 'Abdu'l-Bahá, *Bahá'í Prayers*, Baha'i Publishing Trust, 2002.

Conservation of the Earth's Resources, Research Dept. Universal House of Justice.

Consultation: A Compilation. Extracts from the Writings and Utterances of Bahá'u'lláh, Economics, Agriculture and Related Subjects. Comp. The Research Department of the Universal House of Justice, May 1 1997, 6.

Extracts from the *Bahá'í Writings on the Subject of Agriculture and Related Subjects*. Comp. The Research Department of the Universal House of Justice, Revised November 12, 2001.

Hanley, Paul, *Eleven*, Friesen Press, 2014.

Huqúqu'lláh — The Right of God. A Compilation prepared by the Research Department of The Universal House of Justice.

https://www.bahai.org/library/authoritative-texts/compilations/huququllah-right-god/.

Lights of Guidance: A Bahá'í Reference File, 1988 https://bahailibrary.com/hornby_lights_guidance.

Nakhjavani, Bahiyyih. *Response*. Oxford: George Ronald, 1981.

Poostchi, Iraj, 'Adasiyyah: "A Study in Agriculture and Rural Development," Bahá'í Studies Review 16, 2010, 61–105 doi: 10.1386/bsr.16 61/7.

Pyne, Stephen J., *The Pyrocene: How We Created an Age of Fire, and What Happens Next*, University of California Press, 2021.

The Redistribution of Wealth. Extracts from the Bahá'í Writings and from Letters written by or on behalf of Shoghi Effendi and the Universal House of Justice. Comp. The Research Department of the Universal House of Justice, no date. https://bahailibrary.com/compilation_redistribution_wealth.

Shoghi Effendi, *Citadel of Faith.: Messages to America*, 1947–1957. Wilmette: Bahá'í Publishing Trust, 1980.

Shoghi Effendi, *Directives from the Guardian*. New Delhi: Bahá'í Publishing Trust, 1973.

Shoghi Effendi, *The World Order of Bahá'u'lláh*. Wilmette: Bahá'í Publishing Trust, 1991.

Trustworthiness. A compilation of extracts from the Bahá'í Writings. Comp. Research Department of the Universal House of Justice. London: The Bahá'í Publishing Trust, 1987.

How Can We All Get Along? — A Bahá'í Perspective on Globalization

HAROLD ROSEN

INTRODUCTION

Globalization might be viewed as the multifaceted processes whereby contemporary life — marked by the diffusion of commodities and ideas — is becoming standardized and universalized. There are legitimate concerns that some of these processes are diminishing local traditions and regional distinctions, leading to a homogenized world culture. But are there forms or expressions of Globalization that respect socio-spiritual diversity, while helping to integrate a more dynamic diversity? Perhaps Globalization can be a prelude to a creative 'new world order' — one that preserves regional diversity while fostering planetary unity.

Today's diversity of outlooks and worldviews poses significant challenges and opportunities. In both local and global contexts we find a stunning variety of belief-groups — identifiable as Religious, Spiritual, Secular or combinations of these. What do these key terms mean — most essentially? How might we view and understand this diversity in realistic, hopeful and practically cooperative ways? Can effective means of integration and progressive activity among diverse belief-groups be identified and nurtured? These are the concerns of the opening sections of this chapter.

To understand where we are today, it is helpful to reflect on how we arrived here across the centuries. What are the most basic historical developments leading to the separation of the Religious, the Spiritual and the Secular spheres? What does an integrative and progressive Secularity look like? What are the dangers of Secularity being completely divorced from Religious and Spiritual foundations? These questions are addressed in the middle sections of this chapter.

What are the basic dynamics of tolerance, respect, understanding and cooperation? Can those who feel reconciled welcome and integrate those who feel unreconciled? Can prejudices leading to conflict ultimately be prevented? How can we contribute to more vibrant spiritual communities and a more united religious world? These issues occupy us in the closing sections of this chapter. I apply a few Bahá'í principles and teachings to these questions, especially to the challenge of unity-building among Religious, Spiritual and Secular belief-groups. Some of the socio-cultural and ideational aspects of Globalization can be legitimately viewed as constructive and progressive.

How can we all get along? This is my overall theme-question, pointing to the quest for unity-in-diversity as a worthy goal for humanity. I do not believe that every single person on earth, in a strictly literal sense, will ever arrive at perfect unity, given that free-will and the choices to be divisive and commit evil acts can never be eliminated from our human condition. However, I assume the developmental nature of human beings and our collective march across time. God has created a providential universe, so human betterment and evolutionary advance are always possible. Ever higher degrees of moral-spiritual excellence call out to us, and humanity will attain ever higher degrees of progress and fulfillment. Globalization need not divide humanity, but rather, it can play a crucial role in uniting us.

VISUALIZING AND DESCRIBING HUMANITY'S DIVERSE BELIEF-GROUPS

We can use a Venn diagram to visualize relations among the Religious, Spiritual and Secular spheres. By the **Religious** sphere I mean humanity's relationship with Divine Power which awakens and nurtures the soul, bringing communion with transcendent realms. Religion is Divine initiative bestowed for our spiritual growth and collective upliftment. It is progressive revelation through Prophets and Saviours, and our human response to their guidance. Religious people focus on a particular Founder or tradition, an oral tradition or scripture, as well as a specific authority structure. Therefore, Indigenous peoples and the major Eastern and Western faith traditions, including Bahá'ís, make up the religious sphere.

By the **Spiritual** sphere I mean humanity's sense of purpose, meaning and connection with Spirit, however conceived. Spirituality is often experienced as inspiration, encompassing experiences of the immanent or transcendent nature of the universe. Spiritual people focus on inner transformation, personal growth, sometimes with a communal orientation, attempting harmony and interdependence with ever-widening reality or consciousness. They may or may not embrace a religious orientation.

And by the **Secular** sphere I mean humanity's attention to the practical needs of daily living, including family life and work, education and the socio-economic order, communication and transportation, legal and governmental concerns, science and technology, medicine, and health issues. Secular people focus on functioning in the workaday world, especially its material aspects. They may or may not embrace Religious or Spiritual orientations. Of course, there is considerable diversity within all three spheres, as people within them show widely varying degrees of integration, cooperation, and ethical commitment.

A note of caution seems necessary in using such categories. Both individuals and belief-groups are fluid, organic mixtures of value-seeking and meaning-making processes. Our beliefs and aspirations are not like static photos, but rather like dynamic motion pictures or unfolding character plots. We are subject to ever-emerging challenges, opportunities, learning, regress, and progress. Nonetheless, we tend to attribute to ourselves and others ideational identities, and if we can develop a wider appreciative understanding of these belief-labels, we can become better diplomats in the interfaith and intercultural arena, contributing to constructive community-building processes. With this caution voiced, I dare to note that seven sectors can be marked out by the overlap of our three spheres, helping us to visualize and describe various categories of belief-systems.

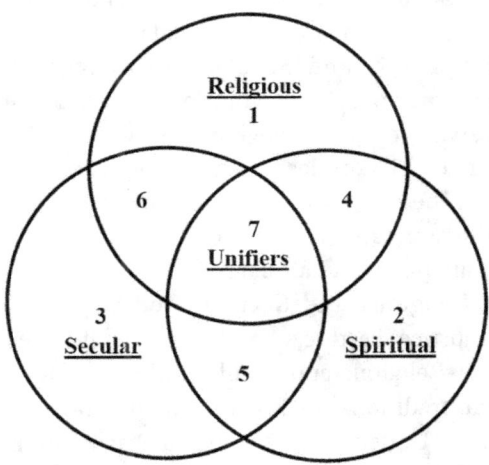

1) **Religious, but not Spiritual or Secular** — focusing on a particular Founder or tradition, scripture, and authority structure, attempting to establish ever-purer communities of faith, while seeking freedom from Secular and Spiritual influences. Examples might include some Amish and some Hasidic Jews.

2) **Spiritual, but not Religious or Secular** — focusing on inner transformation, personal spiritual growth, and communal isolation, while seeking freedom from Religious and Secular influences. Examples might include some Doukhobors, some Scientologists, and the Japanese group once called Aum Shinrikyo.

3) **Secular, but not Religious or Spiritual** — focusing on the workaday world, family life, household and societal economics, education, science, technology, and government, while seeking freedom from Religious and Spiritual influences. Examples might include some Bill 21 advocates in Canada, some Secular Humanists, and some Communists.

4) **Both Religious and Spiritual**—focusing on continual renewal of tradition and moral-spiritual progress, while open to a degree of Inter-Religious and Inter-Spiritual influences. Examples might include the Jewish Renewal movement, the Christian Renewal movement, and modern Universal Sufis.
5) **Both Spiritual and Secular**—focusing on spiritual development, conscious evolution, and planetary advancement, while open to a degree of Secular and Inter-Spiritual influences. Examples might include spiritual activists such as the late Barbara Marx Hubbard and her affiliates, the Emissaries of Divine Light, and Ken Wilber and his Integral Spirituality affiliates.
6) **Both Religious and Secular**—focusing on good works, social justice, earth care and peace, while open to a degree of Inter-Religious and Secular influences. Examples might include traditional mainstream faith communities, such as Jews, the United Church, the Anglican Church, Sunni, and Shia Muslims, as well as most Hindus, Buddhists, and Sikhs.
7) **Unity-Builders: Religious, Secular and Spiritual**—focusing on establishing ever-widening respect, understanding, collaboration and cooperation, while welcoming and integrating Inter-Religious, and varied Secular and Inter-Spiritual influences. Examples might include Bahá'ís, Indigenous peoples, as well as all universalizing, integrative and progressive faith communities within mainstream religions. Our world needs an ever-growing body of Unity-Builders.

Since integration and progressiveness are major emphases in this paper, we look briefly at another typology that is relevant to the question of how we can all get along. What basic attitudes can be taken toward belief-groups other than one's own? What stances or orientations might individuals and groups adopt toward others' views? Here is a five-position breakdown on these matters, an adaptation and development of the three-position scheme offered by Diana Eck—exclusivism, inclusivism, and pluralism.

1) **Exclusivism** — "My view is the only true one."
2) **Inclusivism** — "My view contains the truth of all others."
3) **Pluralism** — "Each view has its own respectable truth and value."
4) **Universalism** — "All views reflect a Common Source."
5) **Progressivism** — "Our Common Source guides us anew, and advancement is continuous."

When Exclusivists enter an inter-belief setting, it is often to convert others to their own perspective. When Inclusivists enter, their main focus may be learning enough to teach others that their view (the Inclusivist's) embraces all others in the most comprehensive and satisfying way. When Pluralists enter, they are usually in a learning mode, perhaps looking for common ground as a basis for cooperation. When Universalists enter, they often wish to show there is little need for inter-belief education or cooperation, because, from their perspective, all belief-systems derive from the same Divine grounding. And when Progressivists enter, they try to appreciate and identify the universal principles being shared, offer relevant guidance from the latest Divine Revelation, seeking to establish a deeper unity than has thus far been attained in human history.

This five-part schema suggests that Pluralists and Progressivists are probably more genuinely interested in inter-belief understanding, respect and cooperation. Exclusivists, Inclusivists and Universalists bring challenging elements to the table, but in my view, they should always be welcome in the inter-belief arena. While Pluralists may have a relativistic view of Truth and adopt a more theoretical orientation, Progressivists affirm Divine authority for their view, but try to avoid any tone of finalism or triumphalism, placing the emphasis on unity-building toward a more just, peaceful, and prosperous humanity. And they have faith that God will send other Revealers in the distant future, who will further integrate diverse belief-groups, abrogating teachings no longer relevant.

INTERPRETING TODAY'S WORLD THROUGH A BRIEF OVERVIEW OF RELIGIOUS HISTORY

Below is a suggestive and thematic timeline — not strictly or narrowly factual — offering a broad, synoptic, and progressive interpretation of humanity's religious history. It also offers some factors shaping the present, along with a possible glimpse of the future. It is designed to prepare us for an assessment of major operative worldviews today. In italics are my theorized themes of these traditions. The underlined traditions are those deemed to have more enduring and widespread influence.

A break in the timeline appears at the sixteenth and seventeenth century mark of the Common Era, and I will try to show that this period is when the Secular and the Spiritual spheres began to separate more markedly from the Religious. Another break in the timeline appears before the nineteenth century, to distinguish and name some major developments leading to our world today. A third break comes before the twenty-first century, a pregnant reflection time regarding what might unfold for humanity. A few interpretive comments follow the timeline, attempting to cast light on humanity's current and future maturation process.

- c. 10,000 ⇒ 4000 BCE — pre-historic **Indigenous Spiritualities & Great Goddess Religions**, earth-centered traditions worldwide — *"Earth Reverence & Dependence on Nature."*
- c. 7000 BCE — **African Traditional Religions** — *"Communal Solidarity, Ancestral Spirits & Revering the Source."*
- c. 4000 BCE — **Adam's Revelation** (Mesopotamia) — *"Naming Creatures & Choosing Independence from Nature."*
- c. 3500 BCE — **Mesopotamian Henotheism** — 'high gods': An (creator), Enlil (divine executor) — *"Order in Heaven as a Model for Order on Earth."*
- c. 3200 BCE — **Hermetic Revelation** — other names: Thoth/Enoch/Idris? (Egypt?) — *"As Above, So Below"* & **Egyptian Henotheism** — 'high gods': Ptah (creator of gods),

Amen (creator of heaven & earth), Ra (sun, creator of life) — *"Earthly Stability through Mirroring the Gods."*

c. 3000 BCE — **Noah's Revelation** (Mesopotamia) — *"The Rainbow Promise & Laws for Humanity."*

c. 2700 BCE — **Indus Valley Henotheism** — 'high gods': Dyaus (father of gods), Varuna (lord of justice), Agni (fire, domestic stability) — *"Making Sacrifices to Maintain Cosmic & Social Order."*

c. 2500 BCE — the **Sabaean Prophet's Revelation** (S Arabia & NE Africa)...also called 'Mandeanism' — *"Following Light & Avoiding Darkness."*

c. 2300 BCE — **Chinese Sage-Kings: Yao, Shun & Yu** — *"Fulfilling the Mandate of Heaven & Bringing Prosperity to the People."*

c. 2000 BCE — **Abraham's Revelation** (Mesopotamia & Palestine) — *"Faithfulness to One God."*

c. 1500 BCE — **Moses' Revelation** (Palestine) — *"Obedience to Divine Covenants."*

c. 1400 BCE — **Krishna's Dharma (Wheel of Law)** (NW India) — *"Devotion to the Avatar & Dutiful Action."*

c. 1000 BCE — **Zoroaster's Revelation** (E Persia) — *"Distinguishing Good & Evil, Establishing Heaven on Earth."*

c. 960 BCE — **Solomon's Wisdom Tradition** (E Medit.) — *"Moral Discernment & Practical Sciences."*

c. 700 BCE — **Isaiah's Prophecy** (Palestine) — *"One Righteous God for All Nations."*

c. 550 BCE — **Mahavira's Mission** (N India) — *"Reverence for Life & Self-Mastery."*

c. 540 BCE — **Lao Tzu's Nature Mysticism** (W China) — *"Attaining Balance by Aligning with the Way of Nature."*

c. 520 BCE — **Confucius' Ethical Culture** (N China) — *"Deliberate Cultivation of Character & Social Propriety."*

c. 500 BCE — **Buddha's Dharma (Path of Truth)** (NE India) — *"Compassion for Suffering & Attaining Nirvana."*

c. 420 BCE — **MoTzu's Mission** (C China) — *"Universal Love Brings Peace & Justice for All."*

c. 300 BCE — **Greco-Roman Worldview** (Mediterranean) — *"Cosmic Order Reflected in Cosmopolitan Society."*
30 CE — **Jesus' Revelation** (Palestine) — *"Sacrificial Love & Attaining the Kingdom of Heaven."*
c. 500 CE? — **Quetzalcoatl's Mission** (C America) — *"Building Kind Cities & Becoming God-like."*
c. 500 CE? — **Viracocha's Mission** (S America) — *"Unifying Diverse Peoples into an Empire."*
610 CE — **Muhammad's Revelation** (Arabia) — *"Submission to One God & Building a Spiritual Nation."*
c. 1400 CE — **Deganawida's Mission** (N America) — *"Establishing the Sacred Peace Tree Pact."*
1500 CE — **Nanak's Synthetic Reform** (Sikh Faith, NW India) — *"Remembering God's Name & Building Egalitarian Society."*
16th & 17th Century — Age of Exploration... Colonialism... Printing Revolution... European Renaissance... **Protestant Reformation & Roman Catholic Counter-Reformation... Esoteric Spirituality...** Scientific Revolution... **Wars of Religion...** Peace of Westphalia... **State over Church...** Enlightenment... **Early Western Secularization.**
1844 CE — **The Bab's Revelation** (Persia) — *"The Promised One & the Promised Day."*
1863 CE — **Bahá'u'lláh's Revelation** (Middle East) — *"The Unity of God, Religion & Humanity."*
19th & 20th Century — **Decline of the Social-Political Influence of Traditional Religions...** Declining Influence of the 'Great Powers': most especially England, France, Germany, Turkey... **New & Restorationist Spiritual Movements —** *"Personal Enlightenment & Planetary Advance"* — a few representative examples:
    from Judeo-Christian backgrounds — **Jewish Renewal... Latter-Day Saints;**
    from Islamic background — **Ahmadiyyas...** Universal **Sufism;**

from Hindu background — **Theosophy**... **Brahma Kumaris;**
from Buddhist background — **Rissho Kosei Kai**... **Won Buddhism;**
from Chinese Confucian-Taoist background — **Cao Dai**... **Falun Gong**... **Unification Church;**
...World War I... League of Nations... World War II... United Nations... Rise & Fall of Ideologies: Nationalism, Communism, Capitalism... **Rise of Unaffiliated Spirituality**... Communications Revolution... Globalization, both Material and Spiritual... Increasing Global Interdependence.

21st & 22nd Century — Severe Global Environmental, Economic, Political & Health Challenges... Breakdown of the National Sovereignty-based World Order... **Expansion of the Bahá'í Faith**... **Re-Integration of the Religious, Spiritual & Secular Spheres?**... Transition toward Global Governance?... **Humanity's Spiritual Maturation** & World Peace?

Let us consider a few observations on this interpretive sequence as a whole. It is meant to be suggestive rather than specifically explanatory. Not all of these traditions will be familiar to every observer, nor would they necessarily be named as above. We might notice that their themes seem to be complementary, rather than contradictory — as if the same Divine Power were operative throughout human history. Perhaps religions are more like chapters of the same book, than isolated and competing agencies. Later traditions fulfilled some of the prophetic longing of earlier traditions. They all aimed to cultivate such virtues as love, compassion, generosity, truthfulness, service, wisdom, justice, and peace.

I have emphasized the names of the Founders, if reliably known, along with the formative power of Divine Revelation. Like Arnold Toynbee, I believe that religious vision gives rise to advancing culture and civilization. For example, emerging from the underlined revelations above, we might say the Egyptian,

Chinese, Indian, Jewish, Persian, Hellenic, Southeast Asian, Christian, and Islamic civilizations stepped onto the stage of world history. From the Bahá'í Revelation, according to this theoretical schema, a Global civilization will emerge that integrates some of the universal features of previous traditions, while offering new guidance relevant to the building of world unity.

Progressive Revelation is a major teaching of the Bahá'í Faith. It is the view that when a major portion of humanity needs a new religion, when the previous one has lost its potency and guiding power, when decline and corruption have become apparent, and when adherents are disillusioned and adrift, God sends a new Revealer. Each revelation is progressive in that it elevates humanity, propelling us forward after inevitable periods of decline. Each religion at its zenith makes moral, spiritual and social advances over its predecessors. Progressive Revelation is a new paradigm for understanding world religion and world history. Other related principles of the Bahá'í Faith include the elimination of all religious prejudices, the independent investigation of truth, the complementary nature of science and religion, and the necessity of universal education for all people.

The Bahá'í Faith teaches:

> The peoples of the world, of whatever race or religion, derive their inspiration from one heavenly Source, and are the subjects of one God. The difference between the ordinances under which they abide should be attributed to the varying requirements and exigencies of the age in which they were revealed.[1]
> Light is good in whatsoever lamp it is burning.[2]
> A star has the same radiance if it shines from the East or from the West.[3]

---

[1] Bahá'u'lláh, *Gleanings from the Writings of Baha'u'llah*, Bahá'í Publishing Trust, Wilmette, IL, 2005, 111.1.
[2] 'Abdu'l-Bahá, *Paris Talks*, Bahá'í Library Online, 41.9.
[3] Ibid.

> Love the Sun of Truth from whatsoever point (on) the horizon it may arise.[4]
> If the Divine light of truth shone in Jesus Christ, it also shone in Moses and in Buddha.[5] The Prophets of God have been inspired with the message of love and unity.[6]
> See the truth in all religions, for truth is in all, and truth is one.[7]

Progressive Revelation is the claim that all religions are essentially one—having come from the one and only Divine Source—and the differences among them are due to the varying requirements of the cultural and historical contexts in which they were born. This means that Founders such as Moses, Zoroaster, Krishna, Buddha, Christ, Muhammad, and Bahá'u'lláh were united in their divine aspects and spiritual teachings. They were prophetically linked agents of a single providential plan. Their authority was given to them by God, and each had equal access to divine wisdom and power. But they were also distinct in their human temples, historically separate and addressing unique social contexts.

In the next section we look at the question of how the Spiritual and Secular spheres of human life became separated from the Religious in the sixteenth and seventeenth centuries. Here we consider some of the broad developments in the nineteenth and twentieth centuries, followed by some possibilities for the twenty-first and twenty-second centuries. Few would deny that the social and political influence of traditional religions—especially Hinduism, Buddhism, Christianity, and Islam—declined markedly in the nineteenth century. Into this power vacuum stepped the empire-conscious nation-states of England, France, Germany, and Russia. Other attempts to fill the power and direction vacuum

---

[4] Ibid.
[5] Ibid.
[6] 'Abdu'l-Bahá, *Promulgation of Universal Peace*, Bahá'í Publishing Trust, Wilmette, IL, 2007, no. 98.
[7] 'Abdu'l-Bahá, *Paris Talks,* 41.11.

were offered through the ideologies of Nationalism, Communism and Capitalism, which functioned in part as man-made pseudo-religions, becoming aligned in their worst episodes with totalitarian regimes. Because human beings are value-seeking and meaning-making beings, the weakening of religious guidance has palpable collective consequences as we desperately seek a larger orientation and worldview providing purpose and inspiration.

During this same period, humanity's spiritual decline — a relative moral vacuum or void — was partly filled by newer spiritual movements such as the Sikh faith, Theosophy, New Age questing and a wide array of restorationist movements such as those mentioned above. However, the Bahá'í faith is here viewed as a truly Divine initiative, re-casting humanity's understanding of religion and history, while fulfilling prophecies of the Promised Day, and generating a global process toward World Unity.

We can also see the broad pattern of world leaders responding to the two World Wars by establishing international organizations — the League of Nations and the United Nations — seeking at least a minimal degree of global cooperation, peace-making and international human rights. From a Bahá'í perspective, such leaders and initiatives unconsciously reflect the New Light brought to our world in the nineteenth century by Bahá'u'lláh. A growing portion of the world's population, also unconsciously reflecting the New Light, in the closing decades of the twentieth century declared themselves 'Spiritual but not Religious'. Some of them began voicing environmental concerns and working to direct the Communications Revolution toward greater economic interdependence, as well as toward planetary harmony and artistic creativity.

The Coronavirus Pandemic might be viewed as among the consequences of improper earth care, of placing economic desires above science-based healthcare, of the inadequacy of the national sovereignty system, and of our widespread estrangement from Divine Guidance. Global problems require global solutions, which in turn require ever-expanding forms of global governance, which in turn require spiritual humility and receptivity. Aggressive, competitive nation-states are unfit and obsolete in a world that has become so intricately interdependent. Growth of this realization will eventually make the Religious, the Spiritual and Secular more confluent, and in the future — after a few more global calamities — they will become re-integrated at ever higher levels.

However, in the twenty-first and twenty-second centuries, further breakdowns and crises are inevitable — environmentally, economically, politically, and spiritually — until humanity fully recognizes itself as one family created and progressively guided by one God. As this recognition of human solidarity and Divine Oneness deepens, as the unity-promoting principles of the Bahá'í Faith are more widely implemented, and as humanity matures spiritually, the historic attainment of global peace, justice and prosperity will become ever more visible.

HOW THE RELIGIOUS, THE SPIRITUAL, AND THE SECULAR BECAME DIFFERENTIATED

For most of humanity's time on earth, we have not been aware of, nor have we needed to express any serious distinctions between the Religious, the Spiritual and the Secular. Beliefs, rituals, aspirations, family life, means of subsistence, patterns of leadership and social structures were all intimately intertwined. Intercultural contact brought waves of awareness of such distinctions, but rarely in ways that were sustained and historically significant. But this began to change in the sixteenth and seventeenth centuries in the West, with implications for much of the rest of the world. Secularization is the term usually applied to the socio-historical process of drawing away from the Religious and Spiritual spheres. It has been associated with the rise of individualism, of science, and of the modern nation-state.

Here are some of the primary historical factors and developments leading to the rise of the Secular West.

1 — **Islamic Learning Centers** — Baghdad, Damascus, Cairo, Salerno, Cordova, Toledo and Granada — the latter three coveted

by European aristocrats and leaders — leading to European universities.

2 — Collapse of Constantinople — Byzantine Greek scholars moving to Italy, especially after 1453, and sharing their knowledge and manuscripts with Italian scholars.

3 — Economic Developments — ending of Medieval Feudalism with the rise of guild system expertise, middle class leisure, as well as competitive spirit in many fields.

4 — Printing and Book Distribution — invention and improvement of the printing press, especially Gutenberg's, leading to many publications enhancing humanistic education.

5 — Government-supported Exploration — such as those voyages sponsored by Portugal, Spain, Italy, England, France, and Holland — leading to Colonization of much of Africa and Asia.

6 — Independence of Italian Cities — Genoa, Venice, Verona, Padua, Pisa, and Florence — where humanistic studies and attitudes developed, focusing on classical learning.

7 — Renaissance Patrons of Arts and Learning — such as the Medicis in Florence, or more generally, the union of money, leisure, and individual artistic talent.

8 — Creative and Disciplined Individuals — such as Leonardo and Michelangelo in the arts, and Galileo, Boyle, Newton, and Lavoisier in the sciences.

9 — Re-Emergence of Esoteric Spirituality — the Hermetic Tradition ("As Above, So Below"), Alchemy, Neoplatonism and Kabbalism were re-discovered and re-developed by Pico, Ficino, Paracelsus, and Luria — influencing both science and religion, while establishing a kind of Spiritual underground.

10 — Religious Abuses, Challenges to Church Authority, and Reform — influential critiques and reform efforts such as those of Erasmus, More, Luther, Calvin, Loyola, Teresa of Avila, and John of the Cross — encompassing both the Protestant Reformation and the Catholic Counter-Reformation.

11 — Government-supported Science — such as the experimentation proposed by Francis Bacon, and actually funded by England, France, Holland, and Germany.

12 — **The Enlightenment** — a movement of thought and rationality represented by such thinkers as Locke, Hume, Rousseau, Kant, Voltaire, Mendelssohn, and Jefferson — influencing science, religion, politics, the arts and education.

The specific turning-point in the rise of the Secular West was the **Thirty Years War (1618–48)**, a time of tremendous devastation for the people and leadership of Germany. It ended the domination of the Hapsburgs and the Holy Roman Empire, further weakening religious authority, while strengthening secular and national authority. Lutherans and Calvinists gained status in Germany, Spain lost power, Sweden and the Netherlands gained power, while France emerged as the dominant imperial force in the Western hemisphere at that time.

The **Peace of Westphalia (1648)** formally ended hostilities, redrawing the map of Europe, redrafting Western concepts of international relations, while finally establishing that Catholics and Protestants would have to share Europe. Protestantism itself continued to diversify even further. Church and state became much more widely separated, and the church began its long process of decline and marginalization in Western culture. The Secular had clearly parted from the Religious and the Spiritual.

A few other major developments and marking-posts in the rise of the Secular in recent centuries would include the **First Industrial Revolution** (c 1760 ⇒ 1840) which began in England and spread to most of Europe and the United States. This was followed by the **Second Industrial Revolution** (1840 ⇒ 1900) which spread from the Western world to parts of the Eastern world and the Southern Pacific. In these same time periods the social influence of Christianity, Islam, Hinduism, and Buddhism fell precipitously.

In the 1840s came the height of **Millennial Expectation** in Europe and North America, with parallel movements and echoes in the Middle East, India, Southeast Asia, and China in the 1850s. Bahá'ís claim that all of these millennial movements — most directly and discernibly the millennial movement in Iran — were signs of spiritual awareness that a New Day of God was being ushered in by Bahá'u'lláh in the middle and late nineteenth century. Hopefully this major religious turning-point will be more clearly understood by future generations.

1848 is called the **Year of Revolutions**, because there were many public cries for greater equality and human rights in France, Germany, Austria, and Italy. This was also the year that Marx's "Communist Manifesto" appeared. Darwin's "Origin of Species" appeared in 1859, sparking many intense 'science vs religion' debates. And in 1870 the Pope was confined to the Vatican by Italian troops, marking the official end of the Holy Roman Empire. The weakening of traditional Religion set the stage for the differentiation and rise of the Secular sphere in human affairs worldwide.

Globalization became a recognizable phenomenon in the early twentieth century. When rigidly aligned with the ideologies of materialism and nationalism, it become implicated in such ethical violations as racism, sexism, and classism; and even with the genocidal atrocities associated with Nazi Germany, Serbian Bosnia and Hutu Rwanda. But the details of these connected developments are well beyond the scope of this study, which accents the hopeful and constructive side of Globalization.

SECULAR SOCIETY'S ASPECTS THAT OFFER THE PROMISE OF PROGRESS

Secularity, secularization, and secularism are related but not interchangeable terms. **Secularity** is concern with the needs of daily living — whether as individuals or collectives — with or without Religious and Spiritual influence. **Secularization** is the process whereby the religious sphere loses, by degrees, its social significance as described in the previous section. But this process is by no means irreversible, and the re-integration of the Religious and Spiritual seems probable. **Secularism** usually means a deliberate focus on this-worldly matters, and a turning away from, or exclusion of, the Religious and the Spiritual spheres. Here we are concerned with what aspects of the Secular hold promise for societal progress, how an integrative and progressive form of Secularity might function, and whether a strident and imposed secularism presents dangers for humanity.

We might note here that **Globalization** is not merely the worldwide spread of economic Secularization. It is a broader concept containing not only economic and political dimensions, but also social and cultural aspects, family and educational factors, technical and scientific domains, as well as philosophical and spiritual-ideational dimensions. But here we focus on those particular socio-cultural and spiritual-ideational parameters of Globalization which appear to be constructive and progressive.

An expanded concept of the Secular might include such social dimensions as: family and community relations, work and economics, education, and avocation (including the arts and recreation), justice and law, security and order, media and infrastructure, science and technology, health, and medicine, as well as governance and the environment. I believe that these aspects of human life cannot justifiably be ignored by the Religious and Spiritual spheres. They are all needed for a whole society. Highminded citizenship is integral to Religious and Spiritual life. Good citizens embrace ethical concerns for the common good, and this requires constructive participation in some, if not all of these social dimensions of the Secular sphere. Therefore, an integrative and progressive Secularity — in any cultural or national context — would provide productive and creative opportunity in all these areas. Such societies allow a range of Religious and Spiritual expressions, without permitting any single belief-system to dominate all others. A society of this kind, recognizing universal human rights and offering substantial degrees of governmental participation, would inevitably advance, due to the empowerment it affords its citizens.

But Secularism seems to pose a serious threat to human well-being. One might ask: Are there any forms of enforced secularism that would be desirable and sustainable in any geographic or cultural setting? Several such experiments were actually undertaken in the twentieth century: in Italy, Spain, Germany, the Soviet Union, China, Japan, and Korea. They do not appear to have succeeded. Their economies, their cultural expression, and their sense of collective fulfillment ground to a halt. These nations resumed making progress only to the extent that they modified and diversified their dictatorial regimes of imposed secularism. Given that human nature contains non-material or spiritual capacities which clamor for expression, the attempt to constitutionalize secularism is doomed to failure. Human consciousness requires a larger sense of purpose and aspiration than materialistic secularism can provide. However, the integration of spiritual purposes and appropriate material means yields progress and fulfillment.

ENGAGING EXCLUSIVE BELIEF-GROUPS IN WIDER LEARNING AND COOPERATION

In my interfaith work over the decades, I have developed a formula that guides me: Better than conflict between belief-groups is tolerance; better than tolerance is acceptance; better than acceptance is respect; better than respect is understanding; better than understanding is cooperation; and better than cooperation is unity-building. Of course, this developmental sequence is easier said than done. There are usually painful dynamics — progress and regress and renewal — as we grow through these relational stages.

1 — **Tolerance** is a situational virtue, a major step forward when there have been hostilities between belief-groups, for it means living side by side with people and value-orientations that feel difficult to accept.

2 — **Acceptance** means suspending one's criticisms and prejudices and choosing to get along.

3 — **Respect** means giving others full attention and consideration.

4 — **Understanding** means seeing the basic rationale behind others' beliefs and empathizing with their conduct.

5 — **Cooperation** means planning and working with others on projects of mutual interest.

6 — Unity-building means establishing together with others a better community, society and world, in accordance with Divine guidance.

In this section we focus on understanding, and in the next section we focus on cooperation and unity-building. Exclusive belief-groups pose the greatest challenge for interfaith understanding, cooperation, and unity-building. What are the most constructive responses to those who declare, in effect, "Our view is the only true one"? Can such views and persons be sincerely welcomed and integrated into cooperative activity? Can prejudices leading to conflict — prejudices on both sides of the argument — be ultimately overcome?

I agree with Harvey Cox that attempting to reconcile the universal and the particular aspects of major faith traditions is both vexing and essential. As I have tried to show elsewhere ("Founders of Faith") each of the major religions says, in effect, "We are all one under the Ultimate Reality, fellow family members of one Creator". This is the universal claim. But each of the major faith traditions also says, in effect, "You must recognize and obey our Divine Teacher in order to attain fulfillment." This is the particular claim. If only one set of claims is shared and emphasized — the universal or the particular — then dialogue and cooperation are blocked and interfaith progress grinds to a halt. Sharing the universal and particular dimensions of our traditions takes courage, intellectual capacity, as well as humility and perseverance.

Bahá'u'lláh, the founder of the Bahá'í Faith, offered several strategies for inter-religious reconciliation. *"The purpose of religion,"* He taught, *"is to establish unity and concord amongst the peoples of the world; make it not the cause of dissension and strife."*[8] Moojan Momen analyzed Bahá'u'lláh's strategies of reconciliation, and I attempt to summarize these strategies briefly. Sincere

---

[8] Bahá'u'lláh, *Tablets of Bahá'u'lláh Revealed after the Kitab-i-Aqdas*, Bahá'í Library Online, no. 14.

participants in interfaith discussions should recognize certain general truths, because each of these principles contributes to resolving divergent beliefs:

1) There is some truth in all major theological-philosophical views.
2) Human beings have finite minds and cannot comprehend Ultimate Reality.
3) Each can discern a portion of truth, relative to the individual's viewpoint and framework.
4) Human concepts of Ultimate Reality refer to impersonal or personal manifestations of God.
5) Unity-building, virtue-development, establishing universal justice — these practical considerations override theoretical and conceptual debates.

The fourth principle here is the recognition that Eastern religions often depict Ultimate Reality in impersonal, abstract terms such as the Beyond or the Transcendent, while Western religions often use more personal, concrete terms such our Lord and Savior. But overall, moral and practical concerns are more important. When these principles are observed and acted upon, participants enter into a learning mode, and prejudices are reduced as knowledge and understanding replace presumptions and stereotypes. Even exclusivist participants who are treated with respect and understanding, and in a spirit of cooperation, can be drawn into unity-building.

Momen concludes:

> Thus we may describe Bahá'u'lláh's project as a metareligion — a religion that encompasses and provides a theoretical framework within which it is possible to see the truth of all religions. To the contradictory truth claims of the various religions of the world, he does not assert the truth of any particular metaphysical position but rather responds in two stages. The first stage is the relativist

statement that religious metaphysical truth is an individual truth which each person sees from his or her own viewpoint. The second stage is to deny that metaphysics itself is the core of religion. Although throughout the history of religion, religions have tended to define themselves in terms of certain metaphysical positions, Bahá'u'lláh denies that this is either the central point or purpose of religion. Religion is for the purpose of advancing human spirituality through the acquisition of virtues and of advancing human civilization through the achievement of greater degrees of unity. Whatever advances these goals is true religion.[9]

Here are some teachings of Bahá'u'lláh that promote reconciliation and unity:

The earth is but one country and mankind its citizens.[10]
Let your vision be world-embracing.[11]
Ye dwell in one world, and have been created through the operation of one Will.[12]
So powerful is the light of unity that it can illuminate the whole earth.[13]
Consort with the followers of all religions in a spirit of friendliness and fellowship.[14]
Ye are the fruit of one tree, and the leaves of one branch.[15]
For the sake of God resolve to root out whatever is the source of contention amongst you.[16]

---

[9] *The Bahá'í Faith and the World's Religions*, ed. Moojan Momen, George Ronald, Publisher, Oxford, 2003, Chapter One, "The God of Bahá'u'lláh," concluding section, final paragraph, p 38.
[10] Bahá'u'lláh, *Gleanings from the Writings of Bahá'u'lláh*, 117.1.
[11] Ibid, 43.5.
[12] Ibid, 156.1.
[13] Ibid, 132.3.
[14] Ibid, 43.6.
[15] Ibid, 132.3.
[16] Ibid, 111.1.

> *Take ye counsel together, and let your concern be only for that which profiteth mankind.*[17]
> *Be a sea for the thirsty, a haven for the distressed, an upholder and defender of the victim of oppression.*[18]
> *Be a luminary above the horizon of virtue... a shining light in the firmament of thy generation.*[19]
> *The well-being of mankind, its peace and security, are unattainable unless and until its unity is firmly established.*[20]
> *That which the Lord hath ordained as the sovereign remedy and mightiest instrument for the healing of all the world, is the union of all its peoples in one universal Cause, one common Faith.*[21]

And here are some teachings of 'Abdu'l-Bahá, the son of Bahá'u'lláh, on reconciliation and unity:

> *Religion is reality, and reality is one. The fundamentals of the religion of God are, therefore, one in reality.*[22]
> *Baha'u'llah has drawn the circle of unity... a design for the uniting of all peoples, and for the gathering of them all under the shelter of the tent of universal unity.*[23]
> *In the eye of the Creator all His children are equal; His goodness is poured forth on all.*
> *He does not favor this nation nor that nation, all alike are His creatures.*
> *This being so, why should we make divisions, separating one race from another?*

---

[17] Ibid, 120.1.
[18] Ibid, 130.1.
[19] Ibid.
[20] Ibid, 131.2.
[21] Ibid, 120.3.
[22] 'Abdu'l-Bahá, *The Promulgation of Universal Peace*, no. 47.
[23] 'Abdu'l-Bahá, *Paris Talks*, 15.12.

> Why should we create barriers of superstition and tradition bringing discord and hatred among people?[24]
> All men are of one family; the crown of humanity rests on the head of every human being.[25]

FOSTERING TRANSFORMATIVE COMMUNITY-BUILDING IN EVER-WIDER CIRCLES

In closing this chapter I attempt to briefly describe some Bahá'í-inspired methods of community-building. I generalize my terminology hoping to be more applicable to, and recognizable by other faith communities, as well as by unaffiliated spiritual activists and high-minded secular justice advocates. Bahá'ís are attempting to implement the guidance of their highest authoritative body, the Universal House of Justice. This agency is believed to be divinely guided, and to be correctly interpreting the teachings of Bahá'u'lláh, the Manifestation of God for this era of world unity. The current plan includes a worldwide process of transformative community-building in ever wider circles, seeking to engage ever-larger portions of humanity. Transformation is understood as more than positive change; rather, it is a process of moving toward a higher mode of being, an advance in evolutionary development, or even a breakthrough in humanity's spiritual maturation. The ultimate aim is co-establishing an ever-advancing global civilization, bringing peace, justice, and prosperity for all people.

A Bahá'í-inspired approach to community-building might include sequential categories of activities or processes, which could be called the four Ps. This is a way of learning through spiritual and practical experience, as well as by study of guidance, discerning surrounding conditions, and implementing plans.

1 — **Praying** — devotion or worship — spiritual conversation with our Creator through a Divine Intermediary (for Bahá'ís this is Bahá'u'lláh)... praising and drawing closer to Divine Reality... puri-

---

[24] Ibid, 42.3.
[25] Ibid, 42.2.

fying the insistent and egocentric self... quickening spiritual energies... cultivating receptivity to and conforming with Divine Will.

2 — **Pondering** — meditation or discernment — considering the import of sacred verses... setting the heart toward Higher Truth... posing questions to the Spirit and receiving guidance... reflecting on what has been learned from experience... reading contextual realities or conditions... disclosing more comprehensive meanings... discovering realities previously unknown.

3 — **Planning** — consultation or deliberation and designating steps — identifying practical means, both individually and with others... proposing a proper order of their implementation... scheduling time, space, and resources... determining the immediate path to be taken... mustering decisive resolve.

4 — **Performing** — action or implementation — reaping the fruits of pondering and planning... translating Divine guidance into action... arising to serve the Divine Cause... carrying out inspired and selfless deeds... offering service projects... engaging in elevated discourses on the major issues of the day... persevering with audacity, wisdom, and humility.

After one cycle or sequence of these activities ends, a new one begins, attempting to build upon the learnings of previous cycles. Integration among the four Ps is a sign of spiritual growth. 'Abdu'l-Bahá referred to this integration of spiritual and volitional practices, or prayerful serving in ever-wider circles:

> Strive that your actions day by day may be beautiful prayers. Turn towards God and seek always to do that which is right and noble. Enrich the poor, raise the fallen, comfort the sorrowful, bring healing to the sick, reassure the fearful, rescue the oppressed, bring hope to the hopeless, shelter the destitute![26]

Also in the current global Bahá'í plan, there are four kinds of small groups — covering the lifespan — and the above-mentioned four moral-spiritual processes take place in each of these groups:

---

[26] Ibid, 26.7.

1) children's classes, 2) junior youth empowerment groups, 3) devotional gatherings, and 4) adult study-and-action circles. Bahá'ís have developed a Training Institute that systematically fosters capacities, attitudes, spiritual knowledge, and skills to enable ever-expanding numbers to take ownership of their own community-building. The emphasis is on moral-spiritual empowerment and community service. When all of these groups and processes are operating coherently in a community, integrated with effective social action and public discourse on prevalent issues, facilitated by thoughtful administration, supported by material means, enriched by the arts, supplemented by good outreach and public relations — then a significant contribution is made to the building of a more united and spiritually globalized world.

If Revelation generates advanced learning and higher cultural expression — as Bahá'í Writings claim — then this progressive pattern has operated in the past to generate the great civilizations of world history. Processes similar to the four Ps, but perhaps less widespread and systematic, bore significant cultural fruit in the course of world history when royal patrons of learning and progress helped implement Divine guidance. High-points of civilization became manifest and visible, for example, in Jerusalem under David and Solomon, in ancient Persia under Cyrus and Darius, in India under the Guptas, in China under the Tang rulers, in Constantinople under Justinian, and in Baghdad and Cordova under high-minded caliphs.

Authentic and original religious inspiration has the power to engender cultural advancement and moral-spiritual maturation for humanity. God willing, our world family will attain another Golden Age, but one much more global in scope than in ages past. But we should not expect this evolution to take place without sacrificial suffering, perseverance, a perplexing blend of disintegrating and integrating forces, and widespread embracing of the unifying power of Divine guidance.

Elena Mustakova identified some of the main collective capacities — or skills of social evolution — that humanity seems poised to develop in the twenty-first and twenty-second centuries if we can add the necessary moral-spiritual dimensions of Globalization:

a) Recognition of our oneness;
b) Rethinking of freedom in the age of maturity, as honoring interdependence;
c) Rethinking the role of authority and governance in regulating planetary life;
d) Ability to develop meaningful collaborative relationships with different science and faith communities, and to work together toward the spiritual and social evolution of society, creating collective centers of illumination;
e) Vast grassroots consultative processes and initiatives;
f) Building consultative governing bodies representative of human diversity;
g) New social, political, and economic structures that reflect unity in diversity;
h) Collective service to the advancement of human and planetary wellbeing.[27]

CONCLUSION

We can almost all get along! Those who identify with widely diverging Spiritual, Religious and Secular circles — and their various combinations — can get along. There are constructive and progressive aspects of the here-to-stay Globalization process. Humanity can grow ever more loving, capable, and unified as the created family of God. But manifesting our glorious potential — both individually and collectively — will probably require several more centuries of patient discipline such as the four Ps, cultivating virtues, interfaith understanding and cooperation, resilience in the face of calamities, breakdowns which ultimately

---

[27] Elena Mustakova, *Global Unitive Healing: Integral Skills for Personal and Collective Transformation*, Light on Light Press, Fort Lauderdale, FL, 2021, pp 161–2.

yield breakthroughs, socio-cultural evolution, or in one phrase: transformative unity-building in ever-wider circles. We close with words drawn from a prayer conveying the aspiration to fulfill our calling to be worthy of humanity's Divine blessings:

> O Thou kind Lord! Unite all. Let the religions agree and make the nations one, so that we may see each other as one family and the whole earth as one home.
> May we all live together in perfect harmony...
> Gladden our hearts through the fragrance of Thy love.
> Brighten our eyes through the Light of Thy Guidance.
> Delight our ears with the melody of Thy Word, and shelter us all in the Stronghold of Thy Providence.
> Thou art the Mighty and Powerful, Thou art the Forgiving and Thou art the One Who overlooks the shortcomings of all mankind.[28]

REFERENCES AND SOURCES

'Abdu'l-Bahá, *Some Answered Questions*, Bahá'í World Centre, Haifa, Israel, 2014

———, *The Promulgation of Universal Peace*, Bahá'í Publishing Trust, Wilmette, IL, 2007

———, *Paris Talks*, Bahá'í Library Online, https://www.bahai.org/library/ authoritative-texts/abdul-baha/paris-talks/.

Alexander, Fran, editor, *Oxford Encyclopedia of World History*, Oxford University Press, New York, 1998.

Armstrong, Karen, *A History of God: The 4000-Year Quest of Judaism, Christianity and Islam*, Ballantine Books, New York, 1993.

Bahá'í worldwide community website — www.bahai.org.

Bahá'u'lláh, *Gleanings from the Writings of Bahá'u'lláh*, Bahá'í Publishing Trust, Wilmette, IL, 2005.

———, *Kitab-i-Iqan: The Book of Certitude*, Bahá'í Publishing Trust, Wilmette, IL, 2003.

---

[28] Abdul-Baha, *The Promulgation of Universal Peace*, no. 41.

———, *Tablets of Bahá'u'lláh Revealed after the Kitab-i-Aqdas*, Bahá'í Library Online, https://www.bahai.org/library/authoritative-texts/bahaullah/tablets-bahaullah/.

Beversluis, Joel, editor, *Sourcebook of the World's Religions: An Interfaith Guide to Religion and Spirituality*, New World Library, Novato, CA, 2000.

Bowker, John, editor, *The Oxford Dictionary of World Religions*, Oxford University Press, New York, 1997.

Braybrooke, Marcus, *Faith and Interfaith in a Global Age*, CoNexus Press, Grand Rapids, MI, 1998.

Canadian Interfaith Conversation — www.interfaithconversation.ca — Box 5885 West Beaver Creek Post Office, Richmond Hill, ON L4B 0B8.

Cohn-Sherbok, Dan, *A Concise Encyclopedia of Judaism*, Oneworld Publications, Oxford, 1998.

Cox, Harvey, *Many Mansions: A Christian's Encounter with Other Faiths*, Beacon Press, Boston, 1988.

Eck, Diana, *Encountering God: A Spiritual Journey from Bozeman to Banaras*, Beacon Press, Boston, 1992.

Gibbs, Charles and Mahe, Sally, *Birth of a Global Community: Appreciative Inquiry in Action*, Lakeshore Communications, Inc, Bedford Heights, OH, 2004.

Hatcher, John, *The Face of God Among Us: How the Creator Educates Humanity*, Bahá'í Publishing Trust, Wilmette, IL 2010.

Klostermaier, Klaus, *A Concise Encyclopedia of Hinduism*, Oneworld Publications, Oxford, 1998.

Mehr, Farhang, *The Zoroastrian Tradition*, Element, Inc, Rockport, MA, 1991.

Momen, Moojan, *The Phenomenon of Religion: A Thematic Approach*, Oneworld Publications, Oxford, 1999.

Momen, Moojan, editor, *The Bahá'í Faith and the World's Religions*, George Ronald, Publisher, Oxford, 2003.

Mustakova, Elena, *Global Unitive Healing: Integral Skills for Personal and Collective Transformation*, Light on Light Press, Fort Lauderdale, FL, 2021.

Newby, Gordon, *A Concise Encyclopedia of Islam*, Oneworld Publications, Oxford, 2002.

Parrinder, Geoffrey, *A Concise Encyclopedia of Christianity*, Oneworld Publications, 1998.

Powers, John, *A Concise Encyclopedia of Buddhism*, Oneworld Publications, Oxford, 2000.

Rosen, Harold, *Founders of Faith: The Parallel Lives of God's Messengers*, Bahá'í Publishing Trust, Wilmette, IL, 2010.

———, *Eye to the Ages: The Rise, Fall and Progressive Renewal of Civilization*, unpublished manuscript, Afnan Library, National Spiritual Assembly of the Bahá'ís of the United Kingdom.

Ruhi Institute — Bahá'í community-building process — www.ruhi.org.

Singh, Harbans, editor, *The Encyclopedia of Sikhism*, Punjabi University, Patiala, India, 1998.

Shoghi Effendi, *The World Order of Bahá'u'lláh*, Bahá'í Publishing Trust, Wilmette, IL, 1991.

Smith, Peter, *A Concise Encyclopedia of the Bahá'í Faith*, Oneworld Publications, Oxford, 2000.

Teeple, John, editor, *Timelines of World History*, Dorling Kindersley Ltd, New York, 2006.

Toynbee, Arnold and Caplan, Jane *A Study of History*, first abridged one-volume edition, Oxford University Press, New York, 1972.

Universal House of Justice, prepared under its supervision two especially relevant documents on the theme of this chapter: *Century of Light*, Bahá'í Canada Publications, Thornhill, Ontario, 2001; and *One Common Faith*, Bahá'í Canada Publications, Thornhill, Ontario, 2005.

Globalization Requires a Bahá'í Foundation

HOOSHMAND BADEE

INTRODUCTION

Justice is one of the fundamental tenets of the Bahá'í Faith, and a wide range of topics are associated with it. Among many, the following two statements from the writings of the Prophet and Founder of the Bahá'í Faith, Bahá'u'lláh reveal the importance of this subject.

> No light can compare with the light of justice. The establishment of order in the world and the tranquillity of the nations depend on it.[1]
>
> We cherish the hope that the light of justice may shine upon the world and sanctify it from tyranny. If the rulers and kings of the earth, the symbols of the power of God, exalted be His glory, arise and resolve to dedicate themselves to whatever will promote the highest interests of the whole of humanity, the reign of justice will assuredly be established amongst the children of men, and the effulgence of its light will envelop the whole earth.[2]

To begin this discussion, a logical and reasonable question is, why is there a need for justice? A sensible answer is that there are injustices of all kinds at all levels of society that become barriers to the creation of meaningful Globalization. For example, injustice arises concerning economic exploitation, the suffering of the poor, the malnourishment of children, child labour, wage

---

[1] Bahá'u'lláh (1988). *Epistle to the Son of the Wolf*, p. 28.
[2] Bahá'u'lláh (1983). *Gleanings from the Writings of Bahá'u'lláh*, p. 218.

discrimination, oppression of women, relentless competition, unfair international trade, corruption, human displacement, and separation from families at a young age. It is manifestly unjust for the nations to spend an increasing amount of their wealth on unnecessary, unethical, and even destructive goods and services instead of eliminating the suffering of millions of people. It is also unjust to damage planet earth to which future generations have the same rights as we do and which we take for granted. In this regard, Bahá'u'lláh states, "Justice is, to this day, bewailing its plight, and equity groaneth beneath the yoke of oppression. The thick clouds of tyranny have darkened the face of the earth and enveloped its peoples."[3] Likewise, 'Abdu'l-Bahá, the Centre of the Covenant of the Bahá'í Faith asserts,

> We ask God to endow human souls with justice so that they may be fair, and may strive to provide for the comfort of all, that each member of humanity may pass his life in the utmost comfort and welfare. Then this material world will become the very paradise of the Kingdom, this elemental earth will be in a heavenly state, and all the servants of God will live in the utmost joy, happiness, and gladness. We must all strive and concentrate all our thoughts so that such happiness may accrue to the world of humanity.[4]

Hence, various wrongdoings have infiltrated people's lives in all strata of society, and only the application of justice can remedy this. Bahá'u'lláh states, "There can be no doubt whatever that if the day-star of justice, which the clouds of tyranny have obscured, were to shed its light upon men, the face of the earth would be completely transformed."[5] The view expressed is that justice is a human virtue that makes a person socially, politically, and economically conscientious and society internally harmonious.

---

[3] Bahá'u'lláh (1983). *Gleanings from the Writings of Bahá'u'lláh*, p. 92.
[4] 'Abdu'l-Bahá (1979). *Foundations of World Unity*, p. 4.
[5] Bahá'u'lláh (1983). *Gleanings from the Writings of Bahá'u'lláh*, p. 218.

THE MEANING AND CONCEPT OF GLOBALIZATION

Globalization is the word used to describe the growing interdependence of the world's economies, cultures, and populations, brought about by cross-border trade in goods and services, technology, and flows of investment, people, and information. Countries have built economic partnerships to facilitate these movements over many centuries. But the term gained popularity after the Cold War in the early 1990s, as these cooperative arrangements shaped modern everyday life.[6] The view of several experts in Globalization is that the current process of Globalization is generating unbalanced outcomes. That wealth is being created, but not many countries and people share its benefits. Most developing countries have little or no voice in shaping the process. These global imbalances are economically unproductive, politically unsustainable, and morally unacceptable. Other factors are essential for reforming and reshaping the current process of Globalization. Several issues need to be considered, including inequality and the democratic deficit in global economic institutions, which weakens democracy in developed and developing countries. For example, the benefits of Globalization have not been distributed fairly and justly among citizens of the world. Although, with current Globalization, millions of people have come out of absolute poverty, which is commendable, not all countries are affected in the process of poverty reduction. Consequently, the problem with the current version of Globalization is that although the idea is good, the process of achieving it is not adequate.

THE SIGNIFICANCE OF BAHÁ'Í GLOBALIZATION

Meaningful Globalization requires a proper foundation. Unity and justice are closely tied together. They are the two funda-

---

[6] "What Is Globalization? And How Has the Global Economy Shaped the United States?" *Peterson Institute for International Economics*, https://www.piie.com/microsites/globalization/what-is-globalization.

mental pillars of establishing enlightened Globalization. There is a significant relationship between oneness and justice. The oneness of humankind is the foundation for establishing a desired economic justice. Bahá'u'lláh states, "The light of men is justice. Quench it not with the contrary winds of oppression and tyranny. The purpose of justice is the appearance of unity among men."[7] This oneness, according to Shoghi Effendi is "the pivot round which all the teachings of Bahá'u'lláh revolve."[8] Therefore, promoting it is the object of life for every Bahá'í. Oneness is such an essential principle that we can call the Bahá'í Faith a religion of oneness. The vision of all Faiths has been the establishment of oneness, but it came in stages of unity of the family, tribes, cities, and nation, and now is the time for establishing the oneness of humankind. Oneness has different levels, stronger the unity, we are closer to oneness.[9] When discussing the principle of the oneness of humankind, Shoghi Effendi upholds that, "Its implications are deeper, its claim greater than any which the Prophets of old were allowed to advance."[10] Unification of humanity came in stages, and each Faith had a vital role to play. Therefore, the oneness of humankind is the main reason for the coming of Bahá'u'lláh and a fundamental prerequisite for enlightened Globalization. Several statements in the Bahá'í writings clearly emphasize the meaning and significance of Globalization concerning the oneness of humankind, including phrases such as "the well-being of mankind"[11], "betterment of the world"[12], and "Let your vision be world-embracing"[13] and "The interde-

---

[7] Bahá'u'lláh (1978). *Tablets of Bahá'u'lláh Revealed after the Kitáb-i-Aqdas*, P. 67.
[8] Shoghi Effendi (1982). *World Order of Bahá'u'lláh*, p. 42.
[9] The author makes contrasts between unity and oneness. Unity is the process; oneness is the outcome. Unity is the catalyst that is the bridge to go into oneness. Unity is the means to an end, but all events and activities should have sufficient follow-up that allows oneness to develop.
[10] Shoghi Effendi (1982). *World Order of Bahá'u'lláh*, p. 42.
[11] Bahá'u'lláh (1983). *Gleanings from the Writings of Bahá'u'lláh*, p. 286.
[12] Bahá'u'lláh. *A Compilation on Trustworthiness*, p. 5.
[13] Bahá'u'lláh (1983). *Gleanings from the Writings of Bahá'u'lláh*, p. 94.

pendence of the peoples and nations of the earth."[14] Similarly, Bahá'u'lláh uses metaphorical expressions such as "the entire human race as one soul and one body"[15] and "ye are the flowers of one garden."[16] He also refers to the catastrophic condition of the world, stating, "The world is encompassed with misery and distress"[17] and "The world is in great turmoil."[18]

'Abdu'l-Bahá confirms that "Today the world of humanity is in need of international unity and conciliation."[19] He then asserts several essential principles for establishing unity.

> To establish these great fundamental principles, a propelling power is needed. It is self-evident that the unity of the human world and the Most Great Peace cannot be accomplished through material means. They cannot be established through political power, for the political interests of nations are various, and the policies of peoples are divergent and conflicting. They cannot be founded through racial or patriotic power, for these are human powers, selfish and weak. The very nature of racial differences and patriotic prejudices prevents the realization of this unity and agreement. Therefore, it is evidenced that the promotion of the oneness of the Kingdom of humanity, which is the essence of the teachings of all the Manifestations of God, is impossible except through the divine power and breaths of the Holy Spirit. Other powers are too weak and are incapable of accomplishing this.[20]

Humans are social beings; hence, just and meaningful Globalization is about the interconnectedness of humans and

---

[14] Shoghi Effendi (1980). *The Promised Day is Come*, p. 122.
[15] Bahá'u'lláh (1983). *Gleanings from the Writings of Bahá'u'lláh*, p. 214.
[16] Bahá'u'lláh. Quoted in *Bahá'u'lláh and the New Era*, p. 209
[17] Bahá'u'lláh (1978). *Tablets of Bahá'u'lláh Revealed after the Kitáb-i-Aqdas*, p. 163.
[18] Bahá'u'lláh (1983). *Gleanings from the Writings of Bahá'u'lláh*, p. 97.
[19] 'Abdu'l-Bahá (2012). *Promulgation of Universal Peace*, pp. 11–12.
[20] Ibid.

the rest of society. We are interconnected from every aspect, politically, socially, economically, environmentally, and morally. A significant subject pertinent to Globalization that has been discussed by 'Abdu'l-Bahá is the interdependence of people and nations. Frequently He emphasizes that "all the members of the human family, whether peoples or governments, cities or villages, have become increasingly interdependent."[21] And in a stronger statement, He continued, "For none is self-sufficiency any longer possible, inasmuch as political ties unite all peoples and nations, and the bonds of trade and industry, of agriculture and education, are being strengthened every day."[22] In light of the above discussion, the following definition given by Bahá'í scholar Suheil Bushrui conveys an appropriate description of understanding the concept of Globalization from a Bahá'í perspective.

> Globalization is a vision of world unity in so deep and broad a sense as to embrace every aspect of human life. However, such a vision of planetary unity and integration bears no relation to the often bland, faceless, and amoral global marketplace that we see operating today. Instead, it recognizes and celebrates the rich diversity of creeds and cultures while at the same time affirming the fundamental oneness of the human race. The Bahá'í approach to Globalization can be summed up as a commitment to the concept of 'unity in diversity' and what this practically entails in the life of the individual and society alike. This definition refers to the fundamental Bahá'í principle of 'world unity', and 'unity in diversity' as practical approaches to ideal Globalization.[23]

The goal of unity is possible because humanity has access to the means necessary to attain it. For example, the revolutionary

---

[21] 'Abdu'l-Bahá (1978). *Selections from the Writings of 'Abdu'l-Bahá*, pp. 31–32.
[22] Ibid. p. 32.
[23] Suheil Bushrui. 'Bahá'í Perspective on Globalization', retrieved at: http://www.onecountry.org/e151/e15102as_Perspective_.htm.

and world-embracing means of communication, transportation, information technology, and global financial interdependency are available as methods of unifying nations. 'Abdu'l-Bahá explains that in the past, "The unity of mankind could not have been achieved..."[24] because the means of coming into contact that is currently available, were not within reach during the past dispensation, thus "...association and interchange of thought were well-nigh impossible."[25] Therefore, it is clear that the features of meaningful Globalization, which are the oneness of humanity, interdependency, and interchange of thoughts, could be facilitated through advanced information and technology. For example, information technology may also promote a faster spread of hate and fear. The embryonic condition for relative hope, integration, and unity is created. Nations increasingly realize that interdependency is a prerequisite for their future prosperity, and consequently, "For none is self-sufficiency any longer possible."[26] The growth of international organizations is evidence of awareness of the interdependency of nations.

It is important to note that the core principle of oneness can be challenged because currently there are many obstacles for the transformation of consciousness, such as doubts, misconceptions, prejudices, suspicions, and narrow self-interest. Such challenges require the society to "... change its attitudes before a solution to social problems can be found."[27]

THE VIEW OF HUMAN FAMILY AND GLOBALIZATION

The phrase 'human family' in the Bahá'í writings shows the entire humanity. It is stated that "The world of humanity has been described as a unit, as one family."[28] Also, it is said, "...we are all inhabiting one globe of the earth. In reality, we are one family

---

[24] 'Abdu'l-Bahá (1978). *Selections from the Writings of 'Abdu'l-Bahá*, p. 31.
[25] Ibid.
[26] 'Abdu'l-Bahá (1978). *Selections from the Writings of 'Abdu'l-Bahá*, p. 32.
[27] Universal House of Justice, 27 April 1988.
[28] 'Abdu'l-Bahá (1979). *Foundation of World Unity*, p. 41.

and each one of us is a member of this family. We must all be in the greatest happiness and comfort."[29] The analogy of the family in Bahá'í globalization and related activities is helpful, given the similarities between the features and structure of a family and those of a global society.

The analogy of the human family described in the Bahá'í writings has a much broader implication in creating unity and justice within humankind. Such an enormous undertaking requires unity and justice within the family and within the world's societies through spiritual and material means. It compels individuals and nations to work together to establish happiness and well-being for all. Today the effects of the gradual application of the spirit of unity, such as the rejection of racial prejudices, the greater awareness of the need to protect the environment, the acceptance of gender equality in many societies, and the greater understanding of human rights, are apparent in the wider society. The application of these would gradually lead to the oneness of humanity.

The analogy of the family in economic activities is also helpful, given the similarities between the features and structure of a family and those of economics. For example, partnership is one of the features of the family. This approach is based on a clear concept of a caring and helping process. It demonstrates how a partnership enables parents and children to overcome their difficulties, build strengths and resilience and fulfil their goals more effectively. The integrity of the family is based on mutual love, trust, service to others, and sacrifices for one another. These qualities are essential for the family to succeed. Otherwise, the family would become dysfunctional and chaotic and will break apart. A family that applies the principles of love, trust, service, and sacrifice can cater to the varied needs of everyone in the family, even with limited resources. In the family unit, division of labour applies too, where each member has a different but complementary function. Thus, the family analogy is the pivot of all

---

[29] Ibid.

economic reciprocal relationships leading to activities of production, distribution, and consumption, be it between the members of the same family, between families or between communities, local, national and international, where we see a logical connection between moral principles and economics.

But contrary to this, the question that should raise is why features working within a family are not working adequately for global society as a human family. 'Abdu'l-Bahá's response is as follows:

> Although the body politic is one family, yet, because of lack of harmonious relations some members are comfortable and some in direst misery; some members are satisfied and some are hungry; some members are clothed in most costly garments and some families are in need of food and shelter. Why? Because this family lacks the necessary reciprocity and symmetry. This household is not well arranged. This household is not living under a perfect law. All the laws which are legislated do not ensure happiness. They do not provide comfort. Therefore, a law must be given to this family by means of which all the members of this family will enjoy equal well-being and happiness.[30]

Now, let us explore and examine the nature of the principle of the family unit and its relationship with the larger society. By looking at those beautiful principles working within a family, we should ask: Why are such principles not working in wider society? For example, in the family unit, with minimal resources, the weaker members of the family, mostly children, are under extreme care. How come currently, as we are speaking, over a billion people in the world go to bed hungry? Or in the family unit, the resources are shared among the members based on equity. How come today, in the wider society, 80% of the world's resources are in the hands of only 20% of the population, increasing the gap? Or

---

[30] 'Abdu'l-Bahá (1982). *Promulgation of Universal Peace*, p. 435.

in the family unit, most activities are based on cooperation. How come in the wider society, it is based on aggressive competition?

It is becoming increasingly clear that the world has been reduced to a global village, and in an ideal sense, the village represents the entire humanity. These changes have made our world smaller. Hence, it was easy for the current pandemic of coronavirus to spread fast throughout the world without consideration of any discrimination and border limitations. With this pandemic, some of the challenges and problems of current Globalization are understood, and the new awareness about globalization based on the concept of unity, cooperation, and compassion is shaping.

THE CONNECTION BETWEEN JUSTICE AND FAIRNESS

Although the two words justice and fairness often appear together or are used interchangeably, there are differences. Justice is the establishment or determination of rights according to the rules of law for the whole of society. It is the maintenance of what is just or right by the exercise of authority or power; assignment of deserved reward or punishment; giving of due deserts.[31] On the other hand, fairness is the quality or state of being fair, and fairness is marked by impartiality, honesty, and mercy, and is free from self-interest and prejudice.[32] Justice is specifically enjoined upon rulers of states to establish order in society, whereas fairness is an ethical principle, and its application is urged to be observed by all. The following extracts from Bahá'u'lláh clarify and distinguish the two terms justice and fairness,

> O son of man! If thine eyes be turned towards mercy, forsake the things that profit thee and cleave unto that which will profit mankind. And if thine eyes be turned

---

[31] "Justice, n.", *Oxford English Dictionary*, https://www.oed.com/view/Entry/102198.
[32] "Fairness, noun," *Merriam-Webster*, https://www.merriam-webster.com/dictionary/fairness.

towards justice, choose thou for thy neighbour that which thou choosest for thyself.[33]

In this verse, Bahá'u'lláh urges us to treat 'mankind' better than ourselves. He focuses on two stations or abilities. Mercy enables a man to forsake his profit for the profit of humankind. And then He says if you set your gaze on justice, apply the Golden Rule.

One of the significant challenges of current Globalization is the disparity between the rich and the poor, particularly the vast accumulation of excessive wealth in the hands of a few. Such disparity, according to the Bahá'í writings, is unjust. 'Abdu'l-Bahá states:

> ...the root cause of these difficulties lies in the law of nature that governs present-day civilization, for it results in a handful of people accumulating vast fortunes that far exceed their needs, while the greater number remain naked, destitute, and helpless. This is at once contrary to justice, to humanity, and to fairness; it is the very height of inequity and runs counter to the good-pleasure of the All-Merciful.[34]

Bearing in mind the meaning of fairness, there is a need for fair-minded policymakers and legislators to set fair and impartial laws for providing equal opportunity for all citizens. This view enables people to discover their hidden talents and capabilities to become productive members of their communities. In other words, humans are equal in the sight of God and laws of the land, however, with different economic capabilities. This way of thinking is a sensible approach for allowing people to become active citizens not only for their own sake but also for contributing to the general well-being. Bahá'u'lláh states: "We exhort the loved

---

[33] Bahá'u'lláh (1978). *Tablets of Bahá'u'lláh Revealed after the Kitáb-i-Aqdas*, p. 68.
[34] 'Abdu'l-Bahá (2014). *Some Answered Questions*, https://www.bahai.org/library/authoritative-texts/abdul-baha/some-answered-questions/, p. 92.

ones of God to observe justice and fairness, and to do that which would prompt the friends of God to evince tender mercy and compassion towards each other."[35]

DEFINING THE CONCEPT OF SPIRITUALITY FOR WELCOMING ALL

To welcome the general population to establish an enlightened Globalization, it is sensible to reconcile the viewpoints of social scientists, theologians, people of Faith, and secular thinkers in embracing and applying a common concept of spirituality. Hence the following working definition is suggested in this paper.

> Spirituality is defined as the all-unifying agency for developing and interconnecting our life with the material world, with other people, with our natural environment, and with the future generation, beyond our human limitations.[36]

Based on this definition and its features of unifying and relational aspects, an alternative interpretation of spirituality is possible for establishing economic justice. This definition contributes to the betterment of external social conditions such as poverty, inequality, population displacement, environmental devastation, and the material side of life. It also refers to the higher nature of human beings represented by qualities of justice and fairness. Justice as a virtue has its place in the higher nature of human beings and is a source of human perfection.

For the subject of Globalization to become meaningful and all-encompassing, the above definition of spirituality is suggested in a way that comprises humanity. This definition includes those who try to distance themselves from religion and consider themselves secular thinkers for various reasons. In other words, they

---

[35] Bahá'u'lláh (1978). *Tablets of Bahá'u'lláh*. p. 132.
[36] Hooshmand Badee (2018). *Economics and the Bahá'í Faith*, p. 34.

consider themselves spiritual but not affiliated with any organized religion. The view of all Holy Scriptures is that humans are gifted with higher nature, but it needs to be nurtured and developed. This "all-unifying agency"[37] or all-unifying function of spirituality helps resolve difficulties when we come face to face with problems. The belief in the higher nature of human beings also closely correlates with the purpose of life. The purpose of life is not simply the satisfaction of one's own needs and enjoyment of material pleasures but also involves service to one's community and the wider society. A similar interpretation of the concept of spirituality as a unifying factor is given by David Hay, a professor of child psychology at Aberdeen University in Scotland. According to him, "secular thinkers and social scientists can recognize spirituality when facing problems."[38] Let us apply this concept of spirituality as an explanation and, to some extent, as a solution to some contemporary challenges we are facing:

- The global financial crisis of 2008 led to the recognition of spiritual principles. It is now believed that the root cause of the global financial crisis was not money but the absence of honesty, trustworthiness, truthfulness, and mismanagement of funds in financial institutions.
- The European economic crisis led to political unity among the member states. The European leaders' coming face-to-face with the financial and political crisis made them realize that the root cause of problems is not the Euro currency but the absence of political unity among the member states.
- As social scientists encounter ecological problems, spiritual principles are recognized. World leaders were invited by the United Nations and gathered several times to consult about the challenges of environmental issues. There is an

---

[37] 'Abdu'l-Bahá (1984). Quoted in *Tablet to August Forel: For the Good of Mankind*, p. 73.
[38] David Hay. *Something There: The Biology of The Human Spirit*, London: Darton — Longman, 2006, p. 28.

agreement that global problems such as the environment require all nations to consult, cooperate, show respect, and take care of the planet earth. The view is that dealing with global challenges requires a great deal of moral and spiritual maturity.

- On the question of refugees, when the rich and developed countries faced with the current surge of population displacement, started to show a level of compassion and welcomed them to have a better life. They have realized a positive potential in refugees. Appropriate policies can harness this rich source of human capital with benefits for everyone.
- Also, coming face to face with the problem of poverty at the global level, the rich people and nations have recognized the need to show compassion and care to bring the poor out of poverty. As a result, absolute poverty has declined in the past few decades, and it is expected by the United Nations to be eliminated soon. Of course, it all depends on how poverty is defined and whether the intention is to eradicate poverty (wipe out totally) or stop it (to reduce) or control it (keep it at the same level).

Therefore, spirituality has a unifying function, and we recognize it when facing problems.

DEFINING THE CONCEPT OF ECONOMICS FOR WELCOMING ALL

Justice issues should be among the key factors when discussing contemporary economic principles. If economics is defined as the optimal use of resources, and justice as giving each one what they are due, then the two principles of economics and justice are partners, both functionally and morally. The term economy comes from the Greek word 'oikonomia', and the word denotes household management.[39] It refers to a person's or orga-

---

[39] "Economics Definition," *WikiEducator*, https://wikieducator.org/Economics_Definition.

nization's skills to ensure the house's management and nation's well-being. Suppose the economy is "...the arrangement...of a general system of the organization."[40] Then, in wider society, we can compare the household to organizations, including governments, responsible for managing a nation's resources for the betterment of the entire population. In several of His writings, 'Abdu'l-Bahá uses this concept when explaining the economic arrangement of society. For example, He said, "This household is not well arranged. This household is not living under perfect law."[41] He, then, refers to a need for legislation to aid the proper functioning of a household, "...to this family by means of which all the members of this family will enjoy equal well-being and happiness."[42] Therefore, the Bahá'í writings support the role of government in establishing legislation to ensure the well-being and prosperity of the whole nation. This symbolic example of the function of a household has direct relevance to the subject of distributive justice with the vital role of governments in creating a balanced economy through the transformation of the consciousness and behaviour of people.

One of the basic assumptions of free-market capitalism is that market actors are rational thinkers, and the market reaches equilibrium by itself. Therefore, there is no need for government intervention. COVID 19 pandemic exposed some of the flaws of this kind of thinking in free-market capitalism and failed to save people's lives and the economy. The main motive is in areas that produce maximum profits, and there are numerous activities in a society, such as various pandemics that do not generate profit. Therefore, as we saw during the current pandemic, active government intervention was needed most urgently.

On the one hand, governments are required to step in and inject financial stimulus packages into the economy and, on the

---

[40] Universal House of Justice. Letter dated 4 June 2013 to the author of this paper.
[41] 'Abdu'l-Bahá (1979). *Foundation of World Unity*, p. 38.
[42] Ibid.

other hand, try to slow the spread of the disease to protect vulnerable populations. By definition, and in a free-market economy that is profit intensive, these are not the kind of activities a capitalist is interested in. As there was too much emphasis on the market to take care of the economy, we noticed that governments were not adequately prepared and equipped to deal with a crisis such as Covid-19. Therefore, the current pandemic is an opportunity to re-think our economy with both government involvement and business models.

MATERIAL AND SPIRITUAL COHERENCE

One of the challenges of current Globalization that humanity is going through is materialism's adverse and harmful consequences. The view in the Bahá'í writing is that "...although material advancement furthers good purposes in life, at the same time it serves evil ends."[43] Examples of 'evil ends' of materialism with its social, moral, and economic consequences include consumerism, damaging the natural environment, and various negative externalities that are destructive to human life. The observations of such challenges and their effects on people's lives are of great significance in understanding and redefining happiness and prosperity. The solution, then, to prevailing economic difficulties is to be sought through applying spiritual principles in the implementation of scientific methods and approaches. Therefore, a one-dimensional solution adopted mainly through monetary instruments would not be sufficient and effective in dealing with numerous injustices formed due to the current market outcomes. 'Abdu'l-Bahá states, "The trouble with our economics [is that] ...its system and application have been purely material, instead of material and spiritual."[44] Economic justice will be attained only when every member of society enjoys a relative degree of materi-

---

[43] 'Abdu'l-Bahá (1982). *Promulgation of Universal Peace*, P. 109.
[44] 'Abdu'l-Bahá (1917). Quoted in Mary Hanford Ford, "The Economic Teaching of Abdul-Baha," *Star of the West*, vol. viii: number 1, p. 5.

al prosperity and gives due regard to acquiring spiritual qualities. Consequently, "No matter how far the material world advances, it cannot establish the happiness of mankind. Only when material and spiritual civilization are linked and coordinated will happiness be assured."[45]

The Bahá'í writings assert the duality of human nature. 'Abdu'l-Bahá, in the following statement, states that the signs of both material and spiritual existence are found in human beings:

> In man, there are two natures; his spiritual or higher nature and his material or lower nature. In one, he approaches God; in the other, he lives for the world alone. Signs of both these natures are to be found in men. In his material aspect, he expresses untruth, cruelty, and injustice; all these are the outcome of his lower nature. The attributes of his Divine nature are shown forth in love, mercy, kindness, truth, and justice, one and all being expressions of his higher nature.[46]

Further, He states that "The impulse of self-interest belongs to the lower nature of human beings."[47] According to Michael Parkin, "In self-interest a choice has to be made and that choice is the best one available for a person. Most people make most of their choices in their own self-interest."[48] A Bahá'í view, on the other hand, would be making choices that promote social interest rather than self-interest. These choices would lead to effective and efficient use of resources and the distribution of goods and services equitably among members of society. The view is that the nature of human beings is altruistic and not egoistic. People who act to further the interests of others ultimately serve

---

[45] 'Abdu'l-Bahá (1982). *Promulgation of Universal Peace*, P. 109.
[46] 'Abdu'l-Bahá (1995). *Paris Talks*, P. 55.
[47] 'Abdu'l-Bahá (1984). Quoted in *Waging Peace*, p. 15.
[48] Michael Parkin (2001). *Economics*, 9th ed., London, Pearson Education, p. 5.

their own interests as well. Human beings should strive to reach this level of thoughtfulness. Bahá'u'lláh deters His followers from egoistic activities and encourages them to pursue behaviours that benefit all. The individual is not merely a self-interested economic unit striving to claim an ever-greater share of the world's material resources. Bahá'u'lláh avers,

> Man's merit lieth in service and virtue and not in the pageantry of wealth and riches...Dissipate not the wealth of your precious lives in the pursuit of evil and corrupt affection, nor let your endeavours be spent in promoting your personal interest ...cling unto that which profiteth mankind.[49]

By consecrating oneself to the service of others, one finds meaning and purpose in life and contributes to the upliftment of society itself.

Knowing that human beings are spiritual, material well-being alone cannot guarantee human happiness. People will be happier if the spiritual aspects of their lives are fulfilled and developed alongside the material. The Bahá'í belief in the principle of material and spiritual coherence advocates that there must be a balance between the two aspects of life. The view is that true happiness is associated with the higher nature of human beings. Consequently, self-interest and self-love belong to the lower nature of human beings. The emphasis is that "human beings must overcome the temptation of this impulse if the common good is to be promoted."[50] At this level of living, there is a need to understand the proper place of material pursuits in one's individual and family life, carrying out meaningful living conditions, transforming self-interest into collective interest, and a quest for true happiness and prosperity.

---

[49] Bahá'u'lláh (1978). *Tablets of Bahá'u'lláh Revealed after the Kitáb-i-Aqdas*, P. 138.
[50] Farhad Rassekh (2001). *The Journal of Bahá'í Studies*, Vol. 11, number 3/4.

THE ECONOMIC VIEW ON EQUALITY, INEQUALITY, AND EQUITY

Irrespective of ideology, culture, and religion, people generally condemn extreme income inequality, and it is not helping enlightened Globalization. Inequality is not acceptable for several reasons: it can signify a lack of opportunity; widening inequality also has significant implications for growth and stability. It can concentrate on political and decision-making power in the hands of a few. Also, high and sustained levels of inequality may divert an individual's efforts toward securing favoured behaviour and protection, resulting in a misallocation of resources. The multiple consequences of social injustices and conditions of extremes of wealth and poverty are addressed by 'Abdu'l-Bahá. He said,

> We see amongst us men who are overburdened with riches on the one hand and on the other those unfortunate ones who starve with nothing; those who possess several stately palaces, and those who have not where to lay their head. Some we find with numerous courses of costly and dainty food; whilst others can scarce find sufficient crusts to keep them alive. Whilst some are clothed in velvets, furs and fine linen, others have insufficient, poor and thin garments with which to protect them from the cold. This condition of affairs is wrong and must be remedied.[51]

There are many advantages to mitigating extremes of wealth and poverty, including the promotion of democracy, as a result of which consumers will be able to participate in economic life and increase the prosperity of an entire society. At the societal level reducing economic inequality leads to eradicating absolute poverty, thus reducing violence both within and between countries. Hence, ending economic inequality is one of the pressing

---

[51] 'Abdu'l-Bahá (1995). *Paris Talks*, pp. 156–157.

issues facing global society. The Bahá'í view is that each individual has different capabilities, knowledge, talent, and eagerness to work. 'Abdu'l-Bahá states:

> It is not meant that all will be equal, for inequality in degree and capacity is a property of nature. Necessarily, there will be rich people and those who will be in want of their livelihood, but in the aggregate community there will be equalization and readjustment of values and interests. In the future there will be no very rich nor extremely poor. There will be an equilibrium of interests, and a condition will be established which will make both rich and poor comfortable and content.[52]

Therefore, equity is preferred to equality when discussing economic justice from a purely monetary standpoint. 'Abdu'l-Bahá elsewhere states, "Equality is a chimera! It is entirely impracticable! Even if equality could be achieved, it could not continue, as if its existence were possible, the whole order of the world would be destroyed."[53] The Bahá'í writings suggest equal opportunity to ensure that material resources are justly distributed. The view is that everyone's talents and abilities are different and hence their economic contribution to society varies, but the opportunity should be there for all. Consequently, human beings are not born the same, aside from equality in dignity and worth. Likewise, Shoghi Effendi states,

> Social inequality is the inevitable outcome of the natural inequality of man. Human beings are different in ability and should, therefore, be different in their social and economic standing. Extremes of wealth and poverty should, however, be abolished..."[54] The view is that all citizens are equal in the sight of the law of the land.

---

[52] 'Abdu'l-Bahá (1982). *Promulgation of Universal Peace*, P. 132.
[53] 'Abdu'l-Bahá (1995). *Paris Talks*, P. 151.
[54] Shoghi Effendi (1973). *Directives from the Guardian*, P. 20.

> And government agencies should ensure that equal opportunity for progress is provided for all. And that "This is the only way in which the deplorable superfluity of great wealth and miserable, demoralizing, degrading poverty can be abolished.[55]

The desired method of wealth redistribution suggests that from each according to one's ability, and to each according to one's productive contribution to society. This method requires "with government responsibility providing social services which would be available equally for all and which would therefore contribute to the lessening of differences in wealth."[56] Consequently, the wage differential exists and is based on an individual's level of education and training, capability, and talents. Shoghi Effendi states,

> It is the duty of those who are in charge of the organization of society to give every individual the opportunity of acquiring the necessary talent in some kind of the profession, and also the means of utilizing such a talent, both for its own sake and for the sake of earning the means of his livelihood.[57]

This approach facilitates the redistribution of income and wealth. The concept of redistribution refers to the transfer of income and wealth from individuals to others through a social mechanism such as taxation, public services, and government welfare program.

There was a claim that inequality and poverty were normal conditions of life and a part of human history in the past. Indeed, short lives, limited education, health challenges, poor nutrition, limited possessions, limited mobility, and inequality suggest that, throughout history, a vast number of people have suffered from

---

[55] 'Abdu'l-Bahá (1995). *Paris Talks*, P. 159.
[56] John Huddleston (1989). *The Search for a Just Society*, p. 439.
[57] Shoghi Effendi (1973). *Directives from the Guardian*, P. 74.

poverty. Responding to such remarks, the Universal House of Justice states:

> However much such conditions are the outcome of history, they do not have to define the future, and even if current approaches to economic life satisfied humanity's stage of adolescence, they are certainly inadequate for its dawning age of maturity. There is no justification for continuing to perpetuate structures, rules, and systems that manifestly fail to serve the interests of all peoples.[58]

The role of government intervention in tackling the challenges of inequality and poverty becomes crucial, and the Bahá'í writings support such intervention. For example, 'Abdu'l-Bahá states that the responsibility of a government is "…establishing just legislation and economics so that all humanity may enjoy a full measure of welfare and privilege, but this will always be according to legal protection and procedure."[59] The overriding priority is that appropriate legislation is required to protect the economically less advantaged people. Aside from government responsibility, the rich are responsible for taking care of the poor. Addressing the rich Bahá'u'lláh states, "O ye rich ones on earth! The poor in your midst are My trust, guard ye My trust, and be not intent only on your own ease."[60] Global wealth has increased substantially in the last one hundred and fifty years. We now have access to a high level of knowledge and information, technological advancement, global financial interdependency, and improved transportation. Thus, allowing poverty and extreme inequality to exist when we can address the problem is morally wrong. The provision of equality of educational and employment opportunities for all enables an adequate standard of living. A fair distribution of resources and eliminating extremes of wealth and poverty are essential parts of Bahá'í distributive justice.

---

[58] Universal House of Justice. Letter dated 1 March 2017.
[59] 'Abdu'l-Bahá (1982). *Promulgation of Universal Peace*, P. 238.
[60] Bahá'u'lláh (1990*). The Hidden Words*, Persian no. 54.

Economic justice involves a fair allocation of financial and economic resources among people. Hence, it is a crucial ethical principle that applies to providing social goods. The focus of distributive justice is the redistribution of income and wealth as an effective method for reducing inequality and taking care of the poor. Taking care of the poor is endorsed in all Faiths and traditions. In Judaism, wealth redistribution includes compassion for those who cannot help themselves, care for the stranger, and charity. The Christian tradition of redistributing income and wealth dealing with poverty is the parable of the 'Good Samaritan', which is helping the stranger, sharing resources, loving the enemy, and helping the poor get back on their feet.

Similarly, the Islamic tradition of dealing with the issue of poverty through income and wealth redistribution includes the basic principles of sharing, the law of 'Zakat', generosity, and Islamic finance, which is the rejection of usury. The spirit of the parable of the Good Samaritan in Christianity, the importance of charity in Judaism, and Zakat in Islam are examples of religious duty with profound spiritual implications. Likewise, in the Bahá'í Faith, the poor have a special place. A fair distribution of resources and eliminating extremes of wealth and poverty are the essential aspects of Bahá'í distributive justice. This is possible through several teachings, including equality of women and men, the provision of equality of education, a consultative method of decision making, work done in a spirit of service is considered as worship, and employment opportunities for enabling an adequate standard of living for all, and numerous other teachings that requires a separate discussion.

THE APPLICATION OF ECONOMIC JUSTICE

The belief that justice has its place in the higher nature of human beings indicates that it is innate in humans. However, efforts are needed to develop necessary virtues for justice to become a reality. The belief in the higher nature of human beings also inspires individuals to act justly and with kindness. This can have significant implications in all aspects of socio-political-economic life. The idea of economic justice also interlinks with the notion of overall economic prosperity. Creating more opportunities for all members of society to earn adequate wages contributes to sustained economic growth. When more citizens can maintain a steady level of income and provide for themselves and their families, they are more likely to spend their earnings on goods and services, which drives demand in various parts of the economy.

An outstanding principle endorsed by Bahá'u'lláh to guarantee a just distribution of resources among the citizens of the world, in the long run, is moderation. It is stated, "In all matters moderation is desirable."[61] Moderation in all aspects of life can be considered the most practical way to maintain economic justice. The principle of moderation maintains a balance in living a spiritual life in a material world. It is a solution to the societal problem of poverty and inequality. The notion of moderation and developing our higher nature and economic activities can enhance human dignity, preserve the natural environment, respect the rights of future generations, and advance the well-being and prosperity of humankind. The idea is to attain economic sustainability and achieve the satisfaction of needs and wants within the limits of moderation. There are numerous Bahá'í writings on the vital role of exercising moderation. For example, in the following warning, Bahá'u'lláh speaks about the evils of materialism,

> Whoso cleaveth to justice, can, under no circumstances, transgress the limits of moderation... If carried to excess, civilization will prove as prolific a source of evil as it had been of goodness when kept within the restraints of moderation.[62]

And addressing those in charge of society, he instructs,

---

[61] Bahá'u'lláh (1978). *Tablets of Bahá'u'lláh Revealed after the Kitáb-i-Aqdas*, P. 69.
[62] Bahá'u'lláh (1983). *Gleanings from the Writings of Bahá'u'lláh*, pp. 342–343.

> Overstep not the bounds of moderation, and deal justly with them that serve thee... Deal with them with undeviating justice, so that none among them may either suffer want, or be pampered with luxuries. This is but manifest justice.[63]

To ensure that economic justice is effectively put into action, the following four elements are suggested: liberty as a fundamental human right, equal opportunity for all citizens, the participation of people from all strata of society, and the provision of necessary means for development. Countries with the greater extent to which these principles are incorporated enjoy higher economic growth with improved living standards for all citizens. In a free society where, equal opportunity is present for all, men and women from all strata of society make maximum participation possible. The provision of necessary means enables skill learning that requires appropriate investment in education and training along with technological advancement and innovation. Opportunities are essential factors that allow the working population to apply their talents and capability. To coordinate the process of upholding the pillars of economic justice and the employment of economic resources more efficiently, the role of both private and public sectors becomes a crucial factor in providing short-term and long-term plans.

CONCLUDING REMARKS

The views presented in this paper were about the issues of social and economic justice and relevant themes that affect globalization with a Bahá'í foundation. Justice has been invoked in the Bahá'í writings frequently and has a special place in the writings of the central figures of the Bahá'í Faith. Social justice is referred to as equality before the law of the land and non-discrimination. Economic justice is referred to as the elimination of extremes of

---

[63] Ibid. p. 235.

wealth and poverty. One of the central themes in the Bahá'í Faith is the view that social structures are constantly changing, so no single economic system, model or theory will always be suitable for the whole world. The fact that today eighty per cent of the world's resources are owned by twenty per cent of the population is an indication that the systems do not meet Bahá'u'lláh's standard. Humanity has reached a level of maturity that is capable of facing the challenges of injustices that humanity is facing and which is "capable of developing an economy with a totally new logic that is not based on greed or false precepts of absolute equality, that allows reasonable freedom yet promotes and safeguards justice."[64] For economic justice to be effective, it requires a contract of individuals, business organizations, and governments based on fairness, compassion, and cooperation. The market will function more sustainably based on these moral and spiritual principles. Once justice is applied in such an economy, every responsible agent in the market will realize that the fundamental principles of economic justice, namely, liberty, equal opportunity, universal participation, cooperation, and the provision of necessary means, are crucial in the efficient functioning of an economy.

The COVID 19 pandemic can be used to convince us that interdependence of the peoples and nations of the world is a fact that no one can deny. The following messages from the people of the world were frequently repeated during the COVID 19 pandemic in the media: "At this moment, we feel more united wherever we live than ever before, even at a distance." Therefore, the truth of cooperation and interconnectedness of humankind is becoming apparent to larger numbers of people. The COVID 19 pandemic is a clear example of the interconnectedness of people and nations. This pandemic signal that we must look at the entire world as one unit, as one body. Therefore, the type of life we will have after this pandemic must consider the interdependence

---

[64] Farzam Arbab (1984). Development — A Challenge to Bahá'í Scholars', *Journal of Bahá'í Studies*, pp. 1–18.

of all people and nations. The most important factor associated with people's interconnectedness can be seen in cooperation and not competition. This pandemic has indeed reminded us of our interconnectedness and has created an opportunity to identify the difficulties and challenges we may face at private and public institutions.

We live in an extraordinary time, and although we want to be optimistic about a better future, we should not be too naïve. With the current pandemic, there are many challenges now, and they may continue in the future. For example, what is done or will be done for millions of refugees living in densely populated areas with deplorable conditions and with minimum or no access to medical care? What about one billion people living in absolute poverty without medical care and vaccination? Several gaps need to be filled, including education, equal opportunity, productivity, wealth, resource allocation, and digital. These and many other challenges require immediate attention to reduce the risk of future pandemics. Therefore, there is a need for restructuring the entire society, restructuring our hospitals, our educational institutions, our agriculture, our politics, our economics, restructuring the way we live, and restructuring our minds. The rights of people must be protected, especially those in the minority, women's rights, the rights of black and ethnic and religious minorities, the rights of children, the rights of disabled people, and the rights of poor people. An enlightened and meaningful Globalization requires a proper foundation to enjoy the greatest happiness possible.

Bibliography

'Abdu'l-Bahá (1978). *Selections from the Writings of 'Abdu'l-Bahá*. Haifa: Bahá'í World Centre.

'Abdu'l-Bahá (1979). *Foundation of World Unity*. Wilmette IL: Bahá'í Publishing Trust, United States.

'Abdu'l-Bahá (1982). *Promulgation of Universal Peace*. Wilmette IL: Bahá'í Publishing Trust, United States.

'Abdu'l-Bahá (2014). *Some Answered Questions*, https://www.bahai.org/library/ authoritative-texts/abdul-baha/some-answered-questions/, p. 92.

'Abdu'l-Bahá (1984). *Tablet to August Forel: For the Good of Mankind*, John Paul Vader (ed.), Oxford: George Ronald.

'Abdu'l-Bahá (1995). *Paris Talks*. London: Bahá'í Publishing Trust, United Kingdom.

Arbab, F. (1984). Development — A Challenge to Bahá'í Scholars', *Journal for Bahá'í Studies*, Association for Bahá'í Studies of North America.

Badee, H. (2018). *Economics and the Bahá'í Faith*, United Kingdom.

Bahá'u'lláh (1988). *Epistle to the Son of the Wolf*, Wilmette, IL: Bahá'í Publishing Trust.

Bahá'u'lláh (1978). *Tablets of Bahá'u'lláh Revealed after the Kitáb-i-Aqdas*. Haifa: Bahá'í World Centre.

Bahá'u'lláh (1983). *Gleanings from the Writings of Bahá'u'lláh*, pocket-size edition. Wilmette IL: Bahá'í Publishing Trust, United States.

Bahá'u'lláh (1990). *The Hidden Words*. Wilmette IL: Bahá'í Publishing Trust, United States.

"Economics Definition," *WikiEducator*, https://wikieducator.org/Economics_Definition.

"Fairness, noun," *Merriam-Webster*, 32 https://www.merriam-webster.com/dictionary/fairness.

Ford, Mary Hanford Ford (1917). "The Economic Teaching of Abdul-Baha," *Star of the West*, vol. viii: number 1, pp. 3–7, 11–16.

Hay, D. *Something There: The Biology of The Human Spirit*, London: Darton — Longman.

"Justice, n.", *Oxford English Dictionary*, https://www.oed.com/view/Entry/102198.

Rassekh, F. (2001). *The Journal of Bahá'í Studies*, Vol. 11, number 3/4.

Shoghi Effendi (1973). *Directives from the Guardian*. Compiled by the National Spiritual Assembly of the Hawaiian Islands, published by the Bahá'í Publishing Trust, India.

Shoghi Effendi (1980). *The Promised Day is Come.* Wilmette IL: Bahá'í Publishing Trust, United States.

Shoghi Effendi (1982). *The World Order of Bahá'u'lláh.* Wilmette IL: Bahá'í Publishing Trust, United States.

What Is Globalization? And How Has the Global Economy Shaped the United States? *Peterson Institute for International Economics,* https://www.piie.com/microsites/globalization/what-is-globalization.

Bahá'í Perspectives on Natural and Social Sciences

A Bahá'í View of Human Rights[1]

PETER SMITH

The concept of human rights has undergone its own complex development and is now both multi-faceted and subject to a variety of philosophical and political interpretations.[2] In its origins it is closely linked to the ideas of Western liberalism and to the protection of the subjective interests of individual persons as against the interests of larger groups and institutions such as the state. Alternative or complementary conceptions of human rights have stressed the contextual and relational nature of individual rights, the role of basic socio-economic needs in the attainment of such rights, and the rights of minority groups and of the social collectivity. The difficulties in resolving these complexities have not stemmed the burgeoning interest in human rights in histori-

---

[1] This is essentially the same paper I presented at an International Symposium on the Conception of Human Rights held under the aegis of the International Sociological Association (Dubrovnik, 1985). I have rearranged a few sentences, 'updated' a few terms (e.g. the 'Global South in place of the 'Third World'), deleted a short summary of Bahá'í history, and replaced or expanded some of the footnotes to incorporate more recent publications.

[2] Alan S. Rosenbaum (ed.), *The Philosophy of Human Rights: International Perspectives* (Westport, Conn.: Greenwood Press, 1980). See also the introductory essays in Walter Laqueur and Barry Rubin (eds.) *The Human Rights Reader* (New York: Meridian Books, 1975. Rev. ed. 1990). More recent introductions include Charles R. Beitz, *The Idea of Human Rights* (Oxford: Oxford University Press, 2009) and Michael Freeman, *Human Rights: An Interdisciplinary Approach* (Cambridge: Polity Press, 2002).

cal debate. International organizations, national governments, and a variety of voluntary organizations have sought to promote particular conceptions of human rights and worked for their defence. Necessarily, particularistic interests have played a significant part in this promotion. Nevertheless, despite continuing contention over the exact scope and nature of human rights, definite areas of consensus have developed. Far though they may be from attainment, certain ideals of human rights are now widely upheld as minimum desiderata in the conduct of national and international life.

Historically, religion has played an important role in the development of human rights thinking. In positive terms, all three major religions in the 'Western' tradition — Judaism, Christianity, and Islam — present images of human beings which may be conducive to the concept of universal human rights. Thus, in each, human beings are regarded as individual moral entities and potential possessors of dignity and worth. Created for a purposeful existence, humans are also accountable to a God who is regarded as both just, loving, and compassionate, and who has inculcated moral commandments for the ordering of human society. More negatively, the 'Western' religions have also borne the conceptions of religious exclusivism and authoritarian orthodoxy. Whilst the modern conception of human rights echoes earlier religious conceptions of moral responsibility, individual worth, and social justice, it also emerged as a reaction against the excesses of religious fanaticism and persecution.

THE BAHÁ'Í FAITH

The Bahá'í Faith represents a new expression of the Western religious tradition.[3] Sharing ideas of justice, responsibility and worth with Judaism, Christianity, and Islam, the Bahá'í scriptures provide their own distinctive basis for conceptions of hu-

---

[3] For a brief introduction to the Bahá'í Faith see Peter Smith, *An Introduction to the Bahá'í Faith* (Cambridge: Cambridge University Press, 2008).

man rights. As such they are worthy of study. Moreover, Bahá'í bears a particular immediacy to the modern world. Whether one accepts Bahá'u'lláh's claims to be a messenger of God, or merely regards him as a creative religious thinker, his message is certainly addressed to the modern world. Again, though they may be relatively few in numbers (perhaps 5 to 7 million people)[4], the Bahá'ís — the followers of the religion's founder Bahá'u'lláh (1817-1892) — represent a dynamic element in world society, who are already established in most of the world's countries, are urgently committed to their particular ideals of internationalism and universal justice and have shown themselves eager to work in collaboration with the international agencies of the United Nations. The ideals that animate such people are at least of wider interest.

THE BAHÁ'Í CONCEPTION OF HUMAN RIGHTS AND RESPONSIBILITIES.

As with other religions in the Western tradition, the Bahá'í conception of human rights is rooted in the beliefs in the moral responsibility and worth of the individual, and in the prophetic challenge of divinely ordained social justice. For Bahá'ís, the purpose of human life on earth is for the individual to develop his or her spiritual capabilities in preparation for the afterlife, and for each to contribute to the spiritualization and development of human society. Human beings are regarded as fundamentally spiritual entities who are created to know and worship God in all the worlds of God. The individual human soul is born into the world in a state of sinlessness but with an inherent capacity for selfishness. Each soul has an infinite capacity for

---

[4] At the time I first wrote this essay in 1984, I estimated that the global Bahá'í population was in the region of 2 to 3 million people. Several more recent sources give estimates of over 5 million Baha'is in the early 2000s (See "Statistics" in the Bahaikipedia website: https://bahaikipedia.org/Statistics. Last accessed 23 February 2018). By contrast, David, B. Barrett, George Thomas Kurian, and Todd M Johnson (eds.), *World Christian Encyclopedia: A Contemporary Survey of Churches and Religions in the Modern World* (2nd ed.) (New York: Oxford University Press, 2001) gives an estimate of over 7 million.

spiritual development, but this can only be begun to be realized through spiritual and moral guidance. Without such guidance, the individual soul is unable to manifest its potential and easily falls into error and wrongdoing. Throughout his or her earthly existence, the individual confronts spiritual and moral challenges. The response to these challenges determines the individual's state of soul in the afterlife. Favourable responses to the challenges enhance spiritual growth, unfavourable responses retard spiritual growth.

This concern with individual spiritual growth and moral responsibility is linked to a strong concern with the affairs of this world. Humanity as a whole is regarded as having been created to carry forward an ever-advancing civilization of increasing spirituality. The periodic decline of religion interrupts this progress, but at an individual level the reality of moral choice remains constant, and all human beings have a responsibility to contribute to the advancement of human society. Religion is concerned with all aspects of human life. Again, a divine standard of guidance is needed.

Guidance in its most perfect form derives from the succession of divine messengers, the 'Manifestations of God'. These individuals periodically renew the pure religion of God, the great religions of the world representing the institutional expression of their teachings. As each institutionalized religion falls victim to human adulteration, a succession of new Manifestations of God appears to revive religion and progressively advance the divine teachings for each new age. Bahá'u'lláh thus represents merely the latest in a line of divine revelators that has included Moses, Zoroaster, Krishna, the Buddha, Jesus Christ, and Muhammad. He is not to be the last. As the conditions of humanity vary throughout its complex history and development, the teachings brought by each Manifestation reflect the potentialities and actualities of the particular age in which he appears. Each Manifestation establishes the standard for morality and justice for his age. These standards subsequently form part of the religious heritage to be revived and extended by the next Manifestation.

Human dignity and honour consist in accepting and trying to live up to the divine standard for the age.

In this context, Bahá'í notions of human rights do not stem from the natural law tradition of Western liberalism. Rather, human rights are God-given rights. Rights represent standards of divinely revealed justice. They entail responsibilities towards God, towards other human beings, and towards the dignity and honour of one's own soul. There is potentially no end to the number and extent of human rights. As humanity progresses, the standards of divine justice are progressively revealed. More is demanded of human beings and more responsibilities are given. In the new age of humanity's religious progress inaugurated by Bahá'u'lláh, the distinctive emphasis is on the unification and wholeness of the human race. New rights and responsibilities stem from that emphasis. Rights and responsibilities established by previous Manifestations of God are reiterated, or, where they are judged to have been specific to only a certain period of human development, they are abrogated.

The various rights and responsibilities established by Bahá'u'lláh or by the authoritative interpreters of his 'revelation' by his appointed successors, 'Abdu'l-Bahá (1844–1921) and Shoghi Effendi (1897–1957), may be conveniently discussed under five headings: economic and political freedoms, human equality, international order, and religion and the family. Although there may be a certain implicit secularization of the material in the way in which I have summarized these ideas, it should be pointed out that the Bahá'í view of divine revelation does not posit a sharp division between spiritual and secular. According to the Bahá'í view, Manifestations of God are well able to address all aspects of human behaviour: there is no purely 'secular' area of life. Moreover, in the manner of their transmission of the divine revelation, Manifestations of God speak and write in the context of their particular era and social (i.e., 'secular') situation.

Sources

The main sources for this discussion are the various writings of the successive leaders of the Bahá'í Faith, many of which have appeared in authorized translations into English from the original Persian and Arabic, or, in the case of Shoghi Effendi, were originally written in English. I have also made use of various transcripts of the oral translations of the talks 'Abdu'l-Bahá gave during his extended visits to Europe and North America in 1911–13, although these are accorded a less authoritative status in the canon of Bahá'í writings.[5]

---

[5] The chief sources used here are as follows.
Of Bahá'u'lláh's writings:
- *Gleanings from the Writings of Bahá'u'lláh*, [comp. and] trans. Shoghi Effendi (London: Bahá'í Publishing Trust, 1978 [Rev. ed.]).
- *Tablets of Bahá'u'lláh Revealed After the Kitab-i-Aqdas*, trans. H. Taherzadeh et al (Haifa: Bahá'í World Centre, 1978). Written in the period after 1873.
- *The Kitab-i-Aqdas: The Most Holy Book* (Haifa: Bahá'í World Centre, 1992). This replaces the old translation I used in the original essay: *Al-Kitab al-Aqdas, or The Most Holy Book*, trans. and ed. E. E. Elder and W. M. Miller (London: Luzac, Royal Asiatic Society, 1961). Bahá'u'lláh's book of laws (c. 1873). See Peter Smith. *A Concise Encyclopedia of the Bahá'í Faith*. 2nd ed. (Oxford: Oneworld, 2002), 43–44.
- *The Proclamation of Bahá'u'lláh to the Kings and Rulers of the World* (Haifa: Bahá'í World Centre, 1967).

Of 'Abdu'l-Bahá's writings:
- *Tablet to the Hague* (London: Bahá'í Publishing Trust, n.d.). 'Abdu'l-Bahá's letter to the Central Organization for a Durable Peace at The Hague (1919). Part of the letter is reproduced in *Selections from the Writings of 'Abdu'l-Bahá*, trans. M. Gail et al (Haifa: Bahá'í World Centre, 1978), 296–307.
- *The Secret of Divine Civilization*, trans. M. Gail (Wilmette, IL: Bahá'í Publishing Trust, 1957). A proposal for Iranian 'modernization' initially circulated anonymously. Written in 1875. See Smith, *Encyclopedia*, 308–9.

Of translations of 'Abdu'l-Bahá's talks:
- *Some Answered Questions*. Collected and trans. L. C. Barney (Wilmette, IL: Bahá'í Publishing Trust, 1981). Talks given in response to questions in 1904–1906. [A new revised edition was published at the Bahá'í World Centre in Haifa in 2014].
- *Paris Talks: Addresses Given by 'Abdu'l-Bahá in Paris in 1911–1912*. 10th ed. (London: Bahá'í Publishing Trust, 1961).

ECONOMIC FREEDOMS

The Bahá'í leaders taught that human beings should free themselves from attachment to the material world. The world was "but a show, vain and empty, a mere nothing, bearing the semblance of reality. Set not your affections upon it."[6] Nevertheless, physical survival depends upon the successful use of the world's resources. God does not create human beings that they should starve, neither does he demand that they should follow a life of asceticism and self-mortification. There is nothing inherently evil about wealth, it is material attachment and the misuse of wealth that is to be morally condemned.

Freedom from Slavery and Economic Want

The Bahá'í writings prohibit both slavery and the slave trade, for to no human being is given the right to lord himself over another.[7] Basic freedom requires more than this, however. As 'Abdu'l-Bahá observed, the struggle for physical survival was "the fountainhead of all calamities." Lack of basic material means was a form of enslavement which reduced human beings to ferocious animals, degrading and demoralizing them.[8] Like chattel slavery, economic slavery had to be abolished.[9] At a basic level, Bahá'u'lláh reaffirmed the Islamic principle of the *zakat*, a tax-levy on behalf of the poor, and made care of the destitute a com-

---

- *The Promulgation of Universal Peace: Talks Delivered by 'Abdu'l-Bahá during His Visit to the United States and Canada in 1912.* Comp. H. MacNutt. 2nd ed. (Wilmette, IL: Bahá'í Publishing Trust, 1982).

Of Shoghi Effendi's writings:
- *The World Order of Bahá'u'lláh.* Rev. ed. (Wilmette, IL: Bahá'í Publishing Trust, 1955). Letters written in 1929-36.

For a general account of Bahá'í texts see Smith, *Introduction,* 99-105. On the writings of 'Abdu'l-Bahá, Bahá'u'lláh and Shoghi Effendi see Smith, *Encyclopedia,* 20, 79-86, 317-18.

[6] Bahá'u'lláh, *Gleanings,* 327.
[7] Bahá'u'lláh, *Aqdas,* 45 v72.
[8] 'Abdu'l-Bahá, *Hague,* 5; *Paris Talks,* 154.
[9] 'Abdu'l-Bahá, *Star of the West,* 7/15 (1916), 147.

munal responsibility.[10] Beyond this, 'Abdu'l-Bahá insisted on the necessity for governments to legislate against extremes of both wealth and poverty.[11] Absolute equality was a chimera, but no one had the right to amass colossal fortunes when millions suffered the miseries of poverty. Such a state of affairs was a sign of the existence of tyranny. All human beings had the right to the basic necessities of life: food, clothing, and rest from labour. All should have some share of comfort and well-being.[12] More specifically, in the industrial context, workers should have legally established rights to an adequate wage and pension, as well as to a share in the profits of the company they worked for. Cases of industrial disputes needed to be settled by independent judicial or governmental arbitration. As strikes were socially and economically destructive, governments had a responsibility to intervene.[13] In the agricultural context, each local community needed to establish a general storehouse out of which those in need might be supported. As in more complex local economies, the main funding for such a storehouse should be provided by a graduated income tax.[14]

Governmental edict was not the only means by which a lot of the poor should be improved. Whilst the Bahá'í leaders regarded begging and giving to beggars as reprehensible, they praised the voluntary sharing of wealth as one of the most meritorious of deeds.[15] Indeed, for the rich to ignore "the midnight sighing of the poor" was a denial of their responsibilities before God. Such heedlessness on their part surely led them to "the path of destruction." Wealth easily became a "mighty barrier" between the

---

[10] Bahá'u'lláh, *Aqdas*, 72 v146–47, 140 q147, 234–5 n161.
[11] 'Abdu'l-Bahá, *Paris Talks*, 151–54; *Promulgation*, 132,216–17; *Questions*, 273–77.
[12] 'Abdu'l-Bahá, *Paris Talks*, 131–32, 151–54.
[13] 'Abdu'l-Bahá, *Questions*, 276.
[14] 'Abdu'l-Bahá, *Promulgation*, 217; National Spiritual Assembly of the Bahá'ís of Canada, *'Abdu'l-Bahá in Canada* (Forest, Ontario: Forest Free Press, 1962), 31–36.
[15] Bahá'u'lláh, *Aqdas*, 30 v33, 72 v146–47, 140 q147, 192 n56, 234–5 n161; *Tablets*, 26; 'Abdu'l-Bahá, *Hague*, 5.

individual and God, leading to the atrophy of spiritual qualities. Thus, "The rich, but for a few, shall in no wise attain the court of His [God's] presence, nor enter the city of content and resignation."[16] Again, human advancement required social reciprocity and cooperation. For human beings not to be concerned with the welfare and interests of others was an abnegation of their responsibilities and status as human beings. It was impossible to win the good pleasure of God as long as exorbitant wealth and dire poverty continued to coexist.[17] Moreover, as all humankind constituted one family, and the world's wealth was provided so that all human beings might live in "perfect happiness and peace", gross global inequalities in wealth constituted a manifest injustice, subject presumably to the same strictures regarding the spiritual consequences of economic injustice.

WORK AND INEQUALITY

The Bahá'í teachings emphasize the necessity for fundamental economic restructuring so as to ensure a more equitable distribution of wealth both in the world as a whole, and within individual societies. Such equity does not entail economic equality, however. Absolute equality was not regarded as an obtainable reality. Even with a similar allocation of resources, economic differences would readily develop. Class differences were to be recognized as a permanent reality of social life (Though a principle such as industrial profit-sharing [above] would undoubtedly modify the nature of class divisions).[18] Social stability and cohesion necessitated that all people (particularly the rich) develop a stronger sense of social responsibility, justice and cooperation, but the bases of inequality were also legitimated, with the rights to both private property and familial inheritance clearly upheld.[19] Again,

---

[16] Bahá'u'lláh, *The Hidden Words* (London: Bahá'í Publishing Trust, 1932), 39, 41.
[17] National Spiritual Assembly of the Bahá'ís of Canada, 31-32, 34-36.
[18] 'Abdu'l-Bahá, *Paris Talks*, 151-54; *Promulgation*, 132, 216-17; *Questions*, 273-77.
[19] Bahá'u'lláh, *Aqdas*, 26-28 v20-28, 106-108 q5-7, 182-88 n38-47.

whilst government intervention in the economy and progressive taxation against the rich were advocated in the interests of social justice, capital accumulation, profit-making, and the receipt of moderate interest payments were all regarded as allowable activities.[20]

Rather than condemning wealth, the Bahá'í teachings seek to revalue its production and use, and to extend its advantages to all human beings. In this regard, the nature of work becomes crucial. In his *Kitáb-i Aqdas*, Bahá'u'lláh had forbidden begging, and given work and the earning of one's living the status of religious obligations. Idleness and the life of religious seclusion were also prohibited.[21] More than this, work was to be regarded as a form of worship, especially when performed in a spirit of service to others.[22] Bahá'ís were instructed to occupy themselves in that which would profit both themselves and others. Again, other people's work was to be respected, and the acquisition of useful skills and knowledge regarded as a source of glory.[23]

EDUCATION AND DEVELOPMENT

If equitably shared and used for the service of humanity rather than only for individual aggrandizement, then wealth was to be positively regarded. From a Bahá'í standpoint, such means as increased the collective wealth of the human race were to be applauded and fostered. Both government action and individual enterprise should be directed to such endeavour. The intelligent development of industry, commerce, technology, science, and (most particularly) agriculture was to be encouraged.[24] All aspects of the social and economic life of a community were intimately linked together.[25]

---

[20] Bahá'u'lláh, *Tablets*, 133–34.
[21] Bahá'u'lláh, *Aqdas*, 30 v33, 72 v 147,192–93 n56, 235 n162, *Tablets*, 24, 71,138.
[22] Bahá'u'lláh, *Tablets*, 26; 'Abdu'l-Bahá, *Promulgation*, 187, 435.
[23] Bahá'u'lláh, *Tablets*, 38, 51–52.
[24] Bahá'u'lláh, *Tablets*, 90; 'Abdu'l-Bahá, *Secret*, 24, 39.
[25] 'Abdu'l-Bahá, *Questions*, 276.

Education constituted a vital aspect of socio-economic development. At an individual level, every child, every adult even, had the right to receive a basic education.[26] Everyone should be taught to read and write. All should be given the basic skills they needed for the acquisition of a trade or profession. Both sexes had this right, but in extreme cases of limited resources, educational priority should be given to the girl in her role as a potential mother and first educator of her children. Although parents had a particular obligation to ensure that their children were educated, the ultimate responsibility for this lay with the community as a whole. Again, children themselves were obliged to apply themselves diligently to their own education. Whilst every individual was encouraged to use education as a means of self-advancement, it was not necessary for all children to receive more than a basic education.

POLITICAL FREEDOMS

Bahá'í views on political freedom are interlinked with the practical responses of the Bahá'í leaders to the political situations of their time. With its messianic vision, the Babi movement (fl. 1844–1853), out of which the Bahá'í religion had initially emerged, had carried a powerful political charge which had quickly led to its suppression by the Iranian state. Part of Bahá'u'lláh's subsequent transformation of the Babi movement had been to command his followers to eschew all such acts as might lead to bloodshed or sedition. The Bahá'ís were further commanded to be loyal to the government of the state in which they resided, and subsequently advised to strictly avoid involvement in party politics. These various commands remain normative for contemporary Bahá'ís.[27]

---

[26] See Universal House of Justice, Research Department (comp.), *Bahá'í Education* (London: Bahá'í Publishing Trust, 1976).
[27] See *Bahá'í World*, vol. 17 (Haifa: Bahá'í World Centre, 1981), 377–83.

JUSTICE AND FREEDOM

For Bahá'u'lláh, unlimited freedom brought with it the danger of sedition, "whose flames none can quench."[28] Constraints on human behaviour were a necessary part of social life, a means of upholding human dignity and guarding against depravity and wickedness. True liberty consisted in submission to the laws of God, and in general religion constituted "the chief instrument for the establishment of order in the world."[29] The fear of God was not an innate human characteristic, however, and for the maintenance of social order, justice needed to be administered. Those who were charged with the administration of justice needed to uphold two principles: the hope of reward and the fear of punishment.[30] Those who made no effort to control their evil inclinations had to be deterred. The actualities of crime and punishment might change over time, however, so the Bahá'í leaders avoided detailing a comprehensive system of crimes and punishments such as that found in the Islamic *sharí'a* (sacred law). Rather, Bahá'u'lláh exhorted the administrators of justice to consider the changing exigencies of their time and to judge with wisdom as to what particular constraints then needed to be employed.[31] With regard to certain crimes, however, he was more specific, advocating graduated fines for physical assault and repeated adultery, progressively more severe punishments for repeated theft, and capital punishment or life imprisonment for murder and arson.[32]

Prevention of crime was more important than punishment, however. Punishment was necessary, but it only affected a superficial discipline. It was a means of protecting the community's right to security, but it did not of itself uplift the morals and character of the criminal and might easily degrade them. It was necessary, therefore, to educate people away from the temptations

---

[28] Bahá'u'lláh, *Aqdas*, 63 v122–23.
[29] Bahá'u'lláh, *Tablets*, 63–64, 125, 129–30.
[30] Bahá'u'lláh, *Tablets*, 27, 66, 126, 129, 164.
[31] Bahá'u'lláh, *Tablets*, 129, 164.
[32] Bahá'u'lláh, *Aqdas*, 35–36 v45, 37 v49, 40 v56, 41 v61, 121 q49, 198 n70–71, 200 n77, 201–2 n81, 203–5 n86–87.

of criminal behaviour and vice, and to attract them towards the acquisition of virtues.[33]

EQUALITY BEFORE THE LAW AND DUE PROCESS

Everyone should be equal before the law.[34] The dignity and equality of all human beings should be respected. All should enjoy the protection of the law and of legal process. Injustice and arbitrary rule were to be censured. Guilt could only be established after the most careful investigation, and severe punishment should never be meted out in haste, nor without the possibility of appeal to a higher judicial authority. To give unbridled authority to provincial governors (as was nineteenth century Iranian practice) was to create the conditions for local despotism.[35]

JUST GOVERNMENT

Those who ruled a nation should fear God. If they ruled oppressively, with injustice and heedlessness, then they would merit divine judgement and chastisement. Absolutist rule laid the basis for tyranny, and it was therefore necessary for there to be constraints upon the exercise of power, both in terms of constitutional legality and by the establishment of constituent assemblies. Although purely republican forms of government profited "all the peoples of the world," constitutional monarchy was advocated as the ideal.[36] Not only was the majesty of kingship one of the "signs of God,"[37] but a permanent non-executive head of state provided a greater measure of political stability than an executive presidency did with its attendant disruptive political contests.[38] Again, republicanism of itself offered no

---

[33] 'Abdu'l-Bahá, *Questions*, 268–72.
[34] 'Abdu'l-Bahá, *Paris Talks*, 132, 154–55.
[35] 'Abdu'l-Bahá, *Secret*, 15, 100–101.
[36] Bahá'u'lláh, *Tablets*, 28, 93.
[37] Bahá'u'lláh, *Tablets*, 28.
[38] This phrase is based on a reported oral statement of 'Abdu'l-Bahá heard by John E. Esslemont, cited in his *Bahá'u'lláh and the New Era* (London: Allen and Unwin, 1923), 123.

certain defence against corrupt government. Universal education and a general moral awareness on the part of the electorate and those who were elected were also essential conditions for the emergence of genuine political freedom.[39] Federalism rather than extreme centralization also constituted a defence against despotism.[40]

PARTICIPATION

Whatever the actual form of the government, there were certain basic requirements of popular participation and freedom. Such political rights should be available to all, regardless of race or sex. Thus, for the well-being and progress of society as a whole it was essential that all its members should be able to enjoy freedom of speech, conscience and thought. As to participation, apart from the endorsement of the general principles of constituent representation on the basis of democratic elections, the Bahá'í principle of consultation seems to provide a paradigm. Thus, Bahá'ís were bidden to: "Settle all things, both great and small, by consultation."[41] Such consultation was intended to transcend the contradictions of individual opinions. Unlike the procedure of a debate, the objective was to arrive at a consensus of opinion as to the truth of a matter rather than to secure the victory of a particular argument. The clash of opinions might yield the spark of truth, but the participants should feel themselves to be contributing to a general process of understanding and not battling for their own particular opinions. The opinions of all participants were to be valued regardless of their social position or rank. In the developing system by which Bahá'ís administer their own affairs this principle is repeatedly stressed. Those who are elected to any post or institution are not mandated by their

---

[39] 'Abdu'l-Bahá, *Secret*, 17–18.
[40] 'Abdu'l-Bahá, *Promulgation*, 167.
[41] The Universal House of Justice (comp.), *The Heaven of Divine Wisdom* [A compilation on consultation] (London: Bahá'í Publishing Trust, 1978), 8. On constituent representation see 'Abdu'l-Bahá, *Secret*, 24.

electors to promote a particular position, but they are charged to consult with them, fully and freely.[42]

The right of political participation is not of itself enough. For such participation to become meaningful, the general populace must have the confidence to participate. In this regard, 'Abdu'l-Bahá argued that universal education was an essential element in fostering genuine participation. An uneducated population lacked the means to complain effectively against injustice or to secure their rights in local government. Such a people might long for justice and happiness, but unless they were educated, they lacked "even the vocabulary to explain what they want."[43] Again, it was necessary for people to become better informed as to the problems and needs of their time.[44] An informed public opinion needed to be created. Newspapers constituted a potent means of informing people about the contemporary world, but journalists needed to be imbued with a strong sense of moral responsibility for what they wrote. Accurate reporting, "fair speech and truthfulness." should be their ideal.[45] Moreover, a free press (an essential adjunct to the freedom of speech) needed both to give "full scope to the expansion of the diversified views and convictions" of humankind, and to be freed from the manipulation of vested interests.[46]

HUMAN EQUALITY

The unity and oneness of the human race is regarded by Bahá'ís as the pivotal teaching of their religion.[47] As a social principle it implies both the radical restructuring of global society and basic changes in human attitudes.

---

[42] On Bahá'í administration see Smith, *Introduction*, 175–86.
[43] 'Abdu'l-Bahá, *Secret*, 18, 110.
[44] 'Abdu'l-Bahá, *Secret*, 109–10.
[45] Bahá'u'lláh, *Tablets*, 39–40.
[46] Shoghi Effendi, *World Order*, 204.
[47] Shoghi Effendi, *World Order*, 36, 42.

GENDER EQUALITY

According to the Bahá'í teachings, men and women were created equally in the image of God, that is, both were endowed with spiritual qualities and enabled to reflect the attributes of God.[48] Both possessed all the potentialities of intelligence, virtue, and human prowess. In the sight of God both were equal, and no distinction was to be made between them. That women were generally prevented from attaining their full potential was to be attributed to their lack of education and the conditions of oppression under which so many of them lived. The injustice of that situation had to change.[49] In the [twentieth] "century of light" the potentialities for women's advancement had become manifest and the forces for change had thus acquired momentum. The attainment of gender equality was a vital necessity for the advancement of the whole human race. Social and political progress for both men and women depended on the acceptance and realization of equality between them.[50] Males and females had been created by God as complementary parts of human society. If one part was wronged and oppressed, and hence unable to develop its perfections, then the progress of human society as a whole was defective and unstable. If men and women were compared to the two wings of a bird, then the bird of humanity could not "wing its way to heights of real attainment" unless both wings were equivalent in strength.[51] Without gender equality, neither international peace nor the unity and oneness of the human race could be attained.[52]

---

[48] 'Abdu'l-Bahá, *Promulgation*, 76, 136, 174. The Bahá'í conception of God is not anthropomorphic, God being thought of as "immeasurably exalted ... above any comparison or human description" (Bahá'u'lláh, *Prayers and Meditations of Bahá'u'lláh*, comp. and trans. Shoghi Effendi (Wilmette, IL.: Bahá'í Publishing Trust, 1938), 128). Nevertheless, Bahá'í writings in English follow the Biblical usage in referring to God as 'He'. On the Bahá'í concept of God in general see Smith, *Introduction*, 106–7.
[49] 'Abdu'l-Bahá, *Promulgation*, 133.
[50] 'Abdu'l-Bahá, *Promulgation*, 76–77, 134.
[51] 'Abdu'l-Bahá, *Promulgation*, 108, 134, 174, 233, 375.
[52] 'Abdu'l-Bahá, *Promulgation*, 77, 134.

The attainment of gender equality required changes in both attitudes and the social opportunities available to women. Men had to abandon their attitude of superiority towards women. Attitudes of male superiority expressed the ignorance of an earlier age when women were regarded as demonic or as inferior to men in mental capacities: in the modern age these were harmful superstitions unworthy of human intelligence. As long as such attitudes persisted, they would continue to depress the ambitions and advancement of women. Women's potentialities were great, but still largely unrealized. To inspire people with hope and ambition, and hence to further their capacity for advancement, it was necessary to encourage them and assure them as to their capacities. If they were told that they were weaker or inferior, this would denude them of hope, and hence handicap their progress. It was necessary to declare the equality, or even the superiority of the capacities of women to men, for thus would their "susceptibilities for advancement" increase.[53] Women themselves should also make such progress as to force men to recognize their equality.[54]

The standard and status of the two sexes had to become equal, not only in the West, where the idea of gender equality had at least become well-established, but also throughout the world. In this regard, universal suffrage was again vital. The electoral and political rights of men and women should be the same. More fundamentally, both sexes needed to gain equal access to education. Education would establish women's equality with men. There should be no difference in the education of the two sexes. Both should follow the same course of study and enjoy the same educational opportunities.[55] Similarly, in social, political, and economic affairs they should be equal. All departments of human life — other than that of the military (see below) — should be open to them both. The economic structure of society should

---

[53] 'Abdu'l-Bahá, *Promulgation*, 76–77, 133–35, 281.
[54] 'Abdu'l-Bahá, *Paris Talks*, 162.
[55] 'Abdu'l-Bahá, *Promulgation*, 175, 233, 281.

be readjusted so as to permit this equality, as well as to enable all human beings to live in the greatest happiness according to their respective degrees of attainment.[56]

GENDER COMPLEMENTARITY AND DIFFERENCES

According to the Bahá'í view, the essential equality of the sexes did not mean that they were identical. This was most clearly seen in the social role of motherhood, itself based on a basic biological difference between women and men. The mother bore a particular importance in the initial care of her children, and whilst both parents shared the responsibility of ensuring that their children were educated, it was the mother who acted as their children's first teacher. It was therefore vitally important that girls — as potential mothers of the future — receive a good education. Indeed, if parents were forced by circumstances to give educational priority to some of their children over others (because of lack of funds, for example), then they should favour their daughters over their sons. If the mother was illiterate and ignorant, then her children were likely to be similarly deficient. She bore the primary responsibility in ensuring the material and spiritual welfare and advancement of her children, and her own education, wisdom and morality would have a significant impact on them.[57]

As a corollary of this vital role of motherhood, the husband had a duty to support his wife and to provide for and protect his family. This might appear to be an endorsement of traditional parental roles, but the roles were not exclusive: both parents had a duty to care for their children, and both were potential breadwinners. Nor had either any right to dominate the other, and women certainly should never be "prisoners of the household."[58]

'Abdu'l-Bahá thought that in certain respects, women were temperamentally superior to men, being more liable to be compassionate, tender-hearted, spiritually receptive, intuitive, and

---

[56] 'Abdu'l-Bahá, *Paris Talks*, 182–83; *Promulgation*, 170, 318.
[57] 'Abdu'l-Bahá, *Paris Talks*, 162; *Promulgation*, 133–34, 175.
[58] The Universal House of Justice, Research Department (comp.), *Family Life* (London: Bahá'í Publishing Trust, 1982), 30–33.

attuned to the necessities of life.⁵⁹ He regarded these 'female' qualities as necessary characteristics of the new age promised in the Bahá'í writings. They provided a balance to the hitherto dominant 'male' qualities of force and aggression. Thus, the attainment of gender equality would not only foster the advancement of women and the proper complementarity between the two sexes, but it would lead to a more even balance between the masculine and feminine elements of civilization.⁶⁰

In this regard, women were destined to play the leading role in the work of peacemaking. The 'feminine' qualities of compassion and tender-heartedness were necessary in the attainment of peace, and those who had mothered children would not readily sacrifice them on the battlefield. When women participated fully and equally with men in law and politics war would cease.⁶¹ A distinction in gender roles should be drawn here, for whilst it was entirely possible to train women to be men's equals in the "military science of slaughter," it was wrong to do so.⁶²

UNITY IN DIVERSITY

For Bahá'ís, all of humanity constitutes a single race. Whilst cultural diversity could be regarded positively as a defence against bland uniformity, national, ethnic, and racial differences are regarded as man-made. Creations of human thought, they are not part of God's creation. Nor did God respect people differently based on the colour of their skin. All human beings were created as the "leaves of one tree and the drops of one ocean." The whole Earth was but one country and all humankind its citizens.⁶³

No one should regard themselves as superior on the basis of their race, religion, or nationality. It was both urgently necessary to overcome the prejudices of the past, and wrong to dis-

---

⁵⁹ 'Abdu'l-Bahá, *Paris Talks*, 161–62.
⁶⁰ Esselemont, *New Era*, 133.
⁶¹ 'Abdu'l-Bahá, *Promulgation*, 108, 134–35, 175, 284.
⁶² 'Abdu'l-Bahá, *Paris Talks*, 183; *Promulgation*, 75.
⁶³ Bahá'u'lláh, *Tablets*, 129; 'Abdu'l-Bahá, *Paris Talks*, 51–54, 129, 131, 138–40, 146–51; *Promulgation*, 232.

criminate against others on the basis of racial, religious, or national differences — unless special consideration needed to be given to those who had been oppressed because of their minority status. Each individual should strive to rid themselves of prejudice against others, associating with the followers of all religions "with joy and radiance," and showing kindness to those of other races and nationalities.[64]

No barriers should exist between people because of race. In those societies in which racial divisions were a major source of confrontation, the work of reconciliation was vital, lest — as in the case of the United States — enmity would increase and lead to hardship and bloodshed.[65] It was useful to have meetings devoted to the subject of inter-racial amity. Interracial marriage was a positive force in the abolition of differences. The exhortation given to the North American Bahá'ís may doubtless also be taken as of general applicability here: that members of the dominant race should abandon even the least sense of superiority and correct any tendency towards patronizing condescension, whilst those of the oppressed race should be ready to forget the past and overcome their suspicions. Neither race should think that 'the solution of so vast a problem' was a matter that exclusively concerned the other. There would be no easy or immediate solution, but the problem could be solved — requiring great tact, love, wisdom, and effort.[66]

INTERNATIONAL ORDER.

COLLECTIVE SECURITY

Basic security can be seen as a human right. For Bahá'u'lláh and 'Abdu'l-Bahá the establishment of peace between the nations was an imperative necessity. The Great Powers should resolve

---

[64] Bahá'u'lláh, *Tablets*, 22, 87; 'Abdu'l-Bahá, *Paris Talks*, 15–17; Shoghi Effendi, *Advent of Divine Justice* (Wilmette, IL.: Bahá'í Publishing Trust, 1963), 32.
[65] Shoghi Effendi, *Advent*, 33.
[66] Shoghi Effendi, *Advent*, 33–34.

"to be fully reconciled among themselves" for the sake of "the tranquillity of the peoples of the world."[67] Differences between nations had to be resolved through an international court of arbitration — not through armed force. An all-embracing assembly of the world's rulers had to be convened in order to work to establish a universal peace treaty which would be binding on all the nations of the world. The terms of this treaty should clearly delineate international boundaries, the obligations and responsibilities between nations, and the size of each nation's military forces. Then, if any nation violated the provisions of the pact, all other states should reduce it to submission.[68]

Armaments

In securing this peace, armament reductions would be essential. Under a system of collective security, such as envisaged by the Bahá'í leaders, each nation would only require sufficient armaments as were necessary to maintain its security and internal order. Armament reduction would only be possible if there was international concurrence and agreement: unilateral disarmament by a single nation would not be effective. All nations had to reduce their armaments simultaneously.[69]

Without such an agreement, there was an arms race between nations. This race had a dynamic of its own: as long as any one nation increased its military expenditure then other nations, through their "natural and supposed interests," would feel forced into "this crazed competition."[70] New inventions would rapidly render older armaments obsolete, thus necessitating further military spending. This had social consequences: the increasing expenditures would lead to an increasing burden of taxation on the mass of the population, and as such could be seen as a form of

---

[67] Bahá'u'lláh, *Tablets*, 165.
[68] Bahá'u'lláh, *Tablets*, 165; 'Abdu'l-Baha, *Secret*, 64–66; 'Abdu'l-Bahá, *Paris Talks*, 155; Esslemont, *New Era*, 147.
[69] National Spiritual Assembly of the Bahá'ís of Canada, 50; Esslemont, *New Era*, 148–49.
[70] Esslemont, *New Era*, 148–49.

oppression. Moreover, the arms industry employed human and financial resources which could be better devoted to fostering development and peace than to devising new means of destruction. Eventually, such spending would reach a point where it was intolerable to humankind, straining nations beyond endurance. Nations would then be forced by economic pressures to come to peace. In the meantime, however, international bellicosity and the arms race were themselves productive of war.[71]

WORK TOWARDS PEACE

The attainment of peace required ceaseless endeavour. At a time when new weapons of destruction could kill ever larger numbers of people, the work for peace became ever more vital.[72] Governments and international organizations had to become fully committed to the work for peace. Peace had to become a genuine concern of governments: lip-service to its ideals was not enough. Countries which were regarded as relatively neutral (such as the United States of America in the years prior to World War I) could play an important mediating role.[73] Whilst peace societies were important, everyone could work to oppose support for war. In this regard, the role of women was crucial in the transformation of public opinion. When women became fully active in the political process, their work for peace would prove decisive.[74]

HUMAN SOLIDARITY

Radical changes in human attitudes needed to be affected in order to build the world envisaged by the Bahá'í leaders. It was essential that prejudices towards other peoples on the basis of race, religion or nationality be abandoned. Such prejudices fos-

---

[71] Bahá'u'lláh, *Tablets*, 89; 'Abdu'l-Bahá, *Secret*, 61–62, 65–67; National Spiritual Assembly of the Bahá'ís of Canada, 42, 51.
[72] 'Abdu'l-Bahá, *Secret*, 66; *Promulgation*, 108, 134–35, 175, 284.
[73] 'Abdu'l-Bahá, *Promulgation*, 121–22.
[74] 'Abdu'l-Bahá, *Promulgation*, 108, 134–35, 175, 284.

tered enmity, and so laid the basis for war.⁷⁵ In place of such sentiments, it was necessary to inculcate the conception that all human beings were members of a single race.

To this end, an international language should be chosen to be taught in all the world's schools as an auxiliary to the children's native languages. This would powerfully reinforce moves to promote understanding between the peoples of the world.⁷⁶

Again, it was necessary to oppose the instinct towards aggression. Thoughts of war and hatred should be overcome by thoughts peace and love. Human beings no longer needed to engage in a savage struggle for survival against wild nature. Instead, their mutual cooperation as a species was now essential for their continued well-being.⁷⁷ The evil of warfare had to be recognized for what it was. To glory in the destruction of other human beings was an abomination. Murder and theft were not altered by being committed as acts of war.⁷⁸ The achievement of gender equality was of crucial importance in affecting all these changes.

WORLD FEDERATION AND THE "MOST GREAT PEACE"

In his writings, Bahá'u'lláh distinguished between what he termed the "Most Great Peace" (*"sulh-e a'zam"*) and a more limited peace between the nations.⁷⁹ For Bahá'ís, the Most Great Peace represents the promised Kingdom of God on Earth, a world united in all the essentials of its life in which all human beings could work unhindered for their collective advancement.⁸⁰ Bahá'ís accept that this millennial vision may be a far distant attainment, however. Nevertheless, they believe that in the meantime, there is a potential in human development which will carry

---

⁷⁵ 'Abdu'l-Bahá, *Hague*, 2–5; *Paris Talks*, 131, 146–51; Eric Hammond, *Abdul Baha in London* (East Sheen: Unity Press, 1912), 4.
⁷⁶ Bahá'u'lláh, *Tablets*, 22, 68, 89, 127, 165–66; 'Abdu'l-Baha, *Promulgation*, 60–61.
⁷⁷ 'Abdu'l-Bahá, *Paris Talks*, 29; Hammond, *Abdul Baha in London*, 4; Shoghi Effendi, *World Order*, 36.
⁷⁸ 'Abdu'l-Bahá, *Promulgation*, 119.
⁷⁹ Bahá'u'lláh, *Proclamation*, 12–13.
⁸⁰ Shoghi Effendi, *World Order*, 203–6.

humankind beyond the ending of international warfare. Political and economic changes have already put an end to local self-sufficiency. The peoples of the world are becoming increasingly interdependent.

In this context, Bahá'ís believe that a federation of all nations becomes ever more necessary in order to adequately deal with the world's social and economic problems. The notion of unfettered national sovereignty has become an outmoded fetish that needs to be abandoned, and the executive power of a world government established. To resist this development is merely to prolong "the anarchy inherent in state sovereignty," with disastrous results for the peace and well-being of the human race.[81] The establishment of a world federation would create the peaceful conditions in which social and economic reconstruction could be adequately pursued, and so should be a goal for present human endeavour.[82]

Such a federation would represent unity but not uniformity. The integrity and traditions of the component nations would be preserved. Full political independence for all component nations (presumably involving decolonialization) would be a necessary recondition for an effective federation.[83]

RELIGION & THE FAMILY

In a framework in which human rights are regarded as God-given rights, the nature of the religious tradition is itself important. In this regard, the Bahá'í conception of the social role of religion is somewhat distinctive. Thus, whilst Bahá'ís are bidden to promote their religion and to ensure that their children are brought up with a strong sense of moral and religious principles, they are also instructed to ensure that ignorant fanaticism and bigotry are avoided. Indeed, "any religion which is not a cause of love and

---

[81] Shoghi Effendi, *World Order*, 202.
[82] Shoghi Effendi, *World Order*, 36–45.
[83] Helen Hornby (comp.), *Lights of Guidance: A Bahá'í Reference File* (New Delhi: Bahá'í Publishing Trust, 1983), 333.

unity" is declared to be "no religion", and that if a religion is the source of division and hatred that "to withdraw from such a religion would be a truly religious act."[84]

RELIGIOUS TOLERANCE AND DIVERSITY

The Bahá'ís represent a distinct religious community with their own scriptures, organization, and criteria of membership. To the present day, there have been numerous Bahá'ís who have been sufficiently committed to their religion to make great personal sacrifices on its behalf, some sadly suffering persecution to the point of accepting death rather than dissimulating their faith. Nevertheless, Bahá'ís have abandoned much of the sense of religious exclusivity generally characteristic of the 'Western' monotheistic religious traditions (i.e., of Judaism, Christianity, and Islam). Bahá'u'lláh was quite specific, bidding his adherents to "Consort with the followers of all religions in a spirit of friendliness and fellowship;" to be tolerant; and to "adhere tenaciously to that which will promote fellowship, kindliness and unity." Again, the Bahá'í leaders commanded the adoption of an irenic attitude to teaching the Bahá'í religion to others, condemning violent controversialism, fanaticism and religious disputation.[85]

In sharp distinction to the then current practices of Iranian Shi'ism all barriers to interpersonal relations between those of different religions based on considerations of ritual purity were abolished. Indeed, the concept of ritual purity was itself almost entirely abandoned in favour of injunctions to practice hygiene and cleanliness.[86]

Moreover, the Bahá'ís were assured by their leaders that their personal religiosity did not of itself guarantee salvation, as at the hour of his or her death, the life-long 'devout believer' might err,

---

[84] 'Abdu'l-Bahá, *Paris Talks*, 130; Universal House of Justice, *Bahá'í Education*, 4–5.
[85] Bahá'u'lláh, *Aqdas*, 72 v144; *Tablets*, 22, 35–36, 72.
[86] E. G. Browne, "The Bábís of Persia," Journal of the Royal Asiatic Society, N.S. 21, 1889, 500.

whilst the 'sinner' attained the essence of faith.[87] For this reason, the believer should never despise the apparently sinful. Again, according to 'Abdu'l-Bahá, to be a true Bahá'í meant simply "to love all the world; to love humanity and try to serve it; [and] to work for universal peace and universal brotherhood." By such a measure, an individual might be a Bahá'í in spirit even though they had never heard of Bahá'u'lláh, whilst someone might call themselves a Bahá'í "for fifty years", but if they did not lead their life according to the Faith's spiritual and moral principles then they were not Bahá'ís.[88]

Religious authority

The Bahá'ís have a strong sense of religious authority centring on the authority claims of the successive leaders of their Faith. Acceptance of this succession (Bahá'u'lláh, 'Abdu'l-Bahá, Shoghi Effendi, and the Universal House of Justice) constitutes what they term "firmness in the Covenant", whilst opposition to the succession is labelled as "Covenant-breaking", leading ultimately to expulsion from the Faith.[89] Again, Bahá'ís ascribe an absolute authoritative status — or even infallibility — to the authenticated writings of their leaders, employ a temporary system of official review of Bahá'í literature, and emphasize the authority of their 'Administrative Order'. At the same time, however, the actual exercise of this authority within the Bahá'í community is relatively non-authoritarian. The Covenant is seen as a means of ensuring communal unity rather than of imposing uniformity. Apart from accepting the authority and official succession of leaders, the religious freedom and autonomy of individual belief are recognized and upheld.[90] The style of leadership is generally consultative and exhortatory rather than commandeering.

---

[87] Bahá'u'lláh, *The Kitab-i-Iqan: The Book of Certitude*, trans. Shoghi Effendi (London: Baha'i Publishing Trust, 1946), 124.

[88] Esslemont, *New Era*, 70; Hammond, *Abdul Baha in London*, 109.

[89] See Smith, *Encyclopedia*, 115–16.

[90] Shoghi Effendi, *Citadel of Faith: Messages to America, 1947–1957* (Wilmette, IL.: Bahá'í Publishing Trust, 1965), 130–31, 148.

Some individual Bahá'ís may be dogmatic, but overall, the conception of revelation discourages narrow literalistic dogmatism. A belief in the harmony of religion, science and rationality provides a potent source of authority external to the religious system.[91] The relativity of all human knowledge is asserted and the consequent right of individual doctrinal interpretation is recognized.[92] The "keynote of the Cause" is held to be "humble fellowship" and "a spirit of frank and loving consultation." As to the Administrative Order, it is declared to be rooted in "the undoubted right of the individual to self-expression, his freedom to declare his conscience and set forth his views."[93] Those who are elected to administrative office are warned of the dangers of over-administration, being exhorted not to institute an excessive number of procedural rules in their leadership of the community, and to avoid any tendency towards over-centralization.[94]

MATERIAL AND SPIRITUAL CIVILIZATION

Bahá'ís believe that religion — when both tolerant and non-authoritarian — can play a vital role in the defence of basic rights to security and in the future promotion of social justice, constituting both a powerful defence against social disorder and a potent means of advancing necessary social change.

For Bahá'u'lláh, the true liberty that profited humanity was only to be found in "complete servitude" to God. The precepts laid down by God were "the highest means for the maintenance of order in the world and the security of its peoples."[95] The fear of God was the chief means for the protection of human society. Whilst the fear of worldly punishments might prevent wrongdo-

---

[91] 'Abdu'l-Bahá, *Paris Talks*, 130–31, 141–46.
[92] 'Abdu'l-Bahá, *Promulgation*, 20–22, 253–55; Universal House of Justice, *Wellspring of Guidance: Messages, 1963–1968* (Wilmette, IL.: Bahá'í Publishing Trust, 1969), 88–89.
[93] Shoghi Effendi, *Bahá'í Administration* (Wilmette, IL.: Bahá'í Publishing Trust, 1945 [5th ed.]), 63.
[94] Hornby, *Lights of Guidance*, 36–37, 129.
[95] Bahá'u'lláh, *Aqdas*, 19–20 v2, 63–64 v123–25.

ing, it had no necessary effect on the attitudes of the wrongdoer. By contrast, the fear of God impelled individuals "to hold fast to that which is good and shun all evil." Thus, when "the lamp of religion" was obscured, "chaos and confusion" would ensue, and "the lights of fairness and justice, of tranquillity and peace" would cease to shine. Therefore, those who were concerned with preserving the stability of a country should have the profoundest regard for religion.[96]

The effects of the abandonment of religion were thought to be evidenced in the development of European civilization. For 'Abdu'l-Bahá, writing in 1875, the materialism of contemporary European civilization had produced "a superficial culture, unsupported by a cultivated morality." "Notwithstanding their vaunted civilization," the Europeans sank and drowned in "this terrifying sea of passion and desire." Engaged in a senseless pursuit of conquest and its resultant arms race (the staggering costs of which were borne by their hapless masses), Europe represented only a "nominal civilization."[97] Similarly, Bahá'u'lláh pointed to the contrast between the claims of European civilization and the practice of anti-Semitism, and referred to the destructive impact of European expansion on the peoples and cultures of the rest of the world.[98] It was not European civilization as such that was at fault — the Bahá'í leaders were not anti-European, and they praised many aspects of European civilization, advocating their adoption in the Middle East — but rather the dominance of the material over the spiritual aspects of its culture: "If a thing is carried to excess," wrote Bahá'u'lláh, "it will prove a source of evil."[99] Later, Shoghi Effendi saw materialism as having become a dominant element in the culture of the entire world. The opposing political philosophies of both East and West were now to be "com-

---

[96] Bahá'u'lláh, *Tablets*, 63, 64, 93, 125.
[97] 'Abdu'l-Bahá, *Secret*, 60–64.
[98] Bahá'u'lláh, *Tablets*, 69, 144, 169, 170.
[99] Bahá'u'lláh, *Tablets*, 69.

monly condemned" for their crass materialism and their neglect of spiritual values and eternal verities.[100]

For Bahá'ís, the promotion of 'Divine civilization' did not mean the abandonment of the fruits of material civilization. When infused with the correct moral and spiritual values, the material aspects of civilization would assume a positive role in the future progress of humanity. When inspired by more spiritual objectives, human beings would find the courage and dedication to implement the imperatives of social justice and create a better society. Without such moral and spiritual values, material civilization was like a dead body, devoid of life.[101] To implement the demands of social justice required more than simply reconstructing human institutions, important though that was. In order to accomplish fundamental social change, attitudinal change was also necessary. When people really wanted change, then difficult objectives would become easy to attain. If people were not inspired by spiritual objectives, human selfishness would prevail, and retard the achievement of genuine social change.

Family Life

The importance of family life is much stressed in the Bahá'í writings.[102] The marriage bond is regarded as a potential spiritual union transcending the limitations of earthly life, whilst the institution of the family is regarded as the primary means for the effective moral and religious socialization of children. Thus, Bahá'ís are encouraged to marry (monogamously) and to establish stable and harmonious families. They are also advised that the most stable unions are those which are based on spiritual attraction, comradeship, and companionship between the parties. There are no religious barriers to marriage, and inter-racial marriage is positively regarded.

---

[100] Shoghi Effendi, *Citadel*, 124–25.
[101] 'Abdu'l-Bahá, *Hague*, 6.
[102] See Universal House of Justice, *Family Life*.

As to the regulation of marriage, the choice of partner rests with the couple, but requires the consent of their parents so as to ensure family harmony. Extra-marital unions and concubinage are forbidden. Divorce is discouraged but permitted if the marriage has suffered irreparable breakdown: the couple should first try to resolve any difficulties in their marriage through consultation between themselves, seeking external guidance if helpful.[103] Arbitrary and instant divorce of the wife by the husband (still common in some parts of the world) is forbidden.

Whilst the procreation of children is regarded as the primary purpose of marriage, there is no ban on the use of birth control to limit the number of children. It is up to the couple to decide how best to plan their family life. Abortion for non-medical reasons is forbidden, but effectively treated as a matter of personal conscience.[104]

Within the family, each member is believed to have their own rights and responsibilities. Children have a right to be educated by their parents, but in turn have a duty to respect and serve their parents. Responsibility for providing for the family and bringing up the children rests with both parents, but the mother is regarded as being chiefly responsible for rearing the child and has a corresponding right to be supported by her husband. The actual balance of responsibilities between any particular couple is for them to decide, however. In all cases, all family members should show due consideration for the rest. None have the right to unjustly dominate the others, and each should seek a relationship based on 'frank and loving consultation' rather than arbitrary power.[105] All forms of domestic violence are condemned.

---

[103] Hornby, *Lights of Guidance*, 293–302.
[104] Hornby, *Lights of Guidance*, 260–64.
[105] Universal House of Justice, *Family Life*, 30–33.

PRAXIS

The Bahá'í account of the demands of social justice is essentially informed by a profoundly religious vision of the nature and purpose of human life. That this account readily encompasses areas of social life which many modern Westerners tend to see as 'secular' concerns reflects a lack of a sharp distinction in Bahá'í thinking between sacred and secular. Bahá'ís may emphasize the ultimate otherworldliness of human existence and eschew political involvement, but all areas of human life are regarded as being open to religious commentary and shaping.

Furthermore, it is characteristic of the Bahá'í view of human rights that the attainment of human objectives is seen both in a global context and in spiritual as well as 'practical' terms. Thus, Bahá'ís emphasize that issues such as economic injustice and suffering, the abuse of civil rights, arbitrary rule, racism, sexism, and international conflict can no longer be seen as isolated local problems. They are global issues which impact the stability and development of humanity as a whole and have to be addressed as such. Solutions can only be properly effective if they take account of the increasing integration and interactiveness of global society. Moreover, whilst Bahá'ís insist on the necessity of significant institutional changes to solve social and economic problems, they also emphasize that the spiritual and moral dimension of those problems have to be addressed. Without changes in social attitudes and the acceptance of individual moral responsibility, the full potentialities of social justice cannot be achieved.

Another aspect of the Bahá'í approach to human rights is their 'pragmatic idealism'. Whilst holding to a set of highly idealistic principles and objectives, Baha'is show a willingness to begin with mundane realities and try to work constructively from that base towards their higher goals. In this they follow the example of their leaders. Bahá'u'lláh's distinction between the goal of the desired kingdom of God on Earth and that of the more immediate goal of peace between the nations is a case in point: he inspired his followers with the millennial vision of the 'Most Great Peace', but he also saw fit to outline a proposal for a collective security as a pragmatic response to the international tensions of his day.

Given the dynamism of the global Bahá'í community and the readiness of the Bahá'ís to work with other groups with whom they are in sympathy, the Bahá'í account of human rights represents more than simply a catalogue of idealistic objectives. Although any proper evaluation of the Bahá'ís' endeavour to implement their vision of social justice is premature, in practical terms, the international expansion of the Bahá'í community has undoubtedly served to foster support for basic human rights. In the long run, Bahá'í expansion in the Global South may be particularly significant in this regard.[106] In terms of the rights associated with socio-economic development, there is an evident acceleration of activity. Although the emphasis is on local initiatives by local Bahá'í communities, an international Office of Social and Economic Development (OSED) was established in 1983 at the Bahá'í World Centre to provide general coordination.[107]

Various aspects of development have received attention, most particularly perhaps education, with Bahá'í literacy programs and schools now proliferating in a number of countries. Following Bahá'í principles, these programs are open to all, regardless of religion, and are directed at adults (especially women in those countries where their literacy rates are lower than those of men) as well as children.[108]

In terms of cultural and political rights, the Bahá'í insistence on not getting involved in partisan politics and being obedient to the laws of the countries in which they live have obviously

---

[106] On Bahá'í expansion see Peter Smith, *The Babi and Bahá'í Religions: From Messianic Shi' ism to a World Religion* (Cambridge: Cambridge University Press, 1987), 157–95.

[107] OSED was replaced by the Bahá'í International Development Organization in 2019.

[108] For more detailed accounts see Gregory C. Dahl, "A Bahá'í perspective on economic and social development." In Anthony A. Lee (ed.), *Circle of Unity: Bahá'í Approaches to Current Social Themes* (Los Angeles: Kalimat Press, 1984), 155–89; Smith, *Introduction*, 201–207.

limited their critique of specific cases of injustice. Bahá'í activity is nevertheless potentially significant, particularly in the Global South, where Bahá'ís gain consultative experience through the establishment of their own local administrative bodies in a context which emphasizes the equality of all participants regardless of their gender, race, or ethnic identity.

The empowerment of women and minority group members may be a particularly significant here. Throughout the world, Bahá'í women are playing an increasingly central role in the organization of their religion, whilst the Bahá'í stress on the validity of local indigenous cultures is providing encouragement to members of otherwise despised cultural minorities to take pride in their own identity and cultural achievements. It is also of note that the Faith's international leadership increasingly reflects the preponderant membership of Bahá'ís from the Global South.

Finally, in terms of international order, Bahá'ís are seeking to become increasingly involved in the activities of the United Nations, seeing its goals and objectives as useful and necessary contributions to the attainment of their own vision of the future of human society.

Whatever the future potential and success of the Bahá'ís endeavours to implement their vision of social justice, their underlying conception of human rights and responsibilities is neither closed nor exclusive. For Bahá'ís, the implementation of their principles is an objective that transcends their own activities as a religious community. They would see the onward progress of the human race as having a dynamic of its own, of which the Bahá'ís conceive themselves as being but a necessary part.

BIBLIOGRAPHY

'Abdu'l-Bahá. *Tablet to the Hague* (London: Bahá'í Publishing Trust, n.d.). 'Abdu'l-Bahá's letter to the Central Organization for a Durable Peace at The Hague (1919).

'Abdu'l-Bahá. *Selections from the Writings of 'Abdu'l-Bahá*, trans. M. Gail et al (Haifa: Bahá'í World Centre, 1978).

'Abdu'l-Bahá. *The Secret of Divine Civilization*, trans. M. Gail (Wilmette, IL: Bahá'í Publishing Trust, 1957).

'Abdu'l-Bahá. *Some Answered Questions.* Collected and trans. L. C. Barney (Wilmette, IL: Bahá'í Publishing Trust, 1981). Talks given in response to questions in 1904–1906. [A new revised edition was published at the Bahá'í World Centre in Haifa in 2014].

'Abdu'l-Bahá. *Paris Talks: Addresses Given by 'Abdu'l-Bahá in Paris in 1911–1912.* 10th ed. (London: Bahá'í Publishing Trust, 1961).

'Abdu'l-Bahá. *The Promulgation of Universal Peace: Talks Delivered by 'Abdu'l-Bahá during His Visit to the United States and Canada in 1912.* Comp. H. MacNutt. 2nd ed. (Wilmette, IL: Bahá'í Publishing Trust, 1982).

Bahá'u'lláh. *Gleanings from the Writings of Bahá'u'lláh,* [comp. and] trans. Shoghi Effendi (London: Bahá'í Publishing Trust, 1978 [Rev.ed.]).

Bahá'u'lláh. *Prayers and Meditations of* Bahá'u'lláh, comp. and trans. Shoghi Effendi (Wilmette, IL.: Bahá'í Publishing Trust, 1938).

Bahá'u'lláh. *Tablets of Bahá'u'lláh Revealed After the Kitab-i-Aqdas,* trans. H. Taherzadeh et al (Haifa: Bahá'í World Centre, 1978).

Bahá'u'lláh, *The Hidden Words* (London: Bahá'í Publishing Trust, 1932).

Bahá'u'lláh. *The Kitab-i-Iqan: The Book of Certitude,* trans. Shoghi Effendi (London: Baha'i Publishing Trust, 1946).

Bahá'u'lláh. *The Kitab-i-Aqdas: The Most Holy Book* (Haifa: Bahá'í World Centre, 1992).

Bahá'u'lláh. *The Proclamation of Bahá'u'lláh to the Kings and Rulers of the World* (Haifa: Bahá'í World Centre, 1967).

Barrett, David, B., George Thomas Kurian, and Todd M Johnson (eds.). *World Christian Encyclopedia: A Contemporary Survey of Churches and Religions in the Modern World* (2nd ed.) (New York: Oxford University Press, 2001)

Beitz, Charles R. *The Idea of Human Rights* (Oxford: Oxford University Press, 2009).

Browne, E. G. E. G. Browne, "The Bábís of Persia," Journal of the Royal Asiatic Society, N.S. 21, 1889, pp. 485–526, 881–1009.

Dahl, Gregory C. "A Bahá'í perspective on economic and social development." In Anthony A. Lee (ed.), *Circle of Unity: Bahá'í Approaches to Current Social Themes* (Los Angeles: Kalimat Press, 1984).

Esslemont, John E. *Bahá'u'lláh and the New Era* (London: Allen and Unwin, 1923).

Freeman, Michael. *Human Rights: An Interdisciplinary Approach* (Cambridge: Polity Press, 2002).

Hammond, Eric. *Abdul Baha in London* (East Sheen: Unity Press, 1912).

Hornby, Helen (comp.). *Lights of Guidance: A Bahá'í Reference File* (New Delhi: Bahá'í Publishing Trust, 1983).

Laqueur, Walter and Rubin, Barry (eds.). *The Human Rights Reader* (New York: Meridian Books, 1975. Rev. ed. 1990).

Latimer, George O (comp.). "The Social Teachings of the Bahai Movement," *Star of the West*, 7/15 (1916), pp. 133–139; 145–148.

National Spiritual Assembly of the Bahá'ís of Canada, *'Abdu'l-Bahá in Canada* (Forest, Ontario: Forest Free Press, 1962).

Rosenbaum, Alan S. (ed.), *The Philosophy of Human Rights: International Perspectives* (Westport, Conn.: Greenwood Press, 1980).

Shoghi Effendi, *Advent of Divine Justice* (Wilmette, IL.: Bahá'í Publishing Trust, 1963).

Shoghi Effendi, *Bahá'í Administration* (Wilmette, IL.: Bahá'í Publishing Trust, 1945 [5th ed.]).

Shoghi Effendi, *Citadel of Faith: Messages to America, 1947–1957* (Wilmette, IL.: Bahá'í Publishing Trust, 1965).

Shoghi Effendi. *The World Order of Bahá'u'lláh*. Rev. ed. (Wilmette, IL: Bahá'í Publishing Trust, 1955). Letters written in 1929–36.

Shoghi Effendi. "The Non-Political Character of the Bahá'í Faith. Excerpts from the Writings of Shoghi Effendi," *Bahá'í World*, vol. 17 (Haifa: Bahá'í World Centre, 1981), 377–83.

Smith, Peter. *A Concise Encyclopedia of the Bahá'í Faith.* 2nd ed. (Oxford: Oneworld, 2002).

Smith, Peter. *An Introduction to the Bahá'í Faith* (Cambridge: Cambridge University Press, 2008).

Smith, Peter. *The Babi and Bahá'í Religions: From Messianic Shi'ism to a World Religion* (Cambridge: Cambridge University Press, 1987).

"Statistics," the Bahaikipedia website: **https://bahaikipedia.org/Statistics**. Last accessed 23 February 2018.

The Universal House of Justice, *Wellspring of Guidance: Messages, 1963–1968* (Wilmette, IL.: Bahá'í Publishing Trust, 1969).

The Universal House of Justice, Research Department (comp.), *Bahá'í Education* (London: Bahá'í Publishing Trust, 1976).

The Universal House of Justice (comp.), *The Heaven of Divine Wisdom* [A compilation on consultation] (London: Bahá'í Publishing Trust, 1978).

The Universal House of Justice, Research Department (comp.), *Family Life* (London: Bahá'í Publishing Trust, 1982).

Prophetic Revelation and Sociocultural Evolution:
Some Scientific Perspectives[1]

HARRY P. MASSOTH AND MARILU JENO

> If we understand the processes by which new religions come into being, we should be close to understanding other basic processes of human life...For new religions are, above all else, movements toward the revitalization of man and society.
>
> Anthony F. C. Wallace,
> *Religion: An Anthropological View*, 1966.

> Who, witnessing on one hand the stupendous advance achieved in the realm of human knowledge, of power, of skill and inventiveness, and viewing on the other the unprecedented character of the sufferings that afflict, and the dangers that beset, present-day society, can be so blind as to doubt that the hour has at last struck for the advent of a new Revelation, for a restatement of the Divine Purpose, and for the consequent revival of those spiritual forces that have, at fixed intervals, rehabilitated the fortunes of human society?
>
> Shoghi Effendi,
> *The World Order of Bahá'u'lláh*, 1936.

INTRODUCTION

What is the motive-force behind socio-cultural evolution? What processes working within the universe in general and society in particular enable civilization to progress, to periodically reinte-

---

[1] A study paper prepared by Earthrise Institute, July 1988 Winner of the Multi-Author Category, Association for Bahá'í Studies.

grate its ever-diversifying and often competitive subgroups into more highly-ordered and cooperative systems? To go even further, what processes underlie the 'spiritualization' of society?

The answers to these questions are hardly academic as humanity is presently faced with the awesome challenge of creating a planetary management system capable of guiding the future course of evolution on Earth, establishing world peace, and insuring the continued stability of our global ecosystem. Numerous studies made by social scientists agree that there are two primary and interrelated crises confronting contemporary man. The first and most visible is the population/resource/environment crisis which directly impacts the stability of the Earth's ecosystem. The breakdown of the ozone layer, the pollution of the rivers, oceans and seas, the uncontrolled erosion of our farmlands, and the ruthless exploitation of natural resources all attest that the biosphere of our planet is being threatened by forces unimaginable to man only a century ago. The second crisis is that of man himself — the relationship to himself, to his technological innovations, his institutions, his ideas, and belief systems, to those around him, as well as between the many groups that inhabit the globe; in a word, his relationship to his culture.[2]

Because of the dynamic and often delicate interrelationship between physical and social environments both crises must be resolved or neither will be solved. It is becoming increasingly apparent that there are no technological solutions to the social conflicts confronting the human community. At the same time, technological solutions to environmental problems will never be applied effectively until the human community is sufficiently unified politically, ideologically arid spiritually.

To grasp these relationships more clearly it is helpful to visualize the global ecosystem divided into two subsystems: (1) the biophysical subsystem and (2) the sociocultural subsystem.

---

[2] For a lengthy discussion of this issue see *Beyond Culture* by Edward T. Hall (Anchor Press, N.Y. 1976). The book contains an insightful analysis of the forces which mold human culture and have led to the present dilemma in human affairs.

The biophysical subsystem underlies and sustains the sociocultural subsystem by supplying the basic energies required by living systems. Throughout history human beings have recognized two primary sources of energy which sustain life and society. One is solar energy derived from the sun; the other is metaphysical or spiritual energy derived from the Creator of the universe via prophetic revelation. Solar energy captured by the biophysical systems of the Earth is ultimately harnessed and utilized by man through technology. Spiritual energy, on the other hand is captured by the sociocultural system through religious practices. The balance and coordination between technology and religion appears to be the result of a third human endeavor called governance. In a sense, then, technology, religion and governance constitute three great 'pillars' upholding human culture. When these three pillars are in the proper relationship, the global ecology tends to evolve in a relatively harmonious and gradual way. But if these pillars drift from their proper relationship, the ecosystem grows increasingly unstable and disharmonious until eventually some kind of critical juncture is reached, and a catastrophic episode restores the balance. (See below).

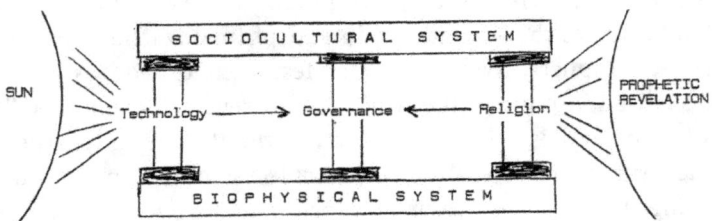

During the last century a scientific and technological revolution has swept through the world. Unfortunately, progress in the realms of religion and governance has been slow and sometimes even retrogressive. This situation has precipitated the various environmental, social, and spiritual crises of our age. Thus, the greatest challenge facing the human community today is to restore the balance between the three pillars of technology, religion, and governance. In essence, our greatest hope lies in a renaissance of religion based on spiritual values which will, in turn, generate a global system of governance capable of directing the awesome powers of modern technology into constructive channels of service to the sociocultural system and the underlying biophysical system.

But just how might such a renaissance of religion occur? This is the central question explored in this essay. In brief, we will reexamine the hypothesis held by all the major world religions that prophetic or 'progressive' revelation is one of the most significant forces underlying sociocultural evolution. It is our hope that some new light will be shed upon this topic and thereby help demonstrate that the theological and naturalistic views of religion's role in human evolution are at last merging. Such a view, we feel, can offer a powerful conceptual tool which may be used to help motivate more people to assume their roles in our emerging planetary guidance system.

DIVINE REVELATION: THE CONCEPT IN RELIGION

The idea that the Creative Force of the Universe (i.e., God, Allah, Brahman) periodically communicated His Will to humankind through the revelation of great spiritual teachers, variously called Prophets, Avatars, or Manifestations of God, is a theme expressed in most of the world's great religious traditions. The Word of God or Logos as revealed by the Prophet is regarded as the primary motive force responsible for transforming human beings from organisms who are primarily materialistic and self-centered into beings who are spiritualized and other-centered. The phenomenon of revelation is said to be 'progressive' because each new outpouring of the Word of God tends to both compliment and expand upon the lessons imparted through previous revelations. Like the rays of the sun which become 'progressively' more intense throughout the spring and summer months and thus provide the necessary energy for the growth and development of life on earth, so do the various revelations of the Word of God energize, revitalize, and provide for the evolution of sociocultural systems. In theological terms this process can be viewed as the unfoldment of the Kingdom of God on Earth.

Although this concept is not universally held or understood in the same way by the followers of different faiths, still it can be found articulated quite clearly in the writings of many theologians and religious philosophers. A few examples should make this point clear.

THE JUDEO-CHRISTIAN TRADITION

The introduction to the *Scofield Reference Bible*, one of the most popular Bibles in circulation, offers the following view of God's progressive revelation to humankind:

> The Bible is a <u>progressive</u> unfoldment of truth. Nothing is told all at once, and once for all. The law is, 'first the blade, then the ear, after that the full corn.' Without the possibility of collusion, often with centuries between, one writer of Scripture takes up an earlier revelation, adds to it, lays down the pen, and in due time another man moved by the Holy Spirit, and another, and another, add new details till the whole is complete...From beginning to end the Bible testifies to one *redemption*...And, finally, these writers, some forty-four in number, writing through twenty centuries, have produces a *perfect harmony* of doctrine in progressive unfolding... (*Emphasis not ours*).[3]

In his book *The Heart of the Gospel*, George Townshend takes a sweeping view of Biblical history and expounds on his theme from an evolutionary perspective. He writes:

> Evolution indeed from its beginning in the distant past to its completion in the distant future is nothing more than the Revelation of God's purpose for mankind. What

---

[3] C. I. Scofield, D.D., ed., *The Scofield Reference Bible*, (Oxford University Press: NY, 1945), p. v.

is being evolved was first created by God, then enfolded by God, then unfolded to man's knowledge by God: the plan, the process, and the substance of the process are all from God. The story of the spiritual evolution of man from his infancy to his maturity, from Genesis to the close of the Apocalypse, is the story of the continuous Self-Revelation of God to man.[4]

Townshend goes on to point out that man's ability to cooperate in his own evolution depends on the extent and the accuracy of his knowledge of God, and the measure of his knowledge is the measure of his progress toward spiritual maturity.

HINDU AND BUDDHIST SCRIPTURES

Both Hindu and Buddhist traditions contain the concept of the Avatar or Divine manifestation whose periodic appearance represents the descent of the Unmanifest Absolute into the contingent realm. These Avatars are likened to spiritual sunbursts and their teachings like the rays of the sun which provide the energy and information through which humanity progresses. The Avatars, also known as Buddhas or Tathagatas, are viewed as unique beings who arise only rarely. As Buddha is purported to have taught in the *Sutta-Nipata*:

> Rarely, O monks, do Tathagatas appear in the world. To the extent that they (men) understand the rarity of a Tathagata's appearance, to that extend will they wonder about His appearance, and sorrow at His disappearance, and when they do not see the Tathagata, they will long for the sight of Him.[5]

Swami Akhilananda, a Hindu philosopher, and member of the Ramakrishna Order, points out that there have been a number of

---

[4] George Townshend, *The Heart of the Gospel*, (George Ronald Press: London, 1960), pp. 43–44.
[5] *Sutta-Nipata*, V. Fausboll, Translator, in Part II, Vol. X of The Sacred Books of the East, (Oxford, 1861), p. 560.

Avatars in the history of the world of whom Krishna, Buddha and Jesus are included. He writes the following explanation of progressive revelation from a Hindu viewpoint:

> There is an interesting and ennobling statement in the teachings of Sri Krishna: "Whenever ...there is decline in Dharma (religion) and the rise of Adharma (evil), then I body Myself forth"... The declaration of the Gita has been fulfilled time and time again, ever since man began to live on this planet. At critical periods in the history of India, when men and women were extremely materialistic and forgot the spirit of religion, such persons have made their appearance every five-hundred or a thousand of years and saved the soul of man from utter degradation and disintegration. It is amazing to note that there is a particular sequence in the events of history in which divine incarnations appear. Study of their lives will reveal the self-same historical reason for every one of them. After observing the facts of history, it seems like the advent of an incarnation can almost be predicted.[6]

Swami Akilinanada's exploration of this subject is penetrating and offers insights on the process of progressive revelation that are rarely found in the writings of Western religious scholars.

ISLAM

Any critical study of the history and teachings of Islam will disclose numerous parallelisms between Islam and the Judeo-Christian tradition. These close relationships find their ground in the common treasury of ideas in which all the 'Semitic' peoples share. Isma'il R. Faruqi, former Professor of Religion at Temple University and a noted Islamic scholar, holds that Judaism,

---

[6] Swami Akhilananda, "Hindu View of Christ," in *Christianity: Some Non-Christian Appraisals*, David W. McCain, ed., (McGraw-Hill: NY, 1964), pp. 39–40.

Christianity and Islam are all complimentary aspects of a developing Semitic religious tradition; or

> better, that they are moments in a developing 'Semitic' consciousness of which the Sumerian, Babylonian, Noahic, Abrahamic, and Mosaic religions are the earlier crystallizations, the Rabbinic and Pauline some of the later, and the Islamic the latest.[7]

Professor Faruqi describes the relationship of Islam to the history of religion in these words:

> Islam's regard for Judaism and Christianity was always one of self-identification with them as predecessor religions founded incontestably upon revelations from God to His prophets...The Qur'an repeatedly declares the Hebrew prophets, including Jesus, as prophets of God and defines the Muslim as the person who believes in all the prophets and does not distinguish among them. All the revelations they brought from God, whether as to credibility or to essential content...are holy, divine, and worthy. The Qur'an gives its own representation of the history—and revelation—content of these prophets. It presents them as moments in a continuing divine revelation whose essence is one and the same, namely, that God is, that He is one, and that man is to serve and obey Him by fulfilling the divine command...[8]

THE BAHÁ'Í FAITH

The Bahá'í Faith is the youngest of the world's independent religions. Arising in Iran in the mid-nineteenth century, it has now virtually spread to every part of the world and is rivaled only by Christianity in the extent of its globality. The prophet-founder

---

[7] Isma'il R, al Faruqi, ed., "Islam," in *Historical Atlas of the Religions of the World*, (Macmillan Publishing Co.: NY, 1974), p. 238.

[8] Ibid., p. 246.

of the Bahá'í Faith, Bahá'u'lláh (1817-1892), particularly emphasized the concept of progressive revelation in His teachings. In their definitive text on the Bahá'í, *The Bahá'í Faith: The Emerging Global Religion*, William Hatcher and Douglass Martin address the question regarding the motive force in humankind's collective evolution. The answer echoes the religious philosophers of other faiths:

> The answer the Bahá'í Faith provides to this question is 'revealed religion.' In one of His major works, the Kitab-i-Iqan, (the Book of Certitude) Bahá'u'lláh explained that God, the Creator, has intervened and will continue to intervene in human history by means of chosen spokesmen or messengers. These messengers, whom Bahá'u'lláh called "Manifestations of God," are principally the founders of the major religions, such as Abraham, Moses, Buddha, Jesus, Muhammad and so forth. It is the spirit released by the coming of these Manifestations, together with the influence of their teachings and the social systems established by their laws and precepts, that enable humankind to progress in its collective evolution. Simply put, the Manifestations of God are the chief educators of humanity.

With regard to the various religious systems that have appeared in human history, Bahá'u'lláh has said:

> These principles and laws, these firmly-established and mighty systems, have proceeded from one Source and are the rays of one Light. That they differ one from another is to be attributed to the various requirements of the age in which they were promulgated...[9]

Thus, in the Bahá'í view there is really only one religion, the religion of God. This one religion is continually evolving, and

---

[9] William S. Hatcher and J. Douglas Martin, *The Bahá'í Faith: The Emerging Global Religion*, (Harper and Row, NY, 1984), pp. 81-82.

each religious system represents a stage in the evolution of the whole. Each revelation is viewed as having taken place at a critical moment in the collective evolution of humankind. Quoting again from Hatcher:

> Though there is much in common among the teachings of these founders of religion, each revelation stressed some particular theme and thereby developed certain particular capacities latent within man: Abraham stressed the oneness of God, Moses the principle of the rule by law, Jesus the importance of love in human interactions, the Buddha the notion of renunciation of egotistical motives, and so forth...The unity of humankind is the primary theme of the Bahá'í revelation, and the promulgation of world unity its primary focus...its special contribution to the collective moral consciousness of humanity.[10]

In summary, it is clear, even through this brief survey, that the concept of an on-going process of divine intervention or 'progressive revelation' is common to each of the major religious faiths. Their various teachings on this theme are both in harmony with each other and complimentary since, when considered together, they shed considerably more light on the topic than when studied separately. Moreover, the phenomenon of revelation is regarded as being essential for sociocultural evolution for without the influx of energy released into the contingent world via this process, human progress would cease, and the spiritualization of humanity simply could not take place.

---

[10] William S. Hatcher, "Human Nature, and Human Society: A Bahá'í Viewpoint," in *The Bahá'í Faith and Marxism*, Bahá'í Studies Publications, Ottawa, 1987, p. 33.

RELIGIOUS REVITALIZATION MOVEMENTS: SCIENTIFIC PERSPECTIVES

While comparative religious studies have been growing in popularity for nearly a century and thus shed a great deal of light on the role of religion in human culture, the scientific study of religious phenomena is relatively recent. One major effort to bring scientific inquiry to religion was begun in 1954 with the establishment of the Institute on Religion in an Age of Science.[11] In 1963 the Institute in collaboration with the Center for Advanced Studies in Religion and Science at the Chicago Cluster of Theological Schools began publishing a quarterly journal, *Zygon*, which has grown to become the foremost scholarly outlet for publication of academic thought and research in the integration of traditional religious concepts with contemporary scientific discovery. What follows is a brief examination of some of the essays published in or referred to by *Zygon* which are particularly relevant to the theme of progressive revelation.

ANTHROPOLOGY

In 1966 the anthropologist Anthony F. C. Wallace published his seminal work, *Religion: An Anthropological View*, in which he set forth a theory on the dynamics of cultural change based on religious revitalization movements. Wallace developed his theory by reviewing a number of religious movements described in historical and anthropological documents along with an indepth study of a religion initiated by Handsome Lake, the Seneca Prophet, among the nineteenth century reservation Iroquois. By "revitalization movement" Wallace means "a deliberate, organized, conscious effort by members of a society to construct a more satisfying culture."[12] Revitalization is thus, from a cultural standpoint, a special kind of culture change phenomenon, and

---

[11] Ralph Wendell Burhoe, "The Institute on Religion in an Age of Science: A Twenty-Year View," *Zygon* 8, (1973), p. 59.

[12] Anthony F. C. Wallace, "Revitalization Movements," *American Anthropologist*, Vol. 58, (1956), p. 265.

implies an organismic analogy. A human society is here regarded as a kind of supra-organism, and its culture is conceived as those patterns of learned behavior which contain certain 'parts' of the social organism or system (including persons or groups of persons) characteristically displayed. In Wallace's words:

> ...the persons involved in the process of revitalization must perceive their culture, or some major areas of it, as a system...; they must feel that this cultural system is unsatisfactory; and they must innovate not merely discrete items, but a new cultural system, specifying new relationships as well as, in some cases, new traits...[13]

In the classic process of cultural change such as acculturation, drift, and diffusion, social change usually occurs gradually over a period of many years or even centuries. In revitalization movements, however, the process is speeded up dramatically mainly because it becomes a conscious and organized effort on the part of those involved.

In general, Wallace suggests that revitalization movements have a three-stage cycle consisting of (1) a steady-state, (2) a period of cultural distortion or disintegration, and (3) a period of revitalization with the various stages being somewhat overlapping. The revitalization stage is characterized by the formation of a code, a new conceptual paradigm, through prophetic revelation or what Wallace calls "mazeway reformulation," and by phases of communication, organization, adaptation, cultural transformation and routinization respectively. (See figure 1).

Wallace suggests that all organized religions are survivals from mazeway reformulations that occurred at an earlier time of cultural crisis and individual stress. The rudiments of religion, he believes, can be traced back at least to the funerary rites of Neanderthal man. At Shinidar, Iraq, some sixty-thousand years ago, Neanderthal people were burying their dead with special medicinal herbs and other grave goods and building small altars

---

[13] Ibid., p. 265.

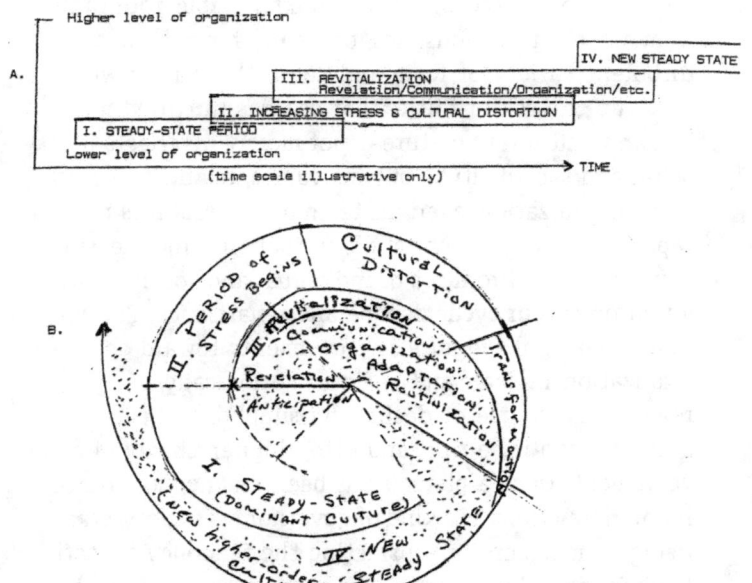

Figure 1. Stages of social change associated with revitalization movements. (Authors' understanding of Wallace's scenario).[14]

of bare bones in caves. Since that time Wallace estimates that humankind has produced on the order of 100 thousand different expressions of religion.

In the introduction of his book, *Religion: An Anthropological View*, he writes:

---

[14] **Note:** Illustration A shows the three major stages associated with Wallace's revitalization model along a linear timeline. Illustration B shows these stages as phases of a cyclic or 'ascending helix.' Cycles occur on higher and higher levels of organization. Notice that the period of increasing stress and cultural distortion tends to occur simultaneously with the period of revitalization. One result of this two-fold process is that the breakdown of the dominant social order usually masks the emergence of the revitalization movement until a critical juncture is reached. At this point, transformation may occur quite rapidly. It is also important to note that the steady state period is much longer than the other two phases.

> New religions have been the inexhaustible fountains from which, for thousands of years, have flowed, in turbulent variety of form and color, the waters which make up the sea of faith. That sea has nurtured much of man's still-infant culture — not merely his theological belief and sacred ritual, but his values, his principles of social organization, even his technology. And it is man's capacity to create new religions that in large measure have made all chronicles of individual and social behavior chronicles of cyclic decline and renaissance. For new religions are, above all else, movements toward the revitalization of man and society. Periodically, religions reverse the course of decline by supplying the energy and direction for a new, and often higher, climax of development. Once a plateau has been reached, of course, religion functions as a kind of governor for society, stabilizing its members and correcting the tendency of institutions to wobble or drift. And even when a religion becomes old and crabbily conservative, it will still, despite the reluctance of its priesthood, provide the cultural building blocks for the next religion. Old religions do not die; they live on in the new religions that follow them.[15]

Looking more closely at Wallace's processual model, we find the "steadystate" phase as a period of moving equilibrium in which the established cultural processes and institutions are able to meet most of the needs of the majority of the population. Varying levels of stress may be experienced by members of the society, but most stress is tolerable. In cases where it is not, deviant coping mechanisms may be employed. Some cultural modification may occur, but at rates which are sufficiently gradual that social stability is not threatened.

If and when a culture is confronted with changes that challenge its stability, it may enter the early phase of the period of

---

[15] Anthony F. C. Wallace, *Religion: An Anthropological View*, Random House: NY, 1966), pp. 3–4.

"cultural distortion." Wallace characterizes this phase as a "period of increased individual stress."

As he explains:

> The sociocultural system is being 'pushed' progressively out of equilibrium by various forces, such as climatic and biotic change, epidemic diseases, war and conquest, social subordination, or acculturation...increasingly large numbers of individuals are placed under what is to them intolerable stress by the failure of the system to accommodate their needs. Anomie and disillusionment become widespread as the culture is perceived to be disorganized and inadequate; crime, illness, and individualistic asocial responses increase sharply in frequency. But the situation is still generally defined as one of fluctuation within the steady state.[16]

If this situation is not corrected by the cultural managers, the social system will enter a period of intensifying cultural distortion. During this period some members of the society usually attempt, piecemeal and ineffectively, to restore personal equilibrium by adopting socially dysfunctional expedients. In Wallace's words:

> Alcoholism (and drug abuse), venality in public officials, the 'black market,' breaches in sexual and kinship morals, hording, gambling for gain, 'scapegoating' by attacking other groups of central bureaucracy, and similar alienated behaviors which, in the preceding period, were still defined as individual deviances, in effect become institutionalized efforts to circumvent the evil effects of 'the system' or of maintaining mutually acceptable inter relationships, may resort to violence in order to coerce others into unilaterally advantageous behaviors. Because of the mal-coordination of cultural

---

[16] Ibid., p. 159.

changes during this period, such changes are rarely able to reduce the impact of the forces that have pushed the society out of equilibrium and, in fact, are likely to lead to a continuous decline in organization.[17]

Wallace suggests that once severe cultural distortion sets in, it is difficult for the society to return to a steady state without the institution of a revitalization process. Indeed, without revitalization the society is apt to disintegrate as a system: the population will either die off, splinter into autonomous groups, or be absorbed into another, more stable, society. Revitalization often begins with a search for alternatives during the period of increased individual stress and thus can be viewed as a process paralleling that of social decline. A truly successful revitalization movement depends, however, on the successful completion of the following functions: mazeway reformulation, communication, organization, adaptation, cultural transformation, and routinization. First, one individual experiences some sort of abrupt and dramatic moment of insight which seems to offer an explanation of the 'real' nature of the culture's problem. A sense of unity and wholeness is perceived by this individual and is described as an inspiration or revelation. This person usually comes to be seen as a prophet who explains the cause of social decline and offers a solution. This solution provides for a new way of thinking or paradigm by which one's experiences in that society seem meaningful.

While the prophet is experiencing his or her revelations, he or she communicates that world view to others and exhorts members of the society to repent and reform. As new converts are made, the beginnings of organization take shape. A small group of devoted disciples often provides the inner circle and the nucleus of the campaign for conversion. Hence, there comes to be a hierarchy of members: the prophet, the disciples, and the followers.

---

[17] Ibid., p. 159.

Quite often the revitalization movement will have a revolutionary or even antiestablishment message. Insofar as the group bears a message which is hostile to the status quo, it will experience resistance and opposition from significant portions of the dominant society. To be widely accepted, the group must gain some measure of legitimacy. In order for this to happen, the original doctrine may need to be modified or adapted by the prophet or his disciples. In response to criticisms and affirmations, various beliefs may be played down and eliminated or emphasized and elaborated. Hence, the original vision may be modified so that it has a better 'fit' to the personality patterns and cultural assumptions of a particular population. The process of adaptation usually occurs over a number of years or even generations especially if the new revelation is regarded as universal. Continual expansion of the new religious movement may thus be dependent upon such adaptation of the world view.

As increasing numbers of people come to accept the new world view, a transformation of attitudes and behavior will gradually take place in the new subculture, and if this transformation is significant enough it will affect the entire culture. The new movement will then come to be routinized or institutionalized, and a new steady-state established.

Wallace's model of religious revitalization does indeed reflect an organic process characterized by a dialectic of crisis and victory, of challenge and response. His own analysis of this drama is similar to that of British historian Arnold Toynbee who arrived at this conclusion after studying some twenty-six civilizations:

> During the disintegration of a civilization, two separate plays with different plots are being performed simultaneously side by side. While an unchanging dominant majority is perpetually rehearsing its own defeat, fresh challenges are perpetually evoking fresh creative responses from newly recruited minorities, which proclaim their own creative power by rising, each time, to the occasion. The drama of challenge-and-response con-

tinues to be performed, but in new circumstances and with new actors.[18]

PSYCHOLOGY

Essential to a revitalization movement is the emergence of a leader or prophet, a person characterized as possessing strong emotional appeal and extraordinary insights about the nature of reality and the social needs of his or her times. Often the prophet is an ordinary individual for whom social or psychological stress personally erupts in an out-of-the-ordinary psychophysiological state that generates the design of a new moral and possibly social order. The new way of life is enunciated in both prescriptions and proscriptions of behaviors and belief. Little detail may be known about the life of a prophet prior to the time of revelation or even for many years afterward because of the very nature of the social conditions out of which such persons arise. Historically, however, if the revitalization movement is successful these events are likely to become apocryphal in retrospect, finding their exegesis in the history and teaching of the movement.

Particularly significant is that the prophet's revelations usually have their genesis in some state of consciousness which appears to differ radically from that of 'ordinary' awareness. Moreover, the content of the revealed instructions for the establishment of a new social and moral order is often complex and elaborately detailed. Defined as a "deliberate, organized, conscious effort by members of a society to construct a more satisfying culture," the revitalization process, according to Wallace, originates in the prophet's "re-synthesized mazeway," or restructured cognitive system.

Thus, the question naturally arises as to just how the phenomenon of revelation actually occurs? Religionists, of course, tend to view revelation as a mysterious or supernatural event, the direct intervention of God into human affairs. Approached from this standpoint, such events would appear to lie outside the

---

[18] Arnold Toynbee, *A Study of History*, (Oxford Univ. Press, 1972), p. 228.

domain of direct scientific scrutiny, nor could they be reduced to simplistic neurophysiological explanations. Nonetheless, it is only through our attempt to understand the psychological dimension of this process that we can begin to appreciate the extraordinary qualities of the religious founders or even accept the credibility of their experiences. As psychologist Barbara Lex states, *"If one accepts the assertion that the structure of one's culture rarely rises to awareness, then these spontaneous emergent capabilities of prophets are indeed exceptional"* (Emphasis ours).[19]

In the last twenty years or so there has been a dramatic revolution of our understanding of the neural organization of the brain and particularly of the functions of the left and right hemispheres.[20] Much of this research has been reviewed by Barbara Lex and Eugene d'Aquili in their own efforts to provide a sound basis for the neurophysiological aspects of the phenomenon of revelation.[21] We can only touch briefly on a few of the profound insights these two psychologists offer.

Lex begins her discussion by speculating on the differences between prophetic revelation and other types of creative inspiration, such as artistic and scientific creativity. She cites the conclusions of Ward H. Goodenough who contends that there is little distinction between the "flash of insight" of the prophet and that of the innovative scientist. Analyzing revelations, he writes:

> Cognitively the sudden conception of a new order or 'key' to all existing problems is no different from that which scholars and scientists experience when they

---

[19] Barbara W. Lex, "Neurological Bases of Revitalization Movements," *Zygon* 13, (1978), p. 278.

[20] See, for example, Roger Sperry, "Changed Concepts of Brain and Consciousness: Some Value Implications," *Zygon* 20, (1985), pp. 41–57; John C, Eccles, "Cerebral Activity and Consciousness," in *Studies in the Philosophy of Biology*, F. J. Ayala, and T. Dobzhansky eds., (University of California Press: Berkley, 1974) pp. 87–107.

[21] Eugene G. d'Aquili, "Senses of Reality in Science and Religion: A Neuroepistomological Perspective," *Zygon* 17, (1982), pp. 361–384; also "Myth, Ritual, and the Archetypal Hypothesis," *Zygon* 21, (1986), pp. 141–160; see also Lex, (n. 19 above).

suddenly perceive a new pattern in their data or get the insight by which everything with which they have been working at last makes sense.[22]

The major difference between scientific creativity and religious revelation, according to Goodenough, lies in the strength of the emotional response in the individual's experience. Resolution of social and moral problems through such an insight, whatever the form, at the same time resolves the inner, emotional conflicts of the revitalization prophet, bringing a therapeutic sense of extreme relief and exalted well-being.[23]

From here Lex examines two promising domains of prophetic experience, the neurobiological substrates of emotion and the neurophysiological functions of the left and right cerebral hemispheres. In her review of the neurobiological aspects of revelation, Lex discusses the emotional impact of symbols, the alteration of body-mind functions involved in ritual trance and other unusual psychophysiological states, the manipulation of the autonomic nervous system by sound, cold, ingestion of certain foods, and sleep deprivation, and individual differences in emotional reactivity. She basically concludes that

> ...emotional reactions involved in prophets' revelations and adherents' conversions fall within the range of behavior typical of contemporary scientific accounts of the human species. Persons who become neither prophets nor converts, despite the highly evocative emotional conditions concomitant with revitalization movements, are unlikely to differ dramatically in genetic makeup from those who do.[24]

For Lex, the more crucial issue on the analysis of revelations is that a prophet announces a complex system for the reorganiza-

---

[22] Ward H, Goodenough, *Cooperation and Change*, (John Wiley and Sons, NY, 1963), p. 293; quoted in Lex, (n. 19 above, p. 280).
[23] See n. 19 above, p. 280.
[24] See n. 19 above, p. 284.

tion of beliefs and behaviors in order to transform an entire society from seemingly intractable chaos to utopian order. "Not only does the prophet's vision surpass ordinary dreams in complexity and vividness," writes Lex,

> but also the content and circumstances of occurrences of this vision frequently attract considerable attention from the persons who become aware of it. Thus, in both intensity and scope of impact the prophetic experience departs from the more private imagery of commonplace dreams. It is also probable that the prophetic experience structurally differs from ordinary dreams. Prophetic dreams are often direct and explicit, with their manifest content contributing the message, and in prophetic dreams there do not appear to be as much displacement of content as those usually identifiable in normal dreams.[25]

Research focusing on the neurophysiological aspects of the differential functions of the right and left hemispheres also shed significant light on the phenomenon of revelation. Considerable evidence now shows that in most humans the left hemisphere is the site of linear analytic thought, sequential information processing, and the assessment of temporal duration. In contrast, the specializations of the right cerebral hemisphere comprise special and tonal perception, recognition of patterns, including emotions and other body states, and holistic, synthetic thought; however, linguistic capability is limited, and the temporal capacity is believed absent. Ordinary task performance requires alternation between the cognitive functions of each hemisphere.[26] Quoting again from Lex:

> According to these analyses in one sense a prophet is a vatic, or seer, who perceives an alternative future be-

---

[25] See n. 19 above, p. 290.
[26] See n. 19 above, p. 291.

cause the state of consciousness generating revelations frees one from the time-bound mode of ordinary, left-hemisphere dominant-sequential thought. Correlatively the unity and cyclical nature of life, including holistic perception of the interrelationships among stress-provoking conditions, rise to a prophet's consciousness because holism is intrinsic to the quality of right-hemisphere cognition. Moreover, symbolism abounds in enunciating the vision, often phrased in metaphor and parable, because ordinary speech — a left-hemisphere activity — cannot render faithfully the functionally ineffable thoughts of the right hemisphere.[27]

Professor d'Aquili in his exploration of the phenomenology of certain mystical states describes nine theoretical and eight actual primary senses of reality. Like Lex, he concludes that the highest sense of reality, which he calls 'absolute unitary being,' arises in some way or other from the gestalt or holistic functioning of the nondominant (right) hemisphere. What exactly triggers this response in the two "computers" comprising the human brain may, d'Aquili admits, lie beyond human conceptualization. For his own part he offers the Buddhist concept of the Void. In his words:

In the terminology we are using today (they would not use this terminology), they (Buddhists) look to what it is that goes into both 'computers', which in one case comes out as the everyday world and in the other case comes out Nirvana, or the Void and is absolute and transcendent. They then suggest it is obvious that whatever is going into both 'computers' is, in fact, *no* thing. Yet this is not 'nothing' as it is understood in everyday parlance, but 'no thing' simply because it cannot be conceptualized outside of the constraints of the mind — and the mind has only two ways of interpreting that 'no thing,'

---

[27] See n. 19 above, pp. 291–292.

namely as absolute unitary being or as the discreet world of everyday living-of chance and causality.[28]

Professor d'Aqili concludes his own exploration of this topic with an observation that perhaps goes as far as science is capable of making, at least at this time. In asking the question: "What can we state about senses of reality in science and religion?" he answers thusly:

> First, it is clear that science as a subset of general human problem-solving arises from what I call the baseline sense of reality, that is the sense of multiple discrete beings with regular relationships permeated with natural effect. This is the primary epistemic state which provides the impetus to, the constraints upon, and the matrix from which Western science is embedded. Religion, however, arises from other primary states. The state of cosmic consciousness certainly facilitates a religious view of the world. Although it is optimistic and although there is a sense of purpose which can easily be translated into religious systems, the individuals who possess cosmic consciousness cannot properly be said to have 'seen God.' *Rather, the most fundamental witness out of which springs the faith of believers is the witness of those who have experienced absolute unitary being. This witness, reinforced by the experience of those who have experienced cosmic consciousness, provides* the authoritative affirmation *to those propositions that most people wish desperately to believe*, namely that their lives are purposeful, that the world is purposeful, and that there is no reason to fear death. Out of this state of absolute unitary being, experienced by the very few and affirmed by the slightly more numerous individuals in a state of cosmic consciousness, arise the world's

---

[28] Eugene G. d' Aquili, "Senses of Reality in Science and Religion: A Neuroepistomoligical Perspective," *Zygon* 17, (1982), pp. 380–381.

great religions. Those few individuals proclaim to the many the message that almost everyone hopes is true (*Emphasis ours*).[29]

To summarize this section, contemporary research focusing on brain states and various mystical states strongly suggests that certain types of prophetic revelation are indeed extraordinary events. When such revelations embody profound insights about the nature of reality, or a particular social crisis, fused with the charismatic and emotional intensity of the prophet's experience of 'absolute unitary being,' they can become the energizing force behind new religious and revitalization movements.

EVOLUTIONARY PERSPECTIVES

Within the last two decades a whole new understanding of evolution has begun to emerge through the work of general systems theorists. This "grand evolutionary synthesis" as Ervin Laszlo calls it, unites physical, biological, and social evolution into a consistent framework with its own laws and logic. In his book *Evolution: The Grand Synthesis*, Laszlo examines the theoretical and practical implications of the various sciences dealing with the appearance, development, and functioning of complex systems regardless of the domain of investigation to which they belong.[30] He sets forth the hypothesis that the laws governing the evolution of natural systems also govern the development of human societies. These laws do not proscribe the course of evolutionary development but merely set the rules of the game, so to speak — the limits and the possibilities that the players themselves exploit. Thus, the rules for biological evolution have been set by evolution in the cosmos. For sociocultural evolution the rules appear to be set by biological evolution, especially by the evolution of Homo sapiens. As Laszlo points out:

---

[29] Ibid., pp. 381–382.
[30] Ervin Laszlo, *Evolution: The Grand Synthesis*, (Shambala: Boston, 1987). See also Eric Chaisson, "Cosmic Evolution: A Synthesis of Matter and Life," *Zygon* 14, pp. 23–39.

The hypothesis does not mean that human societies are biologically determined. It means only that societies are evolving systems emerging and persisting within the multi-level structure of other systems in the biosphere. Societies follow the rules set by the general laws that govern the evolution of such systems within the limits and possibilities created by human beings, their values, beliefs, habits, and mores. But societies follow these rules on their own, typically societal level, and not on the biological level of their members.[31]

As in Wallace's model, the process of social evolution is not viewed as smooth and gradual. Rather the flight of the arrow may be interrupted at any point; it may be temporarily halted at any point; and it may be made to skip a stage at any point. But it may not, except under the impact of unusually powerful external factors be fully and steadily reversed. Major evolutionary advances usually occur during critical junctures or 'bifurcations.' Bifurcations occur when the steady state can no longer be maintained, and autopoiesis, that is, the normal flow of energy, resources, and information, is replaced by a condition of critical instability. In Wallace's model, this stage is called 'cultural distortion.' Laszlo describes this process in these words:

> If society's information pool (its broadly defined 'culture') is up to date and operational, the production and consumption systems function adequately to maintain society in its milieu. All the essential flows are replenished; all the basic subsystems are repaired or reproduced. Society is sustainable; and the people are in harmony with each other and in balance with their environment. On the other hand, society is critically unstable — and on the point of bifurcation — if it is unable to replenish the flows and repair or reproduce its subsystems. In this

---

[31] Laszlo, p. 92.

unstable and non-sustainable condition, the members of society must update and transform their culture, that is, their collective information pool. They either manage this feat and obtain a new functional mode of social, economic, and political organization, or their society lapses into anarchy and may dissolve in chaos, a ready prey to more stable and powerful adversaries.[32]

A review of the major sociocultural changes in history suggests that there are three principal types of bifurcations: 1) bifurcations due to the destabilizing effect of technological innovations; 2) bifurcations due to instabilities induced by conflicts and conquests, and 3) bifurcations triggered by the internal collapse of the dominant institutions owing to mushrooming economic and social crises. Present society is seen to be challenged by all three types of bifurcations but particularly those triggered by economic and social crises.

Thus, Laszlo has arrived at the conclusion that the greatest hope for the future of humanity is a world-wide revitalization movement which takes into consideration the challenges and possibilities of our particular evolutionary moment. He and his colleagues have written numerous books on this subject which deserve our closest attention[33] (see figures 2 and 3).

Regarding religion, Laszlo states that "... in traditional societies myths and religion create the main kinds of social bonds" and are thereby essential to the preservation of the overall order of society. Yet his concept of technology as the primary motive force behind cultural evolution seems to embrace the possibility of religious revitalization movements. Laszlo defines technology in broad terms as " ...the instrumentality that imbues all human activities and extends human powers to act on nature and interact with others." A technological innovation is not just the invention of a tool, but the stretching of the imagination and the

---

[32] Ibid., p. 104.
[33] See, for example, E. Laszlo, et al., *Goals for Mankind: A Report to the Club of Rome on New Horizons of Global Community*, (E. P. Dutton: NY, 1977).

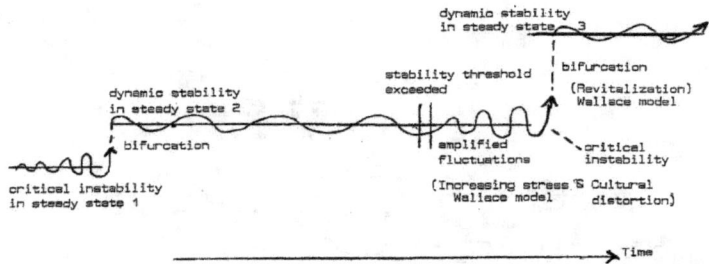

Figure 2. The buildup of dynamic nonequilibrium systems through periodic bifurcations (after Laszlo, note 30, p. 48).[34]

transformation of common sense. A major technological breakthrough makes the supernatural natural — as, for example, with the mastery of fire and then of flight — and renders the abnormal and the unthinkable normal and even commonplace, as with a nuclear reactor or the instantaneous transmission of image and sound. It challenges people's values and practices and shakes the foundations of established institutions.[35]

General systems scientists believe that humankind collectively is in the midst of a catastrophic bifurcation or 'great transition.' It has been caused by the upsurge of revolutionary technological innovations combined by the havoc caused by two world wars and numerous lesser conflicts. It is marked by an explosion of world population, the destabilization of ecosystems and whole societies, the breakdown of traditional values and religious sys

---

[34] **Note:** General systems theory accounts for the buildup of complexity in various systems (physical, biological, sociocultural) through a process of change that leads from one kind of steady state to another. Each phase change in systems behavior represents bifurcations of the trajectory traced by the system states. Bifurcations are, in essence, critical junctures in what Anthony Wallace calls the period of 'increasing stress and cultural distortion.' In addition to a critical instability, the bifurcation is dependent upon an 'attractor' which organizes free energy into a new steady state. In sociocultural evolution attractors may be a new scientific theory, a constitution, or a religious revitalization movement based on a new prophetic revelation.

[35] See n. 30 above, p. 92.

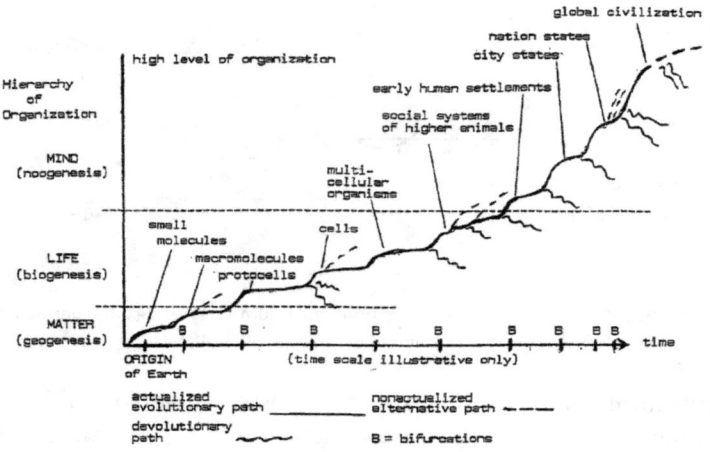

Figure 3. The evolution of successive levels of organization (After Laszlo, note 30, p. 48).[36]

tems, the globalization of problems and the obsolescence of institutions, political systems, and ideologies. This transformation will lead to a 'new world order' — for better or for worse according to our will and capacity to respond to the challenges and possibilities of our present evolutionary moment.

An evolutionary approach to religious knowledge and to human understanding of God has been recently set forth by Karl

---

[36] **Note:** Cosmic evolution has been described as a progressive advance into novelty, complexity of organization and actualization of enfolded possibilities, with matter (geogenesis), life (biogenesis), and mind (noogenesis or genesis of consciousness) as distinct thresholds or boundary conditions separating different ontological levels. Figure 3 attempts to illustrate the continuity of the evolutionary process as lower level systems converge to create higher and higher organizational levels. The actualized evolutionary pathway is not viewed as predestined as certain paths lead to extinction (devolution) while other possibilities are never actualized. Nor is the evolutionary process viewed as gradual; rather stable states are punctuated by critical junctures or bifurcations during which major evolutionary advances may occur.

Peters, editor of *Zygon* and associate professor of philosophy and religion, Rollins College.[37]

In Peters' "Evolutionary Theory of Knowledge" ultimate reality, i.e., God, becomes disclosed to the human mind in two ways, through "general revelation" and "special revelation." In general revelation God discloses His nature and will through the human experience of nature and history and through rational reflection on that experience. Peters argues that the study of God's general revelation to man leads to the development of natural theologies which are quite compatible with the more traditional religious and personal theologies. In special revelation, on the other hand, knowledge of God and God's Will is disclosed through prophetic revelation or the periodic and spectacular emergence of "a complex set of insights about what man ought to think and do, given by a religious genius such as Moses, Jesus, Muhammad, or Buddha."[38]

Peters views special revelation as a subset of general revelation or cosmic evolution. He explains:

> The evolutionary model predicts that under certain conditions of societal stress and breakdown a number of prophets will emerge, but it also predicts that in the long run not all restructurings of religious beliefs, actions, and experiences will be selected as viable or adaptive and hence retained. In short, one expects a separation of true from false prophets, the criterion for which would not be the stated origin of the prophecy (variations are blind, i.e., decoupled from selective criteria)

---

[37] Karl E. Peters, "Religion and an Evolutionary Theory of Knowledge," *Zygon* 17 (1982), pp. 385-415.

[38] Ibid., p. 401. The idea that God manifests Himself through both 'general' and 'special' revelation is a theme developed by Charles E. Hummel in *The Galileo Connection: Resolving Conflicts between Science and the Bible*, (Intervarsity Press, IL, 1986), pp. 260-264. In the scriptures of the world religions, the same theme is discussed by Bahá'u'lláh in *The Kitab-i-Iqan (The Book of Certitude)*, Trans. By Shoghi Effendi, (Bahá'í Publishing Trust: Wilmette, II, 1981), pp. 139-146.

but the ability of the prophetic message and the society following the message to continue to reproduce their biological and cultural systems of knowledge. Expressing this idea derived from the evolutionary model of ultimate reality in terms of the traditional Judeo-Christian personalistic model, we might say that even prophets are subject to the ongoing judgment of the 'Lord of the universe and history'.[39]

Peters goes on to examine the problem raised by religious pluralism. The difficulty arises when we recognize that there are a number of different religious systems each based on the assumption that religious truth revealed through the Word of God is the eternal truth, valid in all times and places. This problem is even more difficult than first indicated, says Peters, because one can add to this the dimension of time to the question of pluralism. When we do this, we become concerned not only with the present diversity of religious options, but also, we begin to wonder at the general fact that over time new cultures with new religions have come into being while other cultures and their religions have died, in much the same way that new biological species come into existence while others perish. Regardless of the conception of ultimate reality, whether personal or impersonal, one is driven to ask, what is ultimate reality doing?

Peters answers this question by reflecting on the fact that the evolutionary perspective recognizes the fact that both genotypes and culture types originally come into being through variation and selection in particular environments. As the environments change the old formulations of the genetic or cultural code may become maladaptive and at least potentially lethal for the species or culture. As one example, he cites the genetically based and culturally supported commandment concerning reproduction: "be fruitful and multiply and fill the earth and subdues it." At one time, when human populations were limited in size, it was

---

[39] Ibid., p. 402.

probably a necessary imperative. However, today, when excessive population growth seems to be taking us beyond the carrying capacity of the earth and thus threatening the balance of our own planet's ecosystem, such an imperative may need revision. In short, the religious revelations of the past represent wisdom about past environments; such knowledge does not seem to be true for all time.

Peters sums up his inquiry in these words:

> In both biological and cultural cases, the mechanisms produce changes that may be detrimental to the existing species or cultural systems: because they alter existing patterns, genotypic and culture typic changes can destabilize a system and lead to its demise. On the other hand, some of the changes produced by the same mechanisms may give rise to new genetic or cultural knowledge that enhances, modifies, or replaces the prior heritage. Our evolutionary outlook suggests that both these phenomena, death and new birth, are nor unusual but are, indeed, consistent with the way the universe works. In short, ultimate reality seems to be dynamically creating ever new systems of order, including ever new systems of knowledge. For this to occur in a finite universe, however, the creation of new order and knowledge can only come about as some prior order or knowledge is destroyed. Creation from the evolutionary perspective is always to some extent death and transformation.[40]

---

[40] Ibid., p. 405. In his essay, "A Thermodynamic Theory of the Origin and Hierarchical Evolution of Living Systems," H. J. Hamilton makes the point that the principles of nonequilibrium thermodynamics coupled with the principles of minimum entropy production "...constitute an a priori assumption about the composition and behavior of matter in the universe, namely, that irreversible processes always give rise simultaneously to the destruction and creation of ordered structures in the universe in such a manner as to cause the entropy to increase at a minimum rate...", *Zygon*, 12, (1977), pp. 289–335.

CONCLUSION

Our purpose in undertaking this exploration was to determine whether or not the phenomenon of special or progressive revelation, as set forth in the world's great religious traditions, might constitute a primary factor or 'motive force' underlying sociocultural evolution. Furthermore, we wished to find out whether this phenomenon could be supported conceptually by solidly grounded scientific studies.

It should be apparent from this survey that the concept of progressive revelation is no longer viewed as a supernatural or simplistic theological notion. Religious revitalization movements are now regarded by social scientists as 'key' events in the revitalization of man and society. Moreover, these movements appear to be both initiated by and essential to the very processes underlying cosmic and particularly sociocultural evolution.

New religious movements tend to arise during critical junctures or bifurcations occurring periodically throughout the history of human evolution. These bifurcations are characterized by a two-fold process each tending, in its own way and with accelerating momentum, to bring to a climax those forces which result in the transformation of cultural systems from simpler to progressively more complex organizational levels. The first is fundamentally a disruptive process while the second is essentially integrative and regenerative. The former, characterized by Anthony Wallace as "cultural distortion," tends to tear down those barriers in a social system that have become blocks to humanity's progress; while the latter, characterized as "revitalization," serves to release creative energies in the form of new ways of thinking, feeling, and acting which frequently bring into being new social systems of a higher order. While not all revitalization movements are religious in nature, some of the most significant in human history definitely are. The rise of Judaism, Hinduism, Buddhism, Christianity, and Islam are typical examples of the religious revitalization movements of the past, while the development of the Bahá'í Faith based on the revelation of

Bahá'u'lláh (1817–1892) is an example of such a movement in our time. (See figure 4.)

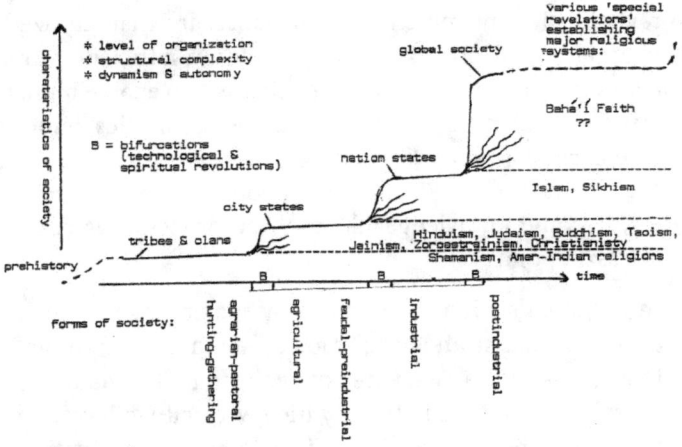

Figure 4. The relationship between sociocultural evolution and special (or progressive) revelation.[41]

Most religious revitalization movements are initiated by the phenomenon of revelation, or the experience of "absolute unitary being," which modern psychologists suggest arises in some way or another from the gestalt or holistic functioning of the nondominant (right) hemisphere of the brain. Prophetic revelation, while not necessarily viewed by psychologists as direct intervention of the Divine into human affairs, is still regarded as a truly extraordinary, emergent capability of certain unique spiritual personages and an event of very rare occurrence. The actual

---

[41] **Note:** Figure 4 illustrates the general process of social evolution and the forms of society and organizational complexity associated with various stages. Periodically, bifurcations or technological revolutions occur which tend to destabilize the social systems and set the stage for spiritual revolutions. New revelations set in motion revitalization movements the success of which depends upon how successfully they address the challenges and opportunities associated with a given 'evolutionary moment.'

force that triggers these revelations is still regarded as a mystery although a number of hypotheses have been advanced.

Of primary interest is the fact that sociocultural evolution and revitalization movements, in particular, are characterized by stages of patterned processes which are now sufficiently understood by social and general systems scientists to enable humanity to meet the challenges and exploit the opportunities associated with the cyclic, or better 'ascending helix,' of organic, social and spiritual development. That more people, especially society's leaders, become knowledgeable of these processes is essential. For as Laszlo points out:

> In a system such as contemporary society, evolution is always a promise and devolution always a threat. No system comes with a guarantee of evolution. The challenge is real. To ignore it is to play dice with all we have. To accept it is not to play God—it is to become an instrument of whatever divine purpose infuses the universe.[42]

Summary

Having begun our exploration with a review of the idea of prophetic revelation as set forth by various religious scholars and then reflecting on the insights of scientists who have been working in the fields of anthropology, psychology, and system theory, we came to the following conclusions.

Presently, the social systems of the world appear to have entered a bifurcation. We are moving from a nation-state, industrial system to a global, post-industrial system. Among the more contemporary religious movements, the Bahá'í Faith is an example of a revitalization movement offering a global vision and agenda.

The emergence of global civilization in our time (though it may take many decades or centuries to accomplish) can be regarded, as far as this planetary life is concerned, as the furthermost limits in the organization of human society. Therefore,

---

[42] See, n. 30 above, p.176.

once this stage has been reached the ensuing steady state phase could be quite long and the bifurcations may be less violent.

When studying the role of religion in human culture, we are reminded of the words of Ralph Wendell Burhoe, a brilliant scientist/theologian and cofounder of the Institute of Religion in an Age of Science. "Religion," said Burhoe, should be reexamined "in the light of the sciences" since, in our age, science has become the dominant method of probing the mysteries of man and the universe. "But, of course, the whole point of getting a creed illuminated in the light of the sciences," Burhoe emphasized, "is to provide the heat, the emotive power of a faith that delivers one and one's society from evil by a new lease on its credibility."[43]

Hopefully, this study will help provide some of the "heat" and "emotive power" that will contribute, in some small way, to an ever-advancing civilization and the establishment of global culture. Thus, we have come full circle and so wish to conclude this journey with a few profound statements drawn from the Holy Scriptures of some of the world's great religious traditions. The subject is, of course, Divine Revelation and the power of the Word of God.

Judaism

...And you shall remember all the way which the Lord your God has led you these forty years in the wilderness, that He might humbled you, testing you to know what was in your heart, whether you would keep His commandments, or not. And He humbled you and let you hunger and fed you with manna, which you did not know, nor did your fathers know; that He might make you know that man does not live by bread alone, but that man lives by everything that proceeds out of the mouth of God.

Deuteronomy 8:2; circa 1300 BCE

---

[43] For an overview of Burhoe's views on the topic of religion and social evolution see Ralph Wendell Burhoe, "Religion's Role in Human Evolution: The Missing Link Between Apeman's Selfish Genes and Civilized Altruism," *Zygon* 14, (1979), pp. 135–162.

Taoism

The Great Tao overflows on every side, right and left. All things depend on it for their being, but without a word it sustains us all. It accomplishes everything but asks for nothing in return. It feeds and clothes all creatures, but never sets itself up as master.

Tao Te Ching, Ch. 34; circa 600 BCE

Christianity

In the beginning was the Word, and the Word was with God, and the Word was God. He was in the beginning with God; and all things were made through him, and without him was not anything made that was made. In him was life, and the life was the light of men. The light shines in the darkness and the darkness has not overcome it.

John 1: 1–5; circa 100 CE

Islam

People of the Book, now there has come to you Our Messenger (Muhammad), making clear to you many things you have been concealing of the Book, and effacing many things. There has come to you from God a light, a Book Manifest whereby God guides whosoever follows His good pleasure in the ways of peace and bring forth from the shadows into light by His leave; and He guides them to His straight path.

Qur'an, The Table: 19; circa 622 CE

Bahá'í

...That which is preeminent above all other gifts, is incorruptible in nature, and pertaineth to God Himself, is the gift of Divine Revelation. Every bounty conferred by the Creator upon man, be it material or spiritual, is subservient unto this. It is, in its essence, and will ever so remain, the Bread which commeth down from Heaven. It is God's supreme testimony, the clearest evidence of His truth, the sign of His consummate bounty, the token of His all-encompassing mercy, the proof of His most loving providence, the symbol of His most perfect grace. He hath indeed partaken of this highest gift of God who hath recognized His Manifestation in this Day.

Gleanings from the Writings of Bahá'u'lláh;
circa 1863 CE

ADDENDUM

In general, the emerging general systems evolution theory coupled with the concept of progressive revelation as synthesized so beautifully in Karl Peter's "Evolutionary Theory of Knowledge" has a number of features which recommend it for further study and application, first as a model of inquiry and second as a model for practical application.

As a model of inquiry, the theory offers the following features which are consistent with both our naturalistic and religious views of reality:

1. The fundamental assumption that there is a transcendent or ultimate reality, i.e., God, underlying all of creation.
2. That this transcendent reality manifests itself to the human mind in two primary ways: through the human experience of the world of nature or 'general revelation,' and through the human experience of religion delivered through unique spiritual personages or 'special revelation.'
3. That both general and special revelation can be approached using scientific method.
4. That both general and special revelation, when properly understood, can be regarded as complimentary expressions of the creative and evolutionary processes set in motion by Ultimate Reality. In theological terms, general and special revelations reflect the Will and Word of God, respectively. In simple terms, they represent God's 'show and tell' method for educating humanity. (See figure 5.)

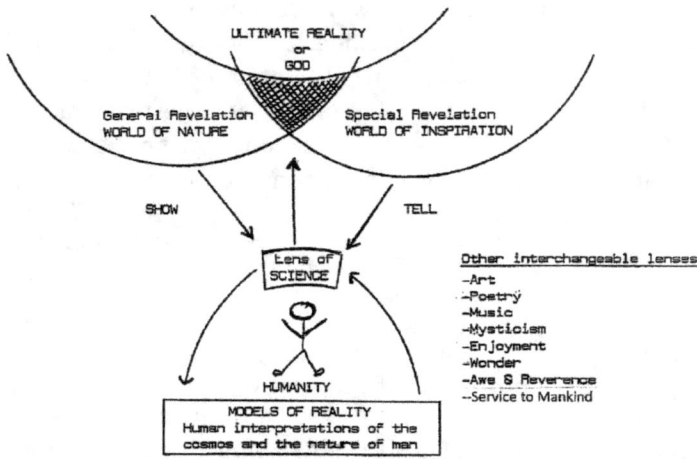

Figure 5. Approach to knowledge and 'Ultimate Reality' based on Karl Peter's "Evolutionary Theory of Knowledge." (Authors' understanding).

In addition to these features, the theory is generative in that it suggests a number of hypotheses for further research, explanatory in that it shed new light on the patterns and processes of social and cultural change, and predictive in that it provides a dynamic paradigmatic approach for the interpretation of contemporary and perhaps future events. This last feature is of special importance as it can help us sort out the management decisions necessary to guide ourselves, and humanity collectively, toward the most viable possibilities open to us and away from those options that could lead to dead-end roads. In theological terms, Peter's model of inquiry offers a dynamic methodology for humankind to seek the "Image of God" within us and work for the "Kingdom of God" at large.

This 'model of inquiry,' based on the concept that God or 'ultimate reality' manifests Himself to man through both 'general' and 'special' revelation, offers a powerful solution to the science and religion dichotomy. It suggests that both types of revelation can be approached using the 'lens of science' as well as other lenses such as art, music, mysticism, and even service to humankind.

When using these various interchangeable lenses to approach ultimate reality, man is involved in a spiritual enterprise.

In very simple terms, general and special revelations are God's 'show and tell' method for educating humankind. Our attempts to interpret these lessons result in various 'models of reality' which, through the arduous task of refinement, allow us to draw ever nearer to the Will of God, i.e., to live in harmony with the laws of Nature.

A Model for Practical Application

Among the most important implications of this study is that humankind is in the midst of a major bifurcation which includes the possibility of an emerging global revitalization movement — an emerging world religion. It is clear that there are many religious and quasi-religious movements occurring throughout the world.[44] These movements, we believe, are reflections of a wide-scale search for purpose, meaning, and new ways of thinking and acting in a world of rapid change and breakdown. Yet they also may well signalize a recent infusion of spiritual energy resulting from the advent of a new revelation from the creative force of the universe. If so, religious movements offering a global agenda — like movements the Baha'i Faith, for example — deserve the serious attention of those leaders of thought who stand in the prominent position of guiding the masses toward the real social and spiritual solutions the peoples of the world so desperately seek. To be sure, if a key to the realization of the spiritual and social unification of humankind does exist and is to be found through human effort, experience suggests that it is far more likely than otherwise to be associated with another

---

[44] One of the best overviews for the search for new values and modes of thinking in contemporary society can be found in Marilyn Furguson's book *The Aquarian Conspiracy: Personal and Social Transformation in the 1980s*, (J. P. Tarcher, Inc.: Los Angeles, 1980). For a discussion of Wallace's revitalization model as applied to contemporary events in Western society see Solomon H. Katz, "The Dehumanization and Rehumanization of Science and Society," *Zygon* 9 (1974), pp. 126–138.

intervention of the Divine in human affairs. Such a possibility, moreover, would seem also to have been anticipated in virtually all the scriptures of the past as expressed in the various concepts of progressive revelation. And it would appear to be entirely in accord with the research findings of scientists like Wallace, Lex, d'Aquili, Laszlo, Peters, and others.

A second practical application of this theory is in the quest for interfaith understanding and unity. It is a well-documented fact that the "exclusivist approach" to religion (i.e., that only one religion is true while all the others are either false or only partially true) has essentially led to religious bigotry and strife. The "pluralistic approach" accepted today by most progressive thinkers has certainly led to greater tolerance and interreligious cooperation. Yet even this approach leaves much to be desired as it ignores certain basic questions. The "evolutionary theory of knowledge" suggested by Peters deals with the issue of religious pluralism much more effectively. It strongly suggests that the various religious traditions can be regarded, at least for the most part, as stages in the eternal history and constant evolution of one Religion whose 'truths' tend to change in accordance with the exigencies of different sociocultural environments.

Furthermore, the concept rests on the fundamental principle that religious truth, like scientific truth, is not absolute but relative, that Divine Revelation is progressive, not final. It supports the basic idea that the major established religions are divine in origin, similar if not identical in their aims, and complimentary in their functions. Most importantly, these mighty systems of faith, when understood as epochal stages of a dynamic, evolving process, appear to remain continuous in their purpose and indispensable in their value to humankind. To be sure, the emerging new paradigm of general systems evolution coupled with progressive revelation offers a fresh approach to comparative religious studies as well as to the psychology and sociology of religion as specifically related to sociocultural development.

References

Bahá'u'lláh, *The Kitab-i-Iqan (The Book of Certitude)*, Trans. By Shoghi Effendi, (Bahá'í Publishing Trust: Wilmette, II, 1981).

Burhoe, Ralph Wendell, "The Institute on Religion in an Age of Science: A Twenty-Year View," *Zygon 8*, (1973), pp. 59-72.

Burhoe, Ralph Wendell, "Religion's Role in Human Evolution: The Missing Link Between Apeman's Selfish Genes and Civilized Altruism," *Zvgon 14*, (1979), pp. 135-162.

Chaisson, Eric, "Cosmic Evolution: A Synthesis of Matter and Life," *Zygon 14*, pp. 23-39.

D'Aquili, Eugene G., "Senses of Reality in Science and Religion: A Neuroepistomological Perspective," *Zygon 17*, (1982), pp. 361-384.

D'Aquili, Eugene G., "Myth, Ritual, and the Archetypal Hypothesis," *Zygon 21*, (1986), pp. 141-160.

Eccles, John C, "Cerebral Activity and Consciousness," in *Studies in the Philosophy of Biology*, F, J. Ayala and T, Dobzhansky eds., (University of California Press: Berkley, 1974), pp. 87-107.

Ferguson, Marilyn, *The Aquarian Conspiracy: Personal and Social Transformation in the 1980s*, (J. P. Tarcher, Inc.: Los Angeles, 1980).

Goodenough, Ward H, *Cooperation and Change*, (John Wiley and Sons, NY, 1963).

Hamilton, H. J., "A Thermodynamic Theory of the Origin and Hierarchical Evolution of Living Systems," *Zygon, 12*, (1977), pp. 289-335.

Hatcher, William S. and Martin, J. Douglas, *The Bahá'í Faith: The Emerging Global Religion*, (Harper and Row, NY, 1984).

Hatcher, William S. "Human Nature and Human Society: A Bahá'í Viewpoint," in *The Bahá'í Faith and Marxism*, (Bahá'í Studies Publications, Ottawa, 1987).

Historical Atlas of the Religions of the World, lsma'il R, al Faruqi, ed., (Macmillan Publishing Co.: NY, 1974).

Hummel, Charles E., *The Galileo Connection: Resolving Conflicts between Science and the Bible*, (lntervarsity Press, IL, 1986).

Katz, Solomon H. "The Dehumanization and Rehumanization of Science and Society," *Zygon 9* (1974), pp. 126–138.

Laszlo, Ervin, et al., *Goals for Mankind: A Report to the Club of Rome on New Horizons of Global Community*, (E. P. Dutton: NY, 1977).

Laszlo, Ervin, *Evolution: The Grand Synthesis*, (Shambala: Boston, 1987).

Lex, Barbara W., "Neurological Bases of Revitalization Movements," *Zygon 13*, (1978), pp. 276–312.

Peters, Karl E., "Religion and an Evolutionary Theory of Knowledge," *Zygon 17* (1982), pp. 385–415.

Scofield, C. I., D.D., ed., *The Scofield Reference Bible*, C. I. Scofield, D.D., ed., (Oxford University Press: NY, 1945).

Sperry, Roger, "Changed Concepts of Brain and Consciousness: Some Value Implications," *Zygon 20*, (1985), pp. 41–57.

Sutta-Nipata, V. Fausboll, Translator, in Part II, Vol. X of The Sacred Books of the East, (Oxford, 1861).

Swami Akhilananda, "Hindu View of Christ," in *Christianity: Some Non-Christian Appraisals*, David W. McCain, ed., (McGraw-Hill: NY, 1964).

Townshend, George, *The Heart of the Gospel*, (George Ronald Press: London, 1960).

Toynbee, Arnold, *A Study of History*, (Oxford University Press, 1972).

Wallace, Anthony F. C. "Revitalization Movements," *American Anthropologist*, Vol. 58, (1956), pp. 264–281.

Wallace, Anthony F. C. Religion: *An Anthropological View*, (Random House: NY, 1966).

Plato, Modern Physics, and Bahá'u'lláh

Vahid Ranjbar

> "What a penetrating vision into philosophy this eminent man had! He is the most distinguished of all philosophers... He (Socrates) it is who perceived a unique, a tempered, and a pervasive nature in things, bearing the closest likeness to the human spirit, and he discovered this nature to be distinct from the substance of things in their refined form. He hath a special pronouncement on this weighty theme. Wert thou to ask from the worldly wise of this generation about this exposition, thou wouldst witness their incapacity to grasp it..." (Bahá'u'lláh, "Tablet of Wisdom.")

Socrates and his pupil Plato are highly praised in the Bahá'í writings. Socrates is the protagonist of Plato's discourses; thus, it is difficult to disentangle Plato's ideas from those of Socrates. Outside of their ideas about political philosophy, Plato was also concerned with the so-called theory of forms, and it is this idea Bahá'u'lláh attributes to Socrates. However, Bahá'u'lláh's appreciation seems to go much further than Plato's theory. The theory of forms claims that non-physical idealized forms or ideas represent the most accurate reality and that physical objects derive their 'essence' from their relationship to these forms. These forms are often

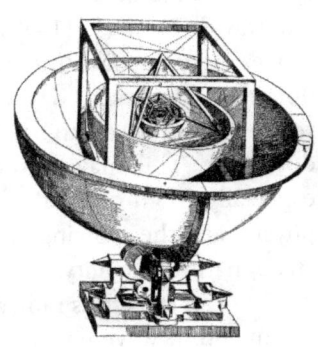

Fig. 1: Kepler's Platonic solid model of the Solar System from Mysterium Cosmographicum (1596).

described as models or templates from which imperfect copies or projections are made in the physical world.

Plato uses the well-known cave analogy to illustrate this relationship. He imagined that there were several prisoners trapped in a cave deep underground. Their bodies and heads are immobile with chains and brackets against one wall, and on the other are projected shadows of objects, which are cast by a large torch behind their heads. The prisoners only know this reality and so mistake the shadows they see projected on the wall for reality itself. Eventually, one of the prisoners escapes and sees the actual objects being projected and realizes the nature of the deception. This freed prisoner is likened to the enlightened philosopher or, as we might say, a spiritually awakened person. The prisoners are all humanity, and the shadows are what we take as physical reality.

Fig 2: Plato's Cave

This idea of a separation between the "essence" of a thing and its actual physical attributes held powerful sway over Christian and Islamic thought since it fits very well within their theologies. However, by the Middle Ages, Nominalists like William of Ockham (of Occam's razor) (1287–1347) began to question this viewpoint. Later, British Empiricists like David Hume (1711–1776) rejected the Platonic notion of essences existing apart from physical reality. This viewpoint is now dominant in present-day scientific thought. The idea of an essence beyond what can be directly measured is looked on as pseudoscience. This may be more a problem of language, however, especially when one reflects on the triumph of math in modern physics and the growing view that math somehow represents the "true" nature of reality.

One can trace this radical view of math to the introduction of the quantum wave equation by Erwin Schrödinger (1887–1961) and the matrix representation by Werner Heisenberg (1901–1976) in the mid-1920s. The new wave function presented a problem: it was explicitly non-physical due to the fact that it was an imaginary or complex-valued object. Additionally, when evaluated to generate measurable quantities, it operated in a probabilistic manner.

The debate over what this wave function represented physically was somewhat resolved by the so-called Copenhagen interpretation. At the heart of this view is Max Born's (1882–1970) thesis that the wave function is simply a mathematical object which can yield a probability density function— thus, it has no physical meaning outside of mathematics and its ability to "predict" a particle's behavior. Needless to say, physicists hated this interpretation, though it has become increasingly accepted in the ensuing eighty years. Yet initially, many clung to the belief that the wave function was masking some other local physics that we just couldn't measure. These were known as the "hidden" variable theories. To try and prove this thesis, Albert Einstein (1879–1955) and others came up with the now famous EPR paradox (Einstein) to expose what was considered an absurd consequence of quantum mechanics; the fact that two particles, after interacting and becoming "entangled" quantum mechanically, could affect the measured state of each other after being separated by a great distance. However, Einstein's 'spooky action at a distance' was subsequently demonstrated through many experiments with quantum entanglement. In 1964, John Bell (1928–1990) put forward his famous theorem, which states, "No physical theory of local hidden variables can ever reproduce all of the predictions of quantum mechanics."[1] He further proposed an approach to test the validity of this theorem by measuring the occurrences of correlations between measured states of particles, which were quantum entangled. Experiments testing Bell's inequality in 1972, 1981, and more recently, 2015 (Hensen) have so far lain to rest any theory of local hidden variables.

---

[1] Bell, J. S. "On the Einstein Podolsky Rosen paradox." *Physics Physique Fizika* 1.3 (1964): 195–200.

Fig. 3: Werner Karl Heisenberg (1901-1976)

It was actually Heisenberg himself who grasped the connection between of quantum mechanics and the Platonic viewpoint: "I think that modern physics has definitely decided in favor of Plato. In fact, the smallest units of matter are not physical objects in the ordinary sense; they are forms, ideas which can be expressed unambiguously only in mathematical language."[2]

There are several important aspects of quantum mechanics that lend themselves to the Platonic interpretation. First, the clear separation between the object measured and the mathematical form, which gives rise to the object. Then there is, as Heisenberg acknowledged, the fact that the "units of matter" are really just mathematical ideas.

Additionally, there is more subtle evidence for the correctness of Plato's view. It flows from the fact that fundamental physical interactions are governed by probability and not pure determinism. If we accept the assumption that the universe is either spatially infinite or eternal, the logical consequence is that all forms are eternal. This is because probabilistic physics operating over any kind of infinity will yield all outcomes that have a non-zero probability of occurring, even if that probability is infinitesimally small. Thus, everything that could exist has a non-zero probability of occurring. This means in a universe with infinite space, all these forms must exist with an infinite number of occurrences, and if the universe is eternal, these forms will occur an infinite number of times.

---

[2] "Quotations: Werner Heisenberg," *MacTutor History of Mathematics Archive*, https://mathshistory.st-andrews.ac.uk/Biographies/Heisenberg/quotations/.

This is the foundation for notions of parallel universes (Greene) so popular with sci-fi writers and analytic philosophers. In fact the only escape from an infinite multiplicity of identities is the conjecture of a unique human soul. Either way the death and decay of forms would seem to be an illusion — a simple product of our limited sampling.

If we now return and reflect on Bahá'u'lláh's praise of Socrates, the innovation he attributes to the Greek philosopher is even more explicitly consistent with modern quantum field theory than Plato's theory of forms as it is usually understood. At the very least, it is much more descriptive. It would seem he is describing, within the limits of the language available to him, the existence of a quantum field. If we reflect on this word "spirit" and what it really means, one can see that it contains both the concepts of non-physicality and pervasiveness, which are the hallmarks of the quantum wave function. In fact, he even uses the word "pervasive" as if to emphasize this aspect.

Finally, he also states that the people of his generation were incapable of grasping the implications of this idea. This is an interesting point, since Plato's theory of forms was, of course, well known and thoroughly studied for millennia. One could understand such a statement in light of what would come some fifty years later, with the important difference, however, that he seems to imply — by using the word "things" — that this type of relationship exists not only between basic particles of matter, but well beyond that.

Interestingly, Bahá'u'lláh's son and appointed interpreter, 'Abdu'l-Bahá, seems to presage important concepts in many of his philosophical talks, often decades before they became current among physicists. For example, in his excellent article "Ether, Quantum Physics, and the Bahá'í Writings," Robin Mihrshahi points out how 'Abdu'l-Bahá used the word 'ether,' commonly understood at that time as the medium for the propagation of electromagnetic waves, in a totally new manner consistent with quantum mechanics. 'Abdu'l-Bahá describes it not as a physical reality but as an intellectual one: "Even the ether, the forces of which are said in natural philosophy to be heat, light, electricity, and magnetism, is an intelligible and not a sensible reality."[3]

In another place, 'Abdu'l-Bahá seems to intuitively understand another profound consequence of quantum mechanics: the non-existence of absolute rest, or the impossibility of reaching absolute zero Kelvin. In several places 'Abdu'l-Bahá makes the statement "that movement is essential to existence." Or later, "All creation, whether of the mineral, vegetable or animal kingdom, is compelled to obey the law of motion;"[4] this idea is repeated in 'Abdu'l-Bahá's Tablet of the Universe.

From a Bahá'í viewpoint, one might understand these Platonic forms or ideas as the words of God.

> ... Word of God which is the Cause of the entire creation, while all else besides His Word are but the creatures and the effects thereof. Verily thy Lord is the Expounder, the All-Wise. Know thou, moreover, that the Word of God — exalted be His glory — is higher and far superior to that which the senses can perceive, for it is sanctified from any property or substance. It transcendeth the limitations of known elements and is exalted above all the essential and recognized substances. It became manifest without any syllable or sound and is none but the Command of God which pervadeth all created things. It hath never been withheld from the world of being."[5]

If we parse this concept of the 'Word of God' more carefully, we conclude that words are containers of ideas or "information" at their simplest level. With the increasing dominance of information technology in our lives, the organizing and creative power possible in information would seem obvious. However, from a physics point of view, the connection between information,

---

[3] 'Abdu'l-Bahá, *Some Answered Questions*, www.bahai.org/r/898497121.
[4] 'Abdu'l-Bahá, *Paris Talks*, www.bahai.org/r/982255238.
[5] Bahá'u'lláh, *Tablets of Bahá'u'lláh*, www.bahai.org/r/893372526.

life, and the rise of order is only now beginning to be understood. This understanding can trace its genesis back to the late nineteenth century. The development of the steam engine helped prompt the new physics of thermodynamics. Thermodynamics was originally concerned with the behavior of gases and heat engines. From this sprung the understanding of physical laws, which governed energy and order. The most important of these were the laws that related the symmetry of the distribution for a given gas to the energy that could be extracted. So, for example, if there was a system where one container held a "hot" gas and another a "cold" gas, the heat differential could be used to drive a so-called heat engine. However, once the system was thermally mixed, no more work could be extracted.

The new concept of entropy quantified this symmetry of mixing. A system was in the highest entropic state when it was most symmetrical — that is, when the hot and cold gases were perfectly mixed. So, if one sampled the gas at any point, one would find an equal number of fast (hot) and slow (cold) particles.

The lowest entropic state was one where the hot and cold particles were distributed as asymmetrically as possible, the fast particles completely separated from the slow. The concept of entropy was introduced along with the second law of thermodynamics, which related the rise of entropy to the extraction of energy from a given system.

It was around this time that James Maxwell (1831–1879) came up with a famous thought experiment that challenged the ideas enshrined in the second law of thermodynamics, specifically the idea that for a system of particles in thermal equilibrium, where all the fast- and slow-moving particles were completely mixed, no more work could be extracted. Maxwell imagined a box containing this distribution with a wall dividing it into two sides. In the wall, there was a door, which was controlled by some demon that would open the door only for fast-moving particles and keep it shut for the slow particles. In this way, over time, all the fast particles would come to reside on one side of the box, leaving the slow particles on the other. In this situation, a heat engine could be run from the differential in temperature and thus extracting work in violation of the second law of thermodynamics.

For many years Maxwell's Demon challenged the understanding of entropy and the second law. Later, statistical mechanics were worked into the existing thermodynamic framework, and entropy was understood as representing the possible states of a given system. Finally, entropy made its way into the new field of information theory when Shannon equated the statistical definition of entropy with information (Shannon). Maxwell's Demon began to be understood as a class of information engines. An information engine is currently understood as a system that can turn information into work. Here information gathered by the demon concerning the velocity of each particle represented a rise in entropy. This is because this information needed to be stored on some physical medium whose initial entropic state had to be considered. So, for example, a magnetic tape, which stores information as zeros and ones, needed to be first initialized to be all zeros. This initialization placed the tape into a lower entropic state, which was then given up as information was recorded. In the end, the work required to reset this memory would consume more energy than was extracted, thus preserving the second law. This is known as Landauer's erasure principle (Landauer). More recently, a physical realization of a type of Maxwell Demon machine has been created using a photon circuit. (M. D. Vidrighin)

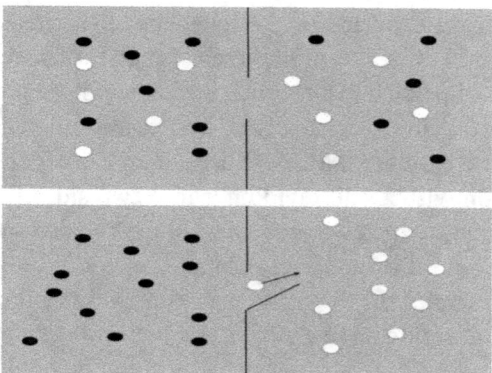

Fig. 4: Fast (white) and slow (black) particles in equilibrium (top). Maxwell's Demon opens the door to sort particles of different speeds (bottom).

However, the implications of Maxwell's Demon are still somewhat unresolved and debated. Some assert there is an important confusion in Shannon's definition of information as entropy. Christoph Adami (b. 1962) professor of Microbiology and Molecular Genetics, as well as professor of Physics and Astronomy, at Michigan State University, has recently pointed this out, claiming that what Shannon called information and equated with entropy was actually a measure of uncertainty, not information as it would be commonly understood.

For example, a coin that can have two defined states, heads or tails, has a defined amount of entropy, which is less entropy than a six-sided dice, which has six possible states. This is what Shannon called information because a six-state system can hold more bits of information than a two-state system.

Adami goes on to define information as "anything, which can give one the ability to predict an outcome better than chance."[6] To my knowledge this new definition of information has yet to be applied to the case of Maxwell's Demon. The existing literature uses the standard Shannon version of the information. It would seem that using the new definition of information wouldn't alter the ultimate implications for the second law of thermodynamics. However, I would argue that it does alter the conclusions about the role of information in generating order.

For example, Shannon's definition relates the rise of entropy with the rise of information. Information defined in this way takes on a "negative" meaning with respect to order. This, I believe, misses the role which the information plays in facilitating the generation of order. If we use the Adami's understanding of information, we can identify the inherent information present in the system. This inherent information is represented in the implied physical assumption that allows the demon to predict the future trajectories of the particles and thus sort them using the trapdoor, or even the fact that faster particles are those that

---

[6] Adami, Christoph. 2016 "What is information?" Phil. Trans. R. Soc. A.37420150230201502302, http://doi.org/10.1098/rsta.2015.0230.

make a system "warmer" and slower make a system "colder." This information inherent in the system is overlooked using the standard definition of information. Further, using this approach permits a better linkage to biological systems, which use the information inherent in DNA to generate order.

Adami argues that this "information" is the real commodity of evolutionary biology. The better an organism is at modeling its environment, the more chance it has of passing on its genes. The process of reflecting or adapting to the environment drives evolution. This concept echoes the common mystical idea that we are "mirrors" of God and the universe: "Dost thou deem thyself a small and puny form, When thou foldest within thyself the greater world?"[7]

Or, as Bahá'u'lláh says:

> He hath entrusted every created thing with a sign of His knowledge, so that none of His creatures may be deprived of its share in expressing, each according to its capacity and rank, this knowledge. This sign is the mirror of His beauty in the world of creation.[8]

In my opinion, we are still on the threshold of understanding the deep connections between the origin of order and information inherent in the laws of nature. Again in the Tablet of Wisdom, Bahá'u'lláh makes another important statement relevant to the origin of order. He also here seems to steer away from the strictly rationalist approach of Plato. Plato famously believed that all knowledge could be arrived at by direct application of the intellect and that this was superior to observation.

> Look at the world and ponder a while upon it. It unveileth the book of its own self before thine eyes and revealeth that which the Pen of thy Lord, the Fashioner,

---

[7] Bahá'u'lláh, *The Call of the Divine Beloved*, www.bahai.org/r/670295484.
[8] Bahá'u'lláh, *Gleanings from the Writings of Bahá'u'lláh*, www.bahai.org/r/384219536.

the All-Informed, hath inscribed therein. It will acquaint thee with that which is within it and upon it and will give thee such clear explanations as to make thee independent of every eloquent expounder."[9]

In this paragraph, Bahá'u'lláh emphasizes what, ironically, is the core idea of empiricism and where one might see a fundamental break with the Platonic approach. He advocates for observation of nature as the basis for deductions. Then, in the next paragraph, Bahá'u'lláh goes on to modify the standard supernatural theory of creation:

> Say: Nature in its essence is the embodiment of My Name, the Maker, the Creator. Its manifestations are diversified by varying causes, and in this diversity, there are signs for men of discernment. Nature is God's Will and is its expression in and through the contingent world. It is a dispensation of Providence ordained by the Ordainer, the All-Wise. Were anyone to affirm that it is the Will of God as manifested in the world of being, no one should question this assertion. It is endowed with a power whose reality men of learning fail to grasp. Indeed a man of insight can perceive naught therein save the effulgent splendor of Our Name, the Creator. Say: This is an existence which knoweth no decay, and Nature itself is lost in bewilderment before its revelations, its compelling evidences and its effulgent glory which have encompassed the universe."[10]

In this paragraph, he breaks with the "traditional" religious narrative, which places supernatural forces as the immediate cause of creation. Here he states that "Nature" creates by virtue of its association with the divine name "Creator." While the ultimate cause of creation is still the divine, its immediate cause is "Nature."

---

[9] Bahá'u'lláh, *Tablets of Bahá'u'lláh*, www.bahai.org/r/131365079.
[10] Bahá'u'lláh, *Tablets of Bahá'u'lláh*, www.bahai.org/r/475103576.

These two paragraphs also form the backbone of the Bahá'í principle of harmony between science and religion, a principle explicitly enunciated by 'Abdu'l-Bahá': "The third principle or teaching of Bahá'u'lláh is the oneness of religion and science. Any religious belief which is not conformable with scientific proof and investigation is superstition."[11] This is because it forces followers of Bahá'u'lláh to always return to the benchmark of the empirical observation of nature and be prepared to subject their interpretations of scripture to the rigors of experimental observation. Ultimately Nature is held up as another "book" of God.

A deeper study of Bahá'í epistemology as elaborated by 'Abdu'l-Bahá reveals a practical viewpoint that values both rationalist and empirical approaches to knowledge. However, it is understood that neither is absolutely free from error. In 'Abdu'l-Bahá's analysis, the only error-free species of knowledge comes from what he terms the "grace of the Holy Spirit." In all cases, the vehicle to correct knowledge is objectivity or detachment. In the opening verses of Bahá'u'lláh's Book of Certitude, he says "No man shall attain the shores of the ocean of true understanding except he be detached from all that is in heaven and on earth."[12]

This paragraph in the Tablet of Wisdom on Nature indicates that Nature continually "creates" and is possessed of a power or force which can bring order. In a letter to the naturalist, Dr. Forel 'Abdu'l-Bahá seems to refer to this as "the Ancient Power." "Nature" is only one term or concept among many that the Bahá'í writings employ to explain what is rather unexplainable to our finite minds. In another place, 'Abdu'l-Bahá identifies "Love" with the power to bring forth life: "Love is the very cause of life." "We declare that love is the cause of the existence of all phenomena and that the absence of love is the cause of dis-

---

[11] 'Abdu'l-Bahá, *The Promulgation of Universal Peace*, www.bahai.org/r/709810346.

[12] Bahá'u'lláh, *The Kitáb-i-Íqán*, www.bahai.org/r/655906123.

integration or nonexistence."[13] He then goes on to relate the "attractive force" to Love.

What is tantalizing is that recent work by Julian Barbour (b. 1937) and his colleagues seems to show that there is something unique about systems under the operation of an attractive force. In this paper, they say, "self-gravitating systems exhibit 'anti-thermodynamic' behavior that is not fully understood."[14] Thermodynamics, as it was originally conceived, didn't consider gravitation. Indeed, the operation of self-attractive forces leads to symmetry breaking and clustering, which is very different from how ideal gases behave. Further, Barbour's work represents a possible solution to the origin of the so-called time's arrow and the asymmetry between matter and antimatter in the universe. Both are important and profound questions in physics. Most physicists have identified the irreversible process described in the second law of thermodynamics as the "arrow of time." So, for example, the process of mixing gases described earlier or breaking glass into many pieces represent physical occurrences that one rarely observes in reverse and so distinguishes the backward from the forward direction of time.

Since the discovery of antimatter in 1932, the question of why normal matter dominates in our universe over antimatter has been unresolved. This is because the laws which govern their production don't seem to exhibit a significant enough preference for matter over antimatter. This question is also deeply related to questions of time directionality since it is understood that antimatter represents matter with reverse time propagation. It is part of what embodies the so-called charge, parity, and time (CPT) violation searches in high-energy physics.

In their studies of simple many-body models of the universe governed by Newtonian laws of gravitational attraction, they

---

[13] 'Abdu'l-Bahá, *The Promulgation of Universal Peace*, www.bahai.org/r/367824701.

[14] Barbour, Julian, Koslowski, Tim and Mercati, Flavio. "Identification of a Gravitational Arrow of Time." *Physical Review Letters* 113.18 (2014): 181101.

have discovered that such systems naturally exhibit modes that both converge and de-converge from what might be considered a type of big-bang singularity. In this case, antimatter represents a kind of anti-time converging on the singularity and normal matter — normal-time divergent from the singularity.

Finally, Bahá'u'lláh also, in his writings, indicates that profound scientific and artistic advances are soon to be revealed in the future. He attributes their imminent discovery to forces released via the revelation of the 'words of God' in his age:

> Through the mere revelation of the word "Fashioner," issuing forth from His lips and proclaiming His attribute to mankind, such power is released as can generate, through successive ages, all the manifold arts which the hands of man can produce. This, verily, is a certain truth. No sooner is this resplendent word uttered, than its animating energies, stirring within all created things, give birth to the means and instruments whereby such arts can be produced and perfected. All the wondrous achievements ye now witness are the direct consequences of the Revelation of this Name. In the days to come, ye will, verily, behold things of which ye have never heard before. Thus hath it been decreed in the Tablets of God, and none can comprehend it except them whose sight is sharp. In like manner, the moment the word expressing My attribute "The Omniscient" issueth forth from My mouth, every created thing will, according to its capacity and limitations, be invested with the power to unfold the knowledge of the most marvelous sciences and will be empowered to manifest them in the course of time at the bidding of Him Who is the Almighty, the All-Knowing.[15]

However, in Bahá'u'lláh's Tablet Kalimat-i-firdawsiyyih (Words of Paradise), he leaves us with several astounding warn-

---

[15] Bahá'u'lláh, *Gleanings from the Writings of Bahá'u'lláh*, www.bahai.org/r/043743455.

ings concerning the progress of civilization and the power of the future scientific discoveries:

> In all matters moderation is desirable. If a thing is carried to excess, it will prove a source of evil. Consider the civilization of the West, how it hath agitated and alarmed the peoples of the world. An infernal engine hath been devised, and hath proved so cruel a weapon of destruction that its like none hath ever witnessed or heard... Strange and astonishing things exist in the earth, but they are hidden from the minds and the understanding of men. These things are capable of changing the whole atmosphere of the earth and their contamination would prove lethal.[16]

Bibliography

'Abdu'l-Bahá. *Paris Talks*. UK Bahá'í Publishing Trust, 1972.

———. "Tablet of the Universe." *Makátib-i 'Abdu'l-Bahá* (1997): 13–32.

———. *Tablet to Dr. Auguste Forel*. Bahá'í World Center, 1976.

———. *Some Answered Questions*. Bahá'í World Center, 2014.

———. *The Promulgation of Universal Peace*. Bahá'í Publishing, 1982.

Adami, Christoph. "What is Information?" 374.2063 (2016).

Bahá'u'lláh. *Gleanings From the Writings of Bahá'u'lláh*. Vol. CXXIV. US Bahá'í Publishing Trust, 1990.

———. *Gleanings From the Writings of Bahá'u'lláh*. Vol. LXXIV. Bahá'í World Center, 1990.

———. "Kalimát-i-Firdawsíyyih (Words of Paradise)." *Tablets of Bahá'u'lláh revealed after the Kitáb-i-Aqdas*. Bahá'í World Center, 1978.

———. "Tablet of Wisdom." *Tablets of Bahá'u'lláh Revealed After the Kitáb-i-Aqdas*. Bahá'í World Center, 1978.

---

[16] Bahá'u'lláh, *Tablets of Bahá'u'lláh*, www.bahai.org/r/062742596.

———. *The Call of the Divine Beloved Selected Mystical Works of Bahá'u'lláh*. Bahá'í World Center: https://www.bahai.org/library/authoritative-texts/bahaullah/call-divine-beloved/, 2019.

———. *The Kitáb-i-Íqán: The Book of Certitude*. Bahá'í World Center, 1931.

Barbour, Julian and Koslowski, Tim and Mercati, Flavio. "Identification of a Gravitational Arrow of Time." *Physical Review Letters* 113.18 (2014): 181101.

Bell, J. S. "On the Einstein Podolsky Rosen paradox." *Physics Physique Fizika* 1.3 (1964): 195–200.

Einstein, A., Podolsky, B. and Rosen, N. "Can Quantum-Mechanical Description of Physical Reality Be Considered Complete?" *Physical Review* 47.10 (193t5): 777–780.

Greene, Brian. *The Hidden Reality: Parallel Universes and the Deep Laws of the Cosmos*. Vintage, 2011.

Heisenberg, Werner. "Quotations," *MacTutor History of Mathematics Archive*, https://mathshistory.st-andrews.ac.uk/Biographies/Heisenberg/quotations/.

Hensen, B., Bernien, H., Dréau, A. et al. "Loophole-free Bell inequality violation using electron spins separated by 1.3 kilometres." *Nature* 526 (2015): 682–686.

Landauer, R. "Irreversibility and Heat generation in the computing process." *IBM Journal of Research and Development* (Volume: 5, Issue: 3, July 1961).

Mihrshahi, Robin. "Ether, Quantum Physics and the Bahá'í Writings." *Australian Bahá'í Studies* (2002/2003): 3–20.

Vidrighin, M. D., et al. 2016. *Physical Review Letters* (American Physical Society) 116 (050401).

Shannon, Claud. "A Mathematical Theory of Communication." *The Bell System Technical Journal*, Vol. 27, pp. 379–423, 623–656, July, October, 1948.

Iterative Theology: Progressive Revelation as the String Theory of Religious Studies

Andres Elvira Espinoza

Some, if not all, of the most important moral, philosophical, and practical questions that human beings can ask can be encompassed by the twin domains of religion and the sciences. The fact that the modern academic and social milieu has declared both domains to be hermetic subjects of interest with no relationship or parallels — or as competing, mutually exclusive beliefs systems between which individuals must necessarily choose — only grants greater urgency in understanding if and how these two domains of investigation, discovery, and action can be reconciled in a constructive and realistic manner. If science and religion are actually two separate domains — as is the current underlying assumption in academic and popular discussion — then is one superior to the other? By what standard? Is science merely another choice of worldview, a religion unto itself? Or is there a truth in religion not found in any of the sciences, or vice versa? Indeed, are both flawed and incomplete, and if this is so, is the choice of being a "believer" in science or God a matter of mere personal preference with no objective truth? As the world moves towards a state of greater racial and religious unity while taking one step back for every two forward, it is also becoming more polarized between two conflicting philosophical stances: one which seems to accept the religion of scientific investigation while rejecting all theological, spiritual, and nonmaterial beliefs as outmoded shibboleths[1] of primitive human-

---

[1] The term "outworn shibboleth" is used several times by the Beloved Guardian, Shoghi Effendi, to describe any custom, principle or belief characterizing some culture or group of people which is regarded as historically valuable, but now outmoded or obsolete. In these cases, He attributes this description to religious laws, ordinances, and dogmas which no longer serve their intended purpose.

ity, and one which seems to adhere to a fundamentalist fideism resisting entropy by reviving old shibboleths and preserving them by rejecting all intellectual inquiry as blasphemous.

The Bahá'í literature of the authoritative Central Figures is unambiguous on its posture regarding the relationship between the sciences and religion. 'Abdu'l-Bahá, the Beloved Master and Exemplar of the Faith, declares that

> [...] we may think of science as one wing and religion as the other; a bird needs two wings for flight, one alone would be useless. Any religion that contradicts science or that is opposed to it, is only ignorance — for ignorance is the opposite of knowledge,

and that "religion *truly* so-called does not oppose knowledge".[2] The implications of this statement are that the two distinct disciplines and viewpoints are complimentary rather than conflicting despite popular assumption, as both are considered to be the repositories of real knowledge rather than a denial of knowledge. While the analogy of the bird makes the concept of "theo-scientific harmony"[3] clear to Bahá'ís, there remains the issue of how such a model can be elucidated in the public and academic discourses, as the concept is new to the modern intellectual paradigm. There are few, if any, examples of science and religion being adequately or satisfactorily reconciled in modern discourse, and no independent school of thought in philosophy or theology which relates to the Bahá'í concept of theo-scientific

---

[2] 'Abdu'l-Bahá. *Paris Talks*. (Wilmette: Bahá'í Publishing Trust, 1912), 207. Original emphasis.

[3] This is my chosen terminology, which I believe to be the most morphologically precise description of the Bahá'í position on the unity of science and religion. Science is descriptive and religion prescriptive, but both share the commonality of emerging from the same reality, necessitating the congruence of conclusions arrived at from the study of both. Ergo a dialogue between them is possible, ergo giving them intrinsic complementarity. May also be called "theo-scientific complementarity", but this may overlook any interactions between the two domians which extend beyond complementarity.

harmony or Progressive Revelation. This is likely due to the fact that most of these attempted reconciliations necessarily emerge from particular religious traditions which are rooted in very ancient — and therefore limited — mindsets and understandings of the world: Abrahamic, Dharmic, and all of the innumerable sects and offshoots thereof. In addition, the domains of science and religion tend — though not exhaustively — to be distinct in seemingly incompatible ways: the domain of science tends to be descriptive and concerned with purely physical realities, while the domain of religion tends to be prescriptive and concerned primarily with intangible and supernatural realities with moral and ritual implications, with some social and relational implications.[4] How, then, can the idea of theo-scientific harmony be introduced into the academic and popular forums in a way which is satisfactory to the scientist, the theologian, and the scholar of all subjects?

One component of Bahá'í theology stands distinct from the majority of the world's major faith traditions: Progressive Revelation. The basic idea of Progressive Revelation is that religion is not static or unique, but changes and evolves in an overall linear fashion through cycles of divine revelation, all originated by a singular God and channeled through a human Manifestation. According to Bahá'ís, these manifestations include Krishna (Hinduism), Buddha (Buddhism), Zarathustra (Zoroastrianism), Moses (Judaism), Christ (Christianity), Muhammad (Islam), and the most recent Twin Manifestations of the Bahá'í Dispensation, the Báb and Bahá'u'lláh.[5] While more about this model of the-

---

[4] This modern dichotomy between science and religion requires two important considerations: 1) the common assumption of the human mind as a primarily (or exhaustively) physical phenomenon, thus categorizing it among the physical sciences, and 2) religion having some descriptive elements, especially in the sense of determining the existence of supernatural phenomena.

[5] 'Abdu'l-Bahá. *The Promulgation of Universal Peace: Talks Delivered by 'Abdu'l-Bahá during His Visit to the United States and Canada in 1912.* Comp. Howard MacNutt. (Wilmette: U. S. Bahá'í Publishing Trust, 1982), 488–9.

ology will be elaborated upon in this article, its immediate implications are clear: a plurality of religions exists not merely by artifice but by jointly divine origin, placing into question the exclusivist idea that only one religion is intrinsically true and the rest are wrong or "traps of the devil." Aside from Islam and some debatable examples in the Dharmic faiths, no other religious tradition, Abrahamic or Dharmic, approaches this broad degree of revelatory acceptance. However, it is exactly this novelty which provides an avenue for the dissemination of the concept of Progressive Revelation.

If science and religion truly are complimentary and harmonious, then there must be some parallel between them, be it methodological, ontological, epistemological, or all three. Progressive Revelation flies in the face of the entrenched idea that the religions of the world possess irreconcilable interests and that either one must be right, or all of them wrong. Yet science possesses a quantum of that reconciliation in the depths of theoretical physics: the ceaseless hunt for a grand unified field theory; a "theory of everything."[6] While physicists seek a fundamental model from which all physical phenomena may be explained, religious studies seek no analogous single point of unity for the religions. This is where the conduit to the academic and popular forums rests: Progressive Revelation as a spiritual analogue to the scientific theory of everything; a "unified field theory of religion." Both remain distinct epistemological domains, but they describe the same reality, and therefore both may affect the execution and conclusions of the other in ways which are congruent with their respective epistemic and ontological concerns (i.e. spiritual and material facets of one underlying Reality). If such a model can be established, then further inquiry into the concept of Progressive Revelation can be pursued beyond the confines of Bahá'í scholarship and begin a new paradigm of mainstream theo-scientific harmony.

---

[6] Stephen Hawking, *The Illustrated Brief History of Time.* New York: Bantam, 1988, 96–7.

Of course, the words "science" and "religion" can mean different things to different people in different contexts. Thus, it will be necessary to elucidate on these two terms before scrutinizing the concept of Progressive Revelation itself.

SCIENCE OVER TIME

The popular understanding of science arose around the thirteenth century as the "scientific method": the study of the natural world through a process of hypothesis, experimentation, analysis, discussion, further hypothesis, and so on.[7] This usually, tacitly assumes a logical positivist position on the definition of science, in which only directly observable and experiential phenomena are regarded as real and true.[8] Bahá'í literature would recognize this as the domain of "material science [...] the investigation of natural phenomena."[9] However, it is important to note that there is more to science than the collection of facts, as understanding of the facts by scientists have changed over time. Practices, such as alchemy, which were regarded as mainstream science in their times are now regarded as obsolete pseudosciences, a phenomenon which logical positivism cannot account for. How science is done, and how science *should* be done, are far more complicated matters than simply gathering data and drawing value-free conclusions devoid of bias. The science of yesterday is not the same as the science of today.

In 1962, Thomas Kuhn introduced a paradigm-based model of scientific evolution, which functioned to describe the changes in the theory and practice of the sciences over time and their implications for the practice of modern science. He argued that all science necessarily takes place within a "paradigm": a de facto collection of theories, models, and underlying assumptions which

---

[7] Hugh G. Gauch Jr., *Scientific Method in Practice*. (Cambridge: Cambridge University Press, 2002), 41.
[8] Helen Longino, *Science as Social Knowledge: Values and Objectivity in Scientific Inquiry*, (Princeton: Princeton University Press, 1990), 22.
[9] *Promulgation*, 195–6.

shape how data is gathered, recorded, and analyzed, within which "normal science" takes place.[10] No paradigm is, nor can it be, perfect and will contain anomalies which accepted theories will fail to explain, but which will be insufficient to outweigh the overwhelming volume of phenomena that the theories can successfully explain. Over time, as data-gathering techniques advance and older generations of theorists are replaced by innovative thinkers, theories are challenged, data interpretation changes, and new theories are discovered which explain the anomalies in the old paradigm while explaining all phenomena encompassed by the now-superseded theories. Thus, a new paradigm of normal science replaces the old.[11] Examples of these "paradigm-shifts" include the replacement of alchemy with inorganic chemistry, phlogistonic chemistry with combustion chemistry, astrology with astronomy, the Ptolemaic solar model with the Copernican, Aristotelian gravity with Newtonian gravity, Lamarckian evolution by Darwinian evolution, and continental drift by plate tectonics. Kuhn's approach emphasized a subjective element of science, in which science was subject to change over time as the "cold facts" of reality were seen through new qualitative and quantitative lenses. It explained why science changes through history, while also explaining science in a normative sense: science is legitimate when it is performed within the current paradigm of normal science, for however long it lasts. If every ongoing paradigm were routinely challenged, then the minutiae of research within that paradigm would never develop, but shifts are nonetheless necessary for science to progress.[12]

However, despite the appeal of a paradigm model of scientific revolutions, Kuhn was never able to explain the idea of scientific progress in anything other than social terms. He emphasized how theories are replaced due less to new and innovative ways

---

[10] Thomas Kuhn, *The Structure of Scientific Revolutions*. (Chicago: University of Chicago Press, 2012), 11.
[11] Ibid, 64, 68.
[12] Alan Chalmers, *What Is This Thing Called Science?* (Indianapolis: Hackett Publishing, 1976), 118.

of gathering data (e.g. telescopes, microscopes, etc.) and more to social changes, such as the death of one generation of theorists whose prestige and employment depended on the truth of a theory. Paradigm shifts become more like religious conversions or political coups than the result of careful, impartial, and dispassionate study.[13] In addition, Kuhn was also devoted to a clause of incommensurability between the theories, and insisted that one characteristic of a paradigm was that it could not simultaneously be true with its predecessor; for example, geocentrism and heliocentrism.[14] If absolute incommensurability is true, then no paradigm could be said to build upon another, no matter how closely their theories are related or how much of a superseded paradigm is explained by its successor. Kuhn was also unable to present an objective, non-relativistic standard by which a paradigm was determined to be truer or better than its predecessor. Whether a paradigm was true depended on a social consensus that it was so, which left the relative truth of paradigms vulnerable to a subjective and fallible "majority rules" standard of scientific revolutions.[15] Other alternatives — such as the "research programmes" of Imre Lakatos — arose as attempts to dampen the social dimension of the Kuhnian model and enhance the objective empirical criterion of assessing the relative superiority of paradigms.[16]

For the purposes of this article, we will overlook the imperfections in Kuhn's model, ignore particular alternatives by other philosophers of science, and focus on its primary strength of being both normative and descriptive. The paradigm model illustrates what science is supposed to be while also explaining why the history of science has progressed in the way that it has. By creating an objective sense of progress towards which scientific theory and experiment is intended, science can then be characterized as relative in the sense of the progressive discovery of physical phenom-

---

[13] Chalmers, 122–3.
[14] Longino, 27.
[15] Chalmers, 122.
[16] Ibid, 141.

ena, but also objective in the sense that this progress is not socially determined, but linear towards an incrementally clearer picture of material truth. Absolute truth is not necessarily possible, but one can continuously approach a near-omniscient state of material understanding without actually attaining it, akin to how the limit of a function infinitely approaches the value of zero without ever actually reaching it. Some literature in the philosophy of science refers to this stance as "realism."[17]

Science, as understood in this manner, is a methodology which serves to understand natural, material reality through observation and experimentation. That is to say, it is an impartial *method* for accomplishing some tasks as opposed to a *worldview* which determines value, meaning, and guidance for action. The idea of science as a worldview diametrically opposed to religion and any spiritual belief system has been referred to as "scientism" and is sometimes considered an overreach or misconstrual of science, as it rests on the claim that anything which cannot be either proven or falsified by empirical analysis is nonexistent or fully relativistic by default (e.g. God, soul, transcendence, morality, meaning, a purpose to life, etc.).[18] However, the purely methodological conception of science precludes a number of ideological qualities which are integral to the practice of scientific inquiry without appeal to a materialist or atheistic worldview. For example, in order to draw conclusions from data, the scientist must accept the validity, and follow the logic of, deductive and inductive rational modalities rather than draw conclusions based upon her emotional urges or ideological needs.[19] The scientist must also assume that there is, in fact, a material reality that exist independently of herself, and that it is possible to gather evidence of this external reality to draw conclusions about how it actually works.[20] The idea that she is the constant victim of a Cartesian

---

[17] Ibid, 238.
[18] Massimo Pigliucci, "New Atheism and the Scientific Turn in the Atheist Movement," *Midwest Studies in Philosophy*, 37, no. 1 (2013): 144.
[19] Gauch, 21–3, 26–7.
[20] Longino, 62.

Evil Genius[21] constantly manipulating her senses and deduction to lead her from the truth, while philosophically interesting, would serve no function in the practice of science and would render her empirical projects meaningless. Most importantly, the scientist must believe that truth statements regarding reality are possible, thus rejecting global skepticism and metaphysical solipsism.[22] These qualities are not a *de jure* litany for scientists, but they follow by implication of the nature of science as a discipline of empirical discovery and inquiry. Thus, while science may be a methodology rather than a worldview, the methodology of science invariably possesses worldview import which normatively guides the conduct of scientists towards practicing science in a manner that is as objective and unbiased as humanly possible, which in turn contributes to the progression of science towards ever-complete pictures of material reality.

For the purposes of this discussion, it is also relevant to note how the worldview import of science encompasses the social paradigm in which it is practiced. Science invariably takes place within some cultural milieu which imports further background assumptions into how data is gathered, experiments set up, and results interpreted, making all theory inextricably value-laden.[23] Experiments, data gathering, data interpretation, and analysis do not occur in an ideological vacuum. The heliocentric solar model was based upon a prescientific cosmology which gave Earth a special position in the whole of physical existence, with the conclusion of circular orbits based upon the background assumption of the circle being an ideal shape to contain energy. The practice of eugenics betrays a philosophical anthropology which determines the value of human lives based upon their

---

[21] In his *Meditations of First Philosophy*, René Descartes proposed the thought-experiment of some malevolent entity who was deceiving him as to the truth of his senses and rational faculties. He concluded that if any truth experience could be forged by this entity, then the only experience that he could be certain of was that he had a self which was experiencing these experiences, leading to his famous declaration: "*Cogito ergo sum.*"

[22] Gauch, 23–5.

[23] Longino, 44.

physiological or genetic health, capabilities, or appearance. To attempt to draw conclusions in a vacuum, from "raw" data, external to a socio-cultural and ideological paradigm, is to perpetuate the background assumptions of that paradigm without conscious awareness, as an ideal absence of assumptions is cognitively impossible.[24] The discussion of worldview above illustrates how even science itself rests on some worldviews import akin to a socio-cultural paradigm. The issue is not the presence of a socio-cultural paradigm within the practice of science, but to determine what socio-cultural background assumptions are the most just and equitable to serve as background assumptions in the interpretation of data.[25] The only question remaining is what assumptions — those unspoken values — are ideal.

It is important to note the paradox of this account of science: because scientific truth is subject to an evolving understanding of the physical world and historically-relative sociocultural background assumptions, it has a relative nature, but still cannot be allowed to deviate from an objectively progressive knowledge base aiming towards greater truth. Therefore, science is both durable and evolutionary simultaneously. Theory is subject to change, but only in one direction. This paradox will become essential to our understanding of Progressive Revelation.

WHOSE RELIGION?

Religion is a more challenging definition to defend. Etymologically, the term "religion" might be drawn from different possible origins. The Latin phrase *"religio"* refers to "respect for what is sacred, reverence for the gods [...] a mode of worship;

---

[24] Ibid, 218.
[25] For more on the idea of "contextual empiricism", see Longino (1990). Her ultimate conclusion is that the notion of objectivity in science must by socially constructed and that to eliminate as much bias as possible, plurality of worldviews and ideologies — within limits — must be involved in the practice of science. While her discussion is highly congruent with the Bahá'í project of unity in diversity, it is far beyond the scope of this passage.

sanctity, holiness."[26] Modern writers seem to favor the term *"religare"*, "to bind."[27] Both of these etymologies imply two distinct definitions of "religion": the former supernatural, the latter social. The broadest definition is described by functionalism, which defines religion as any cultural phenomena which unites adherents into a community independent of geographical region, integrates the individual's conscious will, generates collective sentiment, and provides a meaning — or means to attain a meaning — to the individual's life.[28] This is congruent with the etymology that religion "binds" or unites people with a common interest into a distinctive unit. This is a very broad definition of religion, more concerned with what a religion does to and for its adherents rather than the details of any underlying belief system and can encompass numerous forms of social activity which are not commonly associated with religious practice: philosophies like Confucianism, Stoicism, and Pythagoreanism, political parties, social clubs, college fraternities and sororities, Twitter followings, and fan bases for sports, movies, and television shows. Because of the concern with practice over belief, this definition is more flexible and can expand the range of what constitutes a religion into new precedents.[29]

Alternatively, substantivism defines religion ontologically in terms of the particular belief system shared among its adherents and specifies that the substance of those beliefs must involve supernatural components: if not a God or gods, then souls, ancestral or nature spirits, magic, etc.[30] This definition encompasses all sects of the Dharmic and Abrahamic religions, most cults and new religious movements, ancient polytheism, and all forms of animism, shamanism, fetishism, and totemism. It is concerned

---

[26] "Religion." OED Online, (Oxford: Oxford University Press, March 2021), https://www.oed.com/viewdictionaryentry/Entry/161944.

[27] Sarah F. Hoyt, "The Etymology of Religion," *Journal of the American Oriental Society* 32, no. 2 (1912): 126.

[28] Kevin Schilbrack, "What Isn't Religion?", *Journal of Religion* 93, no. 3, (2013): 293-4.

[29] Ibid, 294.

[30] Ibid.

not with what religious adherents do, but with what they believe in, and qualifies the anthropological definition of religion as "supernaturalism."[31] Naturally, a supernaturalist definition of religion is also intrinsically nonscientific, as it involves entities and forces which cannot be verified — or potentially falsified — by empirical analysis and inquiry.

Interestingly, the Bahá'í literature provides a conception of religion which is congruous with both. One the one hand, when the unity of religions is mentioned, it specifically mentions the "chain of successive Revelations that hath linked the Manifestation of Adam with that of the Báb."[32] The implications are that these religions are supernaturalist in origin and belief, and that "religion" encompasses any and all belief systems created by any such Manifestations as have visited the Earth, although nine major world religions tend to stand out for their modern demographic density and influence.[33] However, one statement by Shoghi Effendi, in *The Promised Day Has Come*, seems to imply that other social, political, or cultural phenomena can fill the role of these religions when their purpose is forgotten or artificially annulled, thus implying at least a normatively conditional functionalist definition:

> The chief idols in the desecrated temple of mankind are none other than the triple gods of Nationalism, Racialism and Communism, at whose altars the governments and peoples, whether democratic or totalitarian, at peace or at war, of the East or of the West, Christian or Islamic, are, in various forms and in different degrees, now worshipping. Their high priests are the politicians and worldly-wise, the so-called sages of the age; their sacrifice, the flesh and blood of the slaughtered multitudes; their incantations outworn shibboleths

---

[31] Clifford Geertz, "Religion," in *Magic, Witchcraft, and Religion*, ed. Pamela A. Moro and James E. Myers (New York: McGraw Hill, 2010), 1.
[32] Bahá'u'lláh, *Gleanings from the Writings of Bahá'u'lláh*, (Wilmette: Bahá'í Publishing Trust, 1952), 74.
[33] *Promulgation*, 276.

and insidious and irreverent formulas; their incense, the smoke of anguish that ascends from the lacerated hearts of the bereaved, the maimed, and the homeless.[34]

However, the tone of this passage emphasizes how such surrogate religions, however much they may analogize the devotion, sentiment, and community characterizing religious membership, are considered metaphysically and morally unworthy substitutes to the original, functional purpose of "true religion": "to safeguard the interests and promote the unity of the human race, and to foster the spirit of love and fellowship amongst men."[35] Thus, the Bahá'í definition is an integrated functionalist-substantivist definition: 1) substantively, religion is exclusively those religions catalyzed by the Manifestations of God towards the divine goal of unity, harmony, and peace among peoples, while 2) functionally, religion — worthy of being considered religion — must unite and promote human welfare universally and non-exclusively, and not divide and compromise human welfare at any scale. A human-created movement or belief system can act analogously to a religion but cannot fulfill the normative moral objectives of the Divine Will and is thus disqualified as "true" religion, whatever its ideological specifics. This will serve as the working definition for the purposes of this passage, as will be essential during the discussion of Progressive Revelation.

SCIENCE AND RELIGION IN TANDEM

There are four basic models for how the domains of science and religion interact: conflict, independence, dialogue, and integration.[36] The conflict model holds that science and religion are inherently contradictory, and that one must necessarily be true and

---

[34] Shoghi Effendi, *The Promised Day Is Come*, (Wilmette: Bahá'í Publishing Trust, 1996), 185–6.
[35] Bahá'u'lláh. *Tablets of Bahá'u'lláh*. (Haifa: Bahá'í World Center, 1978), 168.
[36] Ian Barbour, *When Science Meets Religion: Enemies, Strangers, or Partners?* (San Francisco: HarperOne, 2000), 2–4.

other false, but neither simultaneously. Under this model, one must eventually be proven wrong and the other right, but they describe the same reality, even if in two mutually exclusive ways.[37] The independence model was best exemplified by Stephen Jay Gould in his seminal paper on "non-overlapping magisteria" (NOMA). Under this model, science and religion describe two different realities — one empirical and material, the other moral and transcendent — and thus beliefs based upon them can be simultaneously true without contradiction.[38] Under this model, instances of scientism and fundamentalist accounts of Biblical "Creation science" can be explained as overreach of the two magisteria: one an attempt by science to comment on religious topics (morality and meaning), the other an attempt by religion to comment on the extra-religious topic of scientific cosmology. One may hold both scientific and religious beliefs in juxtaposition, but never the twain shall meet.

The dialogue model proposes that there is common ground between religion and science, and therefore both can strengthen the other through exchanges of ideas and approaches. Notably, both domains are theory-dependent and rely upon approximations of reality — models and metaphors — for individuals to understand truth.[39] For example, the doctrine of Original Sin was never explicitly stated in Genesis but was interpreted from the Genesis story as the result of the temptation of Adam. Likewise, gravity has no tangible substance, and thus the study of gravity has resorted to equations, models of space-time curvature and — more recently — on interferometric measurements.[40] Science and religion remain distinct but overlap. The integration model attempts to unify religion and science partially or completely, blur-

---

[37] Ibid, 10–11.
[38] Stephen Jay Gould, "Nonoverlapping Magisteria", *Natural History* 106, no. 2 (1997): 4.
[39] Barbour, 23–7.
[40] B.P Abbot, et al., "GW170814: A Three-Detector Observation of Gravitational Waves from a Binary Black Hole Coalescence," *Physical Review Letters* 119, no. 14 (2017): 141101–9.

ring the distinctions between them more than the other models. This model proposes that scientific progress may be capable of commenting upon or verifying theological elements through the empirical analysis of clues in the natural world.[41] "Creation science" would fall under this purview: the thesis that proof of non-evolutionary intelligent design can be found in the natural world which are unaccounted for by a Natural Selection model of biological change over time.

The Bahá'í concept of theo-scientific harmony seems to favor a dialogue model, as religion and science share the common ground of a single reality. Bahá'í literature insists that

> there is no contradiction between true religion and science. When a religion is opposed to science it becomes mere superstition: that which is contrary to knowledge is ignorance [...] The Unity of God is logical and this idea is not antagonistic to the conclusions arrived at by scientific study.[42]

They further state that "material science is the investigation of natural phenomena; divine science is the discovery and realization of spiritual verities."[43] Therefore, science and religion/theology remain distinct domains even as they interact, but they retain the common ground of describing the same reality, one from a material and the other from a spiritual standpoint. Bahá'í studies would likely reject a fully integrative model of theo-scientific harmony, as the Writings make clear that God Himself is "sanctified above all comprehension and imagining", and that "Divinity [...] must be unknown with regard to its essence and known only with respect to its attributes."[44] Therefore, the Bahá'í Faith assumes a locally skeptical posture with regards to direct inter-

---
[41] Barbour, 27–8.
[42] 'Abdu'l-Bahá, *Paris Talks*, (Wilmette: Bahá'í Publishing Trust, 1912), 226.
[43] *Promulgation*, 195–6.
[44] 'Abdu'l-Bahá, *Some Answered Questions*, (Haifa: Bahá'í World Center, 2014), 325.

course with God. While the reality of God's Creations (material reality) might be known in their totality, God Himself is beyond the scrutiny of empirical observation and formulation, placing belief in Him exclusively in the domain of faith and not scientific knowledge. This also frees Bahá'ís from dependence on gaps within human knowledge as proof of design in material reality: Kuhn's paradigm model illustrates how those "gaps" or anomalies in theories are not durable phenomena, as superseding paradigms are likely to erase most or all of those anomalies with the advent of greater explanatory power.

Just how integrative the Bahá'í account of theo-scientific harmony can become is beyond the scope of this article. As of now, a significant hurdle in proving this harmoniousness (the plurality of religions) may be overcome by a description of the scientific nature of Progressive Revelation. To begin that process, it is essential to understand how the history of science analogizes the principle of Unity in the Bahá'í Faith in the form of integration from greater diversity to greater harmony.

FROM DIVERSITY TO UNITY

View the natural world from the lens of an ancient mind with no conception of law, order, civilization, or material reality. Your surrounding environment is chaotic and hostile. Hundreds of plants, all of them different in form, scent, and taste. Water flows in river and lakes, the sky is constantly changing with the strange shapes of clouds rolling by, and fluid occasionally falls from the sky. There are animals, all different, with various forms and behaviors, some herbivorous, some carnivorous, some massive and imposing, others tiny and annoying. Countless substances, from rocks of all shapes, sizes, and colors, to the woods and barks of trees, to soil under your feet. This is a world of too much diversity, too many *things*. How do you cope with so much chaos?

As you begin learning how to exist in this world, your cognition begins to systemize and categorize the things around you.

Some plants have specific uses, while others are to be avoided. Animals come as either dangerous or not dangerous, then as meat-eating or plant-eating, then as fur- or scale-covered. Rocks feel different to touch and some break more easily than others. As you satisfy your basic survival needs and begin thriving, you have the cognitive freedom to realize the integration of the world into models or catalogues of increasing simplicity. Whatever their variations, plants are plants and animals are animals. The phenomena of rivers, lakes, rain, and clouds are reduced to the singular phenomenon of "water." Slowly, but surely, you are realizing that the seeming chaos of the forms of Nature are in fact reducible to fewer and smaller sets of explanations.

Millennia passes. You are now part of a complex civilization with technology that enables you a greater understanding of your world than ever before. What seemed like an infinity of substances can be reduced to a single Periodic Table which explains all matter in the universe, and then to a total of three species of subatomic particles. A taxonomic classification system reduces all species of living things at all scales to six biological kingdoms and three major domains. The forces that govern objects on your planet are exactly the same which govern the movements of all the celestial bodies, which can also be categorized in relatively simple classification schemes despite their unthinkable multitude: planets, stars, nebulae, asteroids, galaxies. With the advent of laser interferometry, particle colliders, and electron microscopes, you are approaching the current limit of human understanding, where all objects, phenomena, and fundamental forces in the universe become explicable by two simple scientific theories: General Relativity, and the Standard Model of particle physics.

This is the beauty and power of science: the ability to explain the greatest number and depth of natural phenomena by the most parsimonious theories. Science has reached the limit of explanations for all physical phenomena. Relativity encompasses gravity and galactic-scale space-time, while the Standard Model encompasses all fundamental particles (and by proxy, the electromagnetic force), the strong and weak nuclear forces, and all quantum behaviors thereof. This is why string theory became so well known in theoretical physics: it is an attempt to reconcile the contradictory, but mutually proven, paradigms of the Relativistic and quantum forces, into a single grand unified theory; a "theory of everything."[45,46] Science has reduced the diversity of reality into a few simple explanations, and that has given strength to science since its inception.

Only one impossible task remains: How can this be done for religion?

Look at the domain of religion from the perspective of the modern milieu. The population is divided into adherents of numerous world religions, sects of those religions, and sects within sects, all claiming legitimacy and rightness, oftentimes denying the reality and truth of all others. They are highly divergent, and whatever similarities existent between them are grossly outweighed by the variations. They arose from diverse geographic regions. Their originators came from various cultures and taught different principles of conduct. Even those who can accept the parallels between some of the religious traditions find themselves hard-pressed to find parallels between the overarching paradigms of the Abrahamic and Dharmic traditions. The Abrahamic traditions accept a Creator God separate from material reality, while the Dharmic traditions accept an Absolute power which can be impersonal or pantheist. The Abrahamic traditions teach that evil is "sin" or a violation of divine laws which are punished by God, while the Dharmic traditions teach that evil is ignorance and attachment to materiality, which independently punishes evildoers without external intervention. The *telos* of the Abrahamic traditions is salvation from perdition at the end of life, while the *telos* of the Dharmic traditions is to detach from materi-

---

[45] Hawking, 215–17.

[46] It should be noted that string theory is only one of at least two competing theories of everything, including quantum loop gravity. As it is impossible to know which theory is true at this time, string theory is sometimes used synonymously with "unified field theory" or "grand unified theory."

al existence and break the cycle of reincarnation.[47] Hinduism appears primarily polytheistic, the Abrahamic Faiths monotheistic, while the Catholic Doctrine of the Trinity remains controversial among Christians for its implied pluralism despite the Catholic commitment to monotheism.[48,49] Some schools of Buddhism, notably Theravada Buddhism, even deny any theistic component, placing further into question the meaningfulness of any peripheral parallels between any other faith traditions.[50] The *prima facie* conclusion to be drawn is that the religions possess no relevant similarities and have origins, principles, interests, and objectives far too diverse to ever be considered reconcilable. However, as has been illustrated, this was the *de facto* perceptive of an observable world full of seemingly divergent physical phenomena, now explicable by two major scientific models.

PROGRESSIVE REVELATION

The idea of Progressive Revelation is simple and — perhaps surprisingly to some — not new or exclusive to the Bahá'í Faith. It is the idea that the phenomenon of religion is not static or singular, as it is conventionally regarded in the Western Judeo-Christian paradigm, but evolutionary and relativistic according to the regional culture and time period in which a Manifestation of God visits. This is manifested in the plurality of the religions; there are many, and they are different, because they were meant for different places at different times, each one codifying "such laws and ordinances as conform to the imperative needs, and are dictated by the growing receptivity, of a fast evolving and constantly changing

---

[47] Moojan Momen, "Relativism: A Basis for Bahá'í Metaphysics," In *Studies in the Babi and Bahá'í Religions*, Vol. 5 of *Studies in the Babi and Bahá'í Religions*, (Los Angeles: Kalimat Press), 1988.

[48] Michael C. Rea, "Polytheism and Christian Belief," *The Journal of Theological Studies* 57, no.1 (2006): 133–4.

[49] Dale Tuggy, "The Unfinished Business of Trinitarian Theorizing," *Religious Studies* 39, no. 2 (2003): 165–6.

[50] Schilbrack, 314.

society [...]."⁵¹ A common analogy used among Bahá'ís is that of a schoolteacher with his pupils: the schoolteacher must be highly educated so as to expertly address any educational needs and concerns of the younger, less experienced students. It might appear to the students — as they are of a vastly inferior understanding of the subject — that their teacher understands only as much as he is instructing them, when in fact he knows far more than they can hope to understand at their current stage of life. They may wish to be instructed in calculus, but there is no hope of their competence until they have mastered their arithmetic. As they advance in grade, the students become progressively more aware of, and competent in, a variety of disciplines, again from instructors who have much greater understanding than themselves. In exactly this same way, the various Manifestations of God⁵² serve the roles of teachers guiding humanity towards the goal of greater unity, peace, and justice at incremental grades which are tailored to the "progressive capacity, the ever-increasing spiritual receptiveness, which mankind, in its progress towards maturity, has invariably manifested."⁵³ Even the Bahá'í Dispensation is accepted by its adherents as being one more such grade, distinct only in its adaptation to the current capacities of a world very different from any predecessor, which will eventually be superseded by another far into the future.

Few of the past religions share such a posture regarding other major religious traditions, and perhaps the most important is the Islamic concept of "national prophethood." The Holy Qur'an states

---

⁵¹ Shoghi Effendi, *God Passes By*, (Wilmette: Bahá'í Publishing Trust, 1994), 155.

⁵² While the Bahá'í canon recognizes nine major Manifestations and their respective religions, it does not preclude the possibility that some figures in indigenous religions — including some "cultural heroes" and mythical figures — may have been Manifestations with their histories obscured and embellished by the passage of time. Shoghi Effendi, quoted in Hornby, affirms that Manifestations have existed whose names are (and may remain) unknown, and other Manifestations may be recognized by the historical record who are not explicitly mentioned in the Writings (Hornby 503).

⁵³ Shoghi Effendi, *The World Order of Bahá'u'lláh*, (Wilmette: Bahá'í Publishing Trust, 1938), 166

that "...for every nation there is a messenger."[54] Interestingly, it further states that "Say: We believe in Allah and (in) that which has been revealed to us, and (in) that which was revealed to Abraham, and Ishmael and Isaac and Jacob and the tribes, and (in) that which was given to Moses and Jesus [...] we do not make any distinction between any of them and to him do we submit", and "We make no difference between any of His messengers",

> Those who disbelieve in Allah and His messengers and desire to make a distinction between Allah and His messengers and say: We believe in some and disbelieve in others [...] These are truly disbelievers.[55,56,57]

The Islamic concept of prophethood is manifested on a national scale, whereby Manifestations were sent by God to individual clans, tribes, and nations so as to spiritually uplift and unite the highly tribal humanity of the ancient world, with the goal of the unity of these tribes into a "brotherhood of man."[58] Thus, the religion of Islam accepts all of the prophets of the Judeo-Christian tradition, as well as a number of lesser-known figures named in the Qur'an, and is open to the possibility that other prophets— unrecorded by history or lost to the embellishment of legend— have existed, unrecognized, in other parts of the world. Christianity stops short of Islam, accepting Jesus Christ as having been prophesized by Moses, a concept which is rejected by Judaism.[59,60,.61] The Bahá'í Faith simply extends the

---

[54] Holy Qur'an, 10:47.
[55] Ibid, 2:136
[56] Ibid, 2:285.
[57] Ibid, 4:150–1.
[58] Maulana Muhammad Ali, *The Religion of Islam*, Rowland Heights: S. Chan & Co. (Pvt.) Ltd., 1990). 223-4.
[59] John 1:45.
[60] C. Umhau Wolf, "Moses in Christian and Islamic Tradition," *Journal of Bible and Religion* 27, no. 2 (1959): 106.
[61] John 1:45 specifically reads: 'Philip told Nathaniel, "We have found the one about whom Moses wrote in the law, and also the prophets, Jesus, Jesus, son of Joseph, from Nazareth."'

Progressive Revelation of Islam much further retrogressively, including explicit mention of the Dharmic Faiths of Hinduism and Buddhism, and of future revelation being foretold from its inception. The closest analogues in the Dharmic religions include some Buddhist schools which teach a history of successive Buddhahood, and some Hindu schools acknowledging multiple Avatars who visited (and will visit) humanity but lack direct commentary on the truth of other religions.[62] Bahá'í Progressive Revelation is the only conception of plural prophethood which avows a canon of specific religious lineage in addition to other Manifestations unknown to the historical record.

Can this be proven? An exhaustive study of possible parallels between all of the nine major faiths is not only beyond the scope of this article, but is also largely unavailable, as the idea of Progressive Revelation is not a common area of study in mainstream theology — a status quo which this article is intended to challenge. However, one particular component ubiquitous to the major faiths can be scrutinized as a parallel between all of their belief systems: eschatological prophecy. In every major faith system, there is some sense of anticipation for the advent of a redeeming figure who will revitalize that faith, usually for the entire world, and usually at an "end time" for humanity or material existence. As is commonly known, Christians of all sects and denominations eagerly await the return of Jesus Christ when a Final Judgment is called upon humanity. However, this quality is shared by Muslims and Jews. The Jews await a figure mentioned

---

[62] The Jain concept of *anekantavada* (sometimes translated as "many-pointedness") has been considered a type of spiritual relativism which could accommodate tolerance for other faiths. However, its enablement of tolerance is heavily debated in religious studies, as is its ability to accommodate a progressive revelatory model of iterative religious unfoldment. The concept is more akin to the idea that the fallibility of human knowledge precludes any doctrine or ideology from monopolizing truth. For more information on the Jain concept and the debate, see, John E. Cort, "Intellectual Ahimsa: Jain Tolerance and Intolerance of Others," *University of Hawai'i Press* 50, no. 3 (2000): 234–47.

in the Old Testament referred to as the "Prince of Peace".[63] Sunni Muslims await the Mahdi, the "Rightly Guided One", a descendant of the Prophet Muhammad (p.b.u.m.), who will arrive at the Apocalypse, and fight and defeat the Antichrist alongside the Christ.[64,65] The Shi'a traditions have an analogous prophecy regarding the Occultation of the Twelfth Imam, who is said to have remained in hiding from the 'Abbasid Caliphs for centuries, and will end His Occultation at the end times, similar to the Mahdi.[66] Many schools of Buddhism also await their own redeemer, in the form of the Maitreya or "fifth Buddha."[67,68] The Zoroastrians await the Shah Bahram, another messianic figure.[69] While not exhaustive, this parallel is shockingly similar between faiths which arose in different regions under different circumstances and taught different principles and cosmologies. However, according to Bahá'í Scripture, it is exactly this belief which offers the first quantum of proof that they all share single origins, as the Twin Manifestations of the Bahá'í Dispensation fulfill those prophecies, thus enabling the process of the integration of the religions to begin.[70]

The ontological, epistemological, and moral implications of Progressive Revelation are enormous. Firstly, it would negate

---

[63] "For a child is born to us, a son is given us; upon his shoulder dominion rests. They name him Wonder-Counselor, God-Hero, Father-Forever, Prince of Peace" (Isiah 9:5).

[64] Zeki Saritoprak, "The Mahdi Tradition in Islam: A Socio-Cognitive Approach," *Islamic Studies* 41, no. 4, (2002): 653–4.

[65] It must be noted that the prophecy of the Mahdi does not originate from the Qur'an itself, but from several sources in Hadith, the secondary sources of Muhammad's words and deeds. It is also important to note that the term "Mahdi" has also been used to describe Muslims of exemplary character, analogous, though not identical, to bodhisattvas in Buddhism and saints in Catholicism (Saritoprak 653).

[66] Shi'i Islam.

[67] *God Passes By*, 94–5.

[68] Moojan Momen, "Buddhism and the Bahá'í Faith." Bahá'í Library Online, last modified November 25, 2016, https://bahai-library.com/momen_encyclopedia_buddhism.

[69] Christopher Buck, "Bahá'u'lláh as Zoroastrian Savior," *The Bahá'í Studies Review* 8, (1998): 21.

[70] *Some Answered Questions*, 53–65.

all claims of the superiority of one religion over another, and even subvert the thesis that any of the religions are more right or wrong than any other; all other factors being equal, the religions are merely older and newer, but never right or wrong. Secondly, it would mean that religion has a specific *telos* towards which its adherents are to progress, and thus would introduce objectivity in religious studies via a metric by which to evaluate the claims being made by rival sects, so as to deduce methods of scriptural apologetics congruent with that *telos*. Thirdly, and most essentially for this passage, if every religion was merely one grade in a single curriculum of spiritual evolution, then the numerous existent religions would be reducible to a single religion, revealed iteratively throughout history. This would theologically invalidate all forms of religious conflict and disagreement at all scales, and would establish the Bahá'í Faith, not as superior or inferior, but as timely.

The third implication is also important because it returns us to the role of science in making the world comprehensive through parsimony. The superficial diversity of natural phenomena has finally been reduced to two major theoretical models, all further discoveries necessarily falling into their parameters, leaving the only remaining breakthrough in the current understanding of science to be a theory of everything. Likewise, the diversity of the religions, beautiful in their rendering but regarded as irreconcilable and in perpetual conflict by the mainstream milieu, can be united under a framework of Progressive Revelation. If religion is understood as the means of a singular God to spiritually uplift and guide humanity towards greater degrees of unity, peace, justice, and progress, then the existence of all the religions has been understood by the simplest of explanations. The prescriptive and descriptive nature of the two domains persists, but the intrinsic nature of religious truth becomes identical with that of scientific truth: it is both relative (to the time and place that a religion originates, according to the capacities of humanity), and durable (part of a single, spiritual truth that is One continually unfolding Religion of One God).

Thus, the religions are unified under a single theological theory: a "theory of everything" for comparative theology. The descriptive power of science can be augmented through a dialogue with the cosmology and ethical constraint of religious teachings, while Scriptural exegesis and apologetics, and the execution of ethical laws, can be guided by dialogue with the objective, disinterested study of material reality. Two domains, operating in parallel, both oriented towards greater unity and progress in service of human endeavor. Most importantly, this information is available for all scholars to study freely and will not be limited to adherents to the Bahá'í Faith.

OBJECTIONS TO THE "ONENESS OF RELIGION" CLAUSE

Of course, there are likely to be some disagreements, from the domains of both science and religion, in the way that Progressive Revelation is analogized to scientific theoretical integration, and these disagreements may be similar across the two domains. Firstly, the scale and range of diversity among the religions is likely the first culprit for those who believe in the irreconcilability of the religions. As they are so diverse, oftentimes even having divergent theological accounts, the religions must be fully independent and cannot be regarded as having enough similarities to be part of a single Revelation; trying to make Hinduism one with Christianity is like trying to categorize dogs with cats because both have fur. A believer in Progressive Revelation will be quick to point out that there are several reasons why the religions are diverse both in practice and in substance. In terms of variation, be it moral or supernatural, the Bahá'í literature makes clear that:

> Religion has two main parts: (1) The Spiritual, (2) The Practical. The spiritual part never changes. All the Manifestations of God and His Prophets have taught the same truths and given the same spiritual law [...] The practical part of religion deals with exterior forms and

ceremonies, and with modes of punishment for certain offenses. This is the material side of the law and guides the customs and manners of the people.[71]

Therefore, although the letter of the law might be different, the spirit of the law is the same. Justice is one virtue, but necessity may demand harshness in harsher conditions and more lenience in others. It is justice, nonetheless, decreed by God as the time and place require it. The Master says:

> In the former days the punishment for theft was the cutting off of the right hand; in our time this law could not be so applied [...] It is therefore evident that whilst the spiritual law never alters, the practical rules must change their application with the necessities of the time.[72]

This form of application of universal principles to particular conditions is a form of relativism which is ubiquitous in the Bahá'í literature.

In order to understand this concept of relativism in Progressive Revelation, I propose a schema for the practical and substantive variations among the religions which might be helpful to avoid confusion between enduring spiritual principles and relative social laws:

- 1st order variations: Those laws, practices, customs, beliefs, and shibboleths which are particular to the geographic and historical milieu in which the religion was situated.

Examples include the Hajj in Islam. The annual pilgrimage to the Ka'aba was already practiced in pagan Mecca, so its appropriation by Muhammad made His new religion more acceptable to His first followers.[73] Other practices such as dietary laws, baptism, and all standards of dress and social etiquette apply; dietary necessities change, dress and proper behavior are relative to cul-

---

[71] *Paris Talks*, 226–7.
[72] Ibid, 227–8.
[73] *Encyclopedia Britannica*, s.v. "Kaaba."

ture insofar as it does not violate major moral prohibitions, and foregoing rituals such as baptism are violations of religious law only, not moral laws. The more challenging examples would be variations in theology, especially between the Abrahamic and Dharmic traditions.

Buddhism, in particular, does not appear to be theistic, at least in the sense as understood by the Abrahamic tradition. However, the simplest explanation, congruent with Progressive Revelation, is that an approach to spiritual fulfillment which minimized the role of a conscious Creator being or an interventionist deity may simply have been the most effective way to address the milieu of ancient India and spread the message of the Buddha. Thus, the Buddha, being the expert schoolteacher for the grade of the ancient Asian world, would know this and emphasize a social law of seeking personal enlightenment which fulfilled the spiritual law of rectifying individual conduct for the sake of uplifting the whole of society. Other variations, such as Hindu polytheism, will be discussed at other degrees of variation.

- 2nd order variations: Those laws, practices, customs, beliefs, and shibboleths which were added, abrogated, or modified due to the effects of entropy or complacency on the body of believers.

The Bahá'í literature makes it clear that "the difference in belief which exists is due to dogmatic interpretation and blind imitations which are at variance with the foundations established by the prophets of God."[74] All systems are subject to the encroachment of entropy, which leads to disorder which can only be reversed by the introduction of energy into the repair of weathered systems (i.e. rust never cleans itself). Religions should not be considered an exception to this rule, as the laws of God may be infallible, but they necessarily occur within a preexistent socio-cultural milieu and are executed by inherently fallible human persons who may alter, exclude, or augment belief systems

---

[74] *Promulgation*, 500.

according to outdated understandings of them. The rise of some ascetic orders, especially Christian monasticism[75], may be found to be examples of this phenomenon, as well as many rituals and practices such as the use of rosaries or turbans. That many of these practices did not exist at the onset of the religion, and the fact that disagreement abounds between sects and denominations as to their validity, is characteristic of their status as 2nd order variations.

In terms of theological variations, I offer a personal theory regarding early polytheism, which is easily invoked by detractors of Progressive Revelation as evidence that the religions are irreconcilable. In Islam, there are ninety-nine recorded attributes of God, each with their own given "Name": among them, al-Rahman (the Beneficent), al-Quddus (the Holy), al-Malik (the King), and al-Rabb (the Lord).[76] In the Qur'an, it is made abundantly clear that these Names all belong exclusively to God alone, as they are mere descriptors of the qualities of God. However, imagine these attributes being studied by a more ancient mind. It would appear gratuitous to beseech God the Almighty to solve a minor quotidian problem like getting to school on time, or incongruous to beseech God the Merciful while fighting in a war, even though God is all of those things and more. Thus, an ancient mind may easily simplify the situation by compartmentalizing these attributes to pray to each as is needed. From there, each attribute develops its own prayers, then its own distinct name, persona, and image. An entire pantheon arises from a single God because that was the capacity of humanity at the time. However, this theory would not apply to pre-Abrahamic polytheisms, as it is regarded that Abraham was the first of the major monotheistic Manifestations; His station simply does not preclude the ac-

---

[75] Christian monasticism is believed to have begun around the fourth century with St. Anthony of Egypt (Britannica). The sectarian controversy surrounding many 2nd order practices and customs make it extraordinarily difficult to provide historical data which is satisfactory to all viewpoints.
[76] Muhammad Ali, 61–2.

knowledgement of pre-monotheistic religions as viable sources of divine knowledge when polytheism is understood in this way.[77]

- 3rd order variations: Those laws, practices, customs, beliefs, and shibboleths which arose as a result of ecclesiastic or political control of the body of a religion, motivated by financial concerns or power dynamics over its followers and between its leaders.

These are most often used by detractors of religion who cite the violence and corruption of organizations proclaiming religious motivations. Some can be relatively harmless, though still morally dubious: e.g. the Medieval-era sale of "indulgences" (absolution for crimes and vices) by the Catholic magisterium as a means of financing the construction of cathedrals, which led to the Protestant Reformation.[78] More recent and publicized examples would include the radical sects of Islam responsible for numerous terror attacks across the world, as well as Christian terror groups dedicated to murdering abortion clinic workers or who avow white supremacist ideologies alongside Christian belief, and fighters in the Northern Ireland Conflict who characterized their struggle as one between British Protestantism and Irish Catholicism.[79,80] Arguably, all instances of ecclesiasticism may count, unless unambiguous proof can be found mandating the establishment of priesthoods and clergy in any of the surviving Abrahamic or Dharmic Scriptures. Examples of 3rd order variations abound and include all forms of fundamentalism and sectarianism, but what is significant is that they be recognized as fully artificial modifications to a religion, whatever their mo-

---

[77] 'Abdu'l-Bahá, *Selections from the Writings of 'Abdu'l-Bahá*, (Haifa: Bahá'í World Center, 1978), 81.

[78] *Encyclopedia Britannica*, s.v. "Indulgence."

[79] Donald P. Baker, "Blast at Alabama Abortion Clinic Kills a Policeman, Injures Nurse; Fatality Is the First from Bombing of Such a Facility," *Washington Post*, Jan. 30, 1998.

[80] Patrick Finnegan, "Religious Motivation During the Troubles," *St. Antony's International Review* 12, no. 1 (2016): 70–1.

tivation. While some of these variations may have been derived from certain principles or concepts endemic to a religion, the motivation is always towards some political or financial concern and not by a desire to achieve the goals of spiritual uplift and human unity. Such is the litmus test for the legitimacy of a 3rd order variation.

One distinction between 2nd and 3rd order variations is that, unlike explicitly prescribed 1st order variations, 2nd and 3rd order variations are avoidable because they were never originally part of the religion. The Writings state that "if we set aside these imitations and seek the fundamental reality underlying our beliefs, we reach a basis of agreement because it is one and not multiple."[81] This is how science can be applied to religion under Progressive Revelation: a means of discerning inherent spiritual laws from the three orders of variation.

One other objection that is likely to be shared equally by fundamentalists and materialists alike is the question of why allegory exists at all in the Scripture. The truth of Progressive Revelation depends upon an interpretation of Scripture in a manner which holistically transcends any single religion, but then why would God/Allah/Jehovah/Brahman reveal proofs of this unto His followers which were enmeshed in allegory, metaphor, and parable, forcing their descendants to decipher those proofs instead of having them revealed clearly and without the need for research? This is a legitimate question, but it does make the assumption that human action can be divinely guided in only one way — the way that humans believe they should be guided — and that God cannot work beyond that way despite His omnipotence and omniscience. Perhaps it served a purpose for the truth of Progressive Revelation to be obscured in some way. The most obvious reason for something to be obscured is as a test: for those who sufficiently desire the proof against those who would give up; or for those who find it, that they are mature enough to understand that proof without the bias of their own personal wants

---

[81] *Promulgation*, 224.

and ideological urges. For a teacher to state the obvious would not be conducive to the maturity of the student, as the student must eventually learn to solve problems independently and learn without the promptings of a teacher. Only by meeting challenges can a student grow and mature. By being forced to search for the truth of the religions — and their relationship to science — humanity is forced to choose between a difficult path of discovery and growth towards unity, or an easy path of division and conflict which has been the norm throughout history.

There is also the parallel explanation, compatible with that above, that the obscurity of the proofs of Progressive Revelation were never actually hidden by their Originator but were obscured by human activity. The Bahá'í literature determines the "Qur'an [...] apart from the sacred scriptures of the Bábí and Bahá'í Revelations, constitutes the only book which can be regarded as an absolutely authenticated Repository of the Word of God", as it was dictated directly by Muhammad Himself, unlike any other Scripture in any other pre-Bábí religion.[82] Therefore, Bahá'í theology would more likely accept such exegetical approaches as the "documentary hypothesis" of the authorship of the Old Testament over a doctrine of inerrant Mosaic authorship[83] and, congruent with this quotation from the Beloved Guardian, would reject all claims of Scriptural literacy for any and all pre-Bábí holy texts save the Qur'an. If the texts of all the previous Dispensations — Abrahamic and Dharmic — are untrustworthy as literal sources, then it would be very easy for people to derive divisions between the religions from motivated interpretation of these non-infallible Scriptures, just as the division between science and religion was itself an invented phenomenon. The Manifestations of God appear to humanity to offer spiritual guidance, not to prophesize exhaustively for the

---

[82] Shoghi Effendi, *The Advent of Divine Justice*, (Wilmette: Bahá'í Publishing Trust, 1939), 74.

[83] William W. Hallo, *The Book of the People*, (Providence: Brown Judaic Studies, 2020), 20–1.

sake of human epistemic demands.[84] There must come a point where the student herself assumes the responsibility of learning independently and proves to the teacher that she is ready to make her mark on her own. That is what humanity, as a whole, must now do to find the long-hidden proofs of Progressive Revelation.

CONCLUSION

Progressive Revelation is largely unknown to mainstream academic and popular discussion because it challenges long-held assumptions about the distinctiveness of the major world religions. A better understanding of it can help introduce Progressive Revelation to these discussions, but to do so it must be understood in terms of a paradigm model of the history of science. For science to be understood in relationship to religion, it must be modeled by an evolutionary, paradigm-based account of its changes over history, explaining those changes as the results of an ever-maturing understanding of the world, while maintaining the objectivity of science as an endeavor towards incrementally clearer truth. This gives science, in both a descriptive and normative sense, the seemingly contradictory qualities of durability and evolution, of simultaneous objectivity and relativism, acting to reduce the inherent complexity of the world into a "theory of everything" of ultimate parsimony. Progressive Revelation makes sense when the religions are recognized as successive stages of a single, unfolding Revelation, with all of the theological and moral variations explained in terms of the geo-historically relative capacities of humanity, the effects of entropy on the body of believers, and of more forceful modifications brought about by power dynamics. The many religions become perceptible as one religion, progressively unfolding, teleologically directed towards the iterative spiritual uplift and unity of humanity. Progressive Revelation becomes a religious "theory of every-

---

[84] Momen, 1988.

thing" parsimoniously explaining the diversity of the religions as one religion, and making religion, like science, simultaneously durable and evolutionary, objective and relative. If this dialogue model of theo-scientific harmony could be introduced into the mainstream discussions of science, religion, and both together, then a revolution can take place which will make the Bahá'í principle of unity in diversity a greater possibility than ever in world society.

Bibliography

Abbot, B.P, et al. "GW170814: A Three-Detector Observation of Gravitational Waves from a Binary Black Hole Coalescence." *Physical Review Letters* 119, no. 14 (2017): 141101–16.

'Abdu'l-Bahá. *Paris Talks*. Wilmette: Bahá'í Publishing Trust, 1912.

———. *The Promulgation of Universal Peace: Talks Delivered by 'Abdu'l-Bahá during His Visit to the United States and Canada in 1912*. Comp. Howard MacNutt. Wilmette: U. S. Bahá'í Publishing Trust, 1982.

———. *Selections from the Writings of 'Abdu'l-Bahá*. Haifa: Bahá'í World Center, 1978.

———. *Some Answered Questions*. Haifa: Bahá'í World Center, 2014.

Bahá'u'lláh. *Gleanings from the Writings of Bahá'u'lláh*. Wilmette: Bahá'í Publishing Trust, 1952.

———. *Tablets of Bahá'u'lláh*. Haifa: Bahá'í World Center, 1978.

Baker, Donald P. "Blast at Alabama Abortion Clinic Kills a Policeman, Injures Nurse; Fatality Is the First from Bombing of Such a Facility." *Washington Post*, Jan. 30, 1998.

Barbour, Ian. *When Science Meets Religion: Enemies, Strangers, or Partners?* San Francisco: HarperOne, 2000.

Britannica, T. Editors of Encyclopedia Britannica, "Kaaba." *Encyclopedia Britannica* August 15, 2019. https://www.britannica.com/topic/Kaaba-shrine-Mecca-Saudi-Arabia. (Accessed June 16, 2021)

Britannica, T. Editors of Encyclopedia Britannica. "St. Anthony of Egypt." *Encyclopedia Britannica*, August 5, 2020. https://www.britannica.com/biography/Saint-Anthony-of-Egypt. (Accessed June 16, 2021)

Buck, Christopher. "Bahá'u'lláh as Zoroastrian Savior." *The Baháʼí Studies Review* 8, (1998): 14–33.

Chalmers, Alan. *What Is This Thing Called Science?* Indianapolis: Hackett Publishing, 1976.

Cort, John E. "Intellectual Ahimsa: Jain Tolerance and Intolerance of Others." *University of Hawai'i Press* 50, no. 3 (2000): 234–47.

Descartes, R. (2008). *Meditations on First Philosophy* (M. Moriarty, Trans.). Oxford University Press, 2008.

Duggan, L. G. "Indulgence." *Encyclopedia Britannica*, November 25, 2015. https://www.britannica.com/topic/indulgence. (Accessed June 16, 2021)

Finnegan, Patrick. "Religious Motivation During the Troubles." *St. Antony's International Review* 12, no. 1 (2016): 53–75.

Gauch Jr., Hugh G. *Scientific Method in Practice*. Cambridge: Cambridge University Press, 2002.

Geertz, Clifford. "Religion." In *Magic, Witchcraft, and Religion*, edited by Pamela A. Moro and James E. Myers, 1–5. New York: McGraw Hill, 2010.

Gould, Stephen Jay. Nonoverlapping Magesteria. *Natural History* 106, no. 2 (1997): 16–22.

Hallo, William W. *The Book of the People*. Providence: Brown Judaic Studies, 2020.

Hawking, Stephen. *The Illustrated Brief History of Time*. New York: Bantam, 1988.

Holy Qur'an, The. Trans. By Maulana Muhammad Ali. Ahmadiyya Anjuman Isha'at Islam Lahore Inc., 2002.

Hornby, Helen Bassett, comp. *Lights of Guidance: A Baháʼí Reference File*. Ecuador: National Assembly of the Baháʼís of Ecuador. 1997.

Hoyt, Sarah F. "The Etymology of Religion." *Journal of the American Oriental Society* 32, no. 2 (1912): 126–9.

Kuhn, Thomas. *The Structure of Scientific Revolutions*. Chicago: University of Chicago Press, 2012.

Longino, Helen. *Science as Social Knowledge: Values and Objectivity in Scientific Inquiry*. Princeton: Princeton University Press, 1990.

Momen, Moojan. "Buddhism and the Bahá'í Faith." Bahá'í Library Online. Last Modified November 25, 2016. https://bahai-library.com/momen_encyclopedia_buddhism. Accessed 27 Feb. 2021.

———. "Relativism: A Basis For Bahá'í Metaphysics." In Studies in the Babi and Bahá'í Religions, 185–217. Vol. 5 of *Studies in the Babi and Bahá'í Religions*. Los Angeles: Kalimat Press, 1988.

———. *An Introduction to Shi'a Islam: The History and Doctrines of Twelver Shi'ism*. Yale: Yale University Press, 1987.

Muhammad Ali, Maulana. *The Religion of Islam*. Rowland Heights: S. Chan & Co. (Pvt.) Ltd., 1990.

New American Bible, The. World Bible Publishers, Inc., 1987.

Pigliucci, Massimo. "New Atheism and the Scientistic Turn in the Atheist Movement." *Midwest Studies in Philosophy*, 37, no. 1 (2013): 142–53.

Rea, Michael C. "Polytheism and Christian Belief." *The Journal of Theological Studies* 57, no.1 (2006): 133–48.

"Religion." OED Online, (Oxford: Oxford University Press, March 2021), https://www.oed.com/viewdictionaryentry/Entry/161944. (Accessed 15, May 2021.)

Saritoprak, Zeki. "The Mahdi Tradition in *Islam: A Socio-Cognitive Approach*." Islamic Studies 41, no. 4, (2002): 651–74.

Schilbrack, Kevin. "What Isn't Religion?" *Journal of Religion* 93, no. 3, (2013): 291–318.

Shoghi Effendi. *The Advent of Divine Justice*. Wilmette: Bahá'í Publishing Trust, 1939.

———. *God Passes By*. Wilmette: Bahá'í Publishing Trust, 1994.

———. *The Promised Day Is Come*. Wilmette: Bahá'í Publishing Trust, 1996.

———. *The World Order of Bahá'u'lláh*. Wilmette: Bahá'í Publishing Trust, 1938.

Tuggy, Dale. "The Unfinished Business of Trinitarian Theorizing." *Religious Studies* 39, no. 2 (2003): 165–83.

Wolf, C. Umhau. "Moses in Christian and Islamic Tradition." *Journal of Bible and Religion* 27, no. 2 (1959): 102–8.

Worthington, Francis. *Abraham: One God, Three Wives, Five Religions*. Wilmette: Bahá'í Publishing, 2011.

The Issue of Self-Identity in Transhumanism and the Bahá'í Writings

MIKHAIL SERGEEV

INTRODUCTION

The aim of my article is to examine the problems of human self-identity and immortality as they are approached in Transhumanism and the Bahá'í Writings. Transhumanism or H+ is an intellectual and cultural movement whose ultimate goal is to merge biology with computer technology in order to enhance human capabilities and, in the long run, to make humanity immortal. Transhumanists trace the origin of their undertaking in the inter-civilizational efforts to curb aging and conquer death. Those aspirations go back to ancient Egypt and China and to the search for the Fountain of Youth or the alchemists' Elixir of Life. One of the more immediate precursors to the philosophy of Transhumanism was a nineteenth-century Russian Orthodox thinker Nicholas Fyodorov (1829–1903) who "advocated radical life extension, physical immortality and even resurrection of the dead, using scientific methods."[1]

In 1923 in an essay "Daedalus: Science and the Future" the British geneticist J.B.S. Haldane outlined the basic ideas of

---

[1] "Nikolai Fyodorovich Fyodorov." Wikipedia, the Free Encyclopedia, https://en.wikipedia.org/wiki/Nikolai_Fyodorovich_Fyodorov. For more information on Fyodorov's thought see chapters on him in two American anthologies: (1) *Russian Philosophy*, eds. M. Edie, James P. Scanlan, Mary-Barbara Zeldin, Vol. III, Knoxville, TE: The University of Tennessee Press, 1969, pp. 11–54; and (2) *Ultimate Questions: An Anthology of Modern Russian Religious Thought,* ed. with an Introduction by Alexander Schmemann, Crestwood, N.Y.: St. Vladimir's Seminary Press, 1977, pp. 173–223.

Transhumanism. And in 1957 biologist Julian Huxley who is commonly credited as its founder, coined the term for the movement. In the last decade of the twentieth century the efforts of individual thinkers began to coalesce into a coherent school of thought with the creation of The World Transhumanist Association (WTA) in 1998 and the issuing of Transhumanist Declaration in 2002.[2] According to one of the leading transhumanist thinkers, a contemporary British philosopher Max More,

> Transhumanism is a class of philosophies of life that seek the continuation and acceleration of the evolution of intelligent life beyond its currently human form and human limitations by means of science and technology, guided by life-promoting principles and values.[3]

CONCEPTS AND TERMS

The main philosophical assumption of Transhumanism is that the functioning of the human brain is based on the same principles and is subordinated to the same procedures as the operation of a highly sophisticated computer with advanced capabilities. The supposition that artificial and human intelligence are fundamentally identical is known as the Church—Turing thesis that was independently advanced by an American mathematician and logician Alonzo Church (1903–1995) and a British computer scientist Alan Turing (1912–1954) back in 1937. The strongest and most consistent opponent of the Church—Turing thesis was an American philosopher Hubert Dreyfus (1929–2017) who articulated his systematic critique of artificial intelligence in his now classic work *What Computers Can't Do*, published in 1972.[4]

---

[2] "Transhumanist Declaration," Wikipedia, the Free Encyclopedia, https://hpluspedia.org/wiki/Transhumanist_Declaration.
[3] "What is Transhumanism?" http://whatistranshumanism.org/.
[4] A revised version of Dreyfus' classic was published twenty years later, in 1993, under the title *What Computers Still Can't Do. A Critique of Artificial Intelligence* (Cambridge, MA: The MIT Press).

The substance of Dreyfus' criticism was leveled against the idea that human intelligence in all its forms is based on the collection and analysis of independents atomic facts, which is subject to complete formalization. In his rebuttal of that claim, which Dreyfus dubbed an "ontological assumption," he argued that there existed a philosophical alternative to analytical approach, namely the phenomenological tradition of explaining human intelligence. Pioneered by Martin Heidegger (1889–1976) in the twentieth century, the phenomenological description of intelligent behavior[5] accounted for the indispensable role of the totality of existence — including human bodies, contextual situations as well as purposes and needs — without which such behavior would be impossible. Thus, assessing the prospects of creating artificial intelligence that would match and even surpass what humans are capable of, Dreyfus concluded that there is a "fundamental difference" between the two since human beings do not necessarily operate according to rules and on the basis of independent facts. It is most likely, in fact, that some aspects of human intelligence may never be formalized and reproduced in artificial intelligence in principle.[6]

In spite of the damaging critique of a computer-based model of AI by Dreyfus and his supporters[7], it is still a working hypothesis for many scholars in the field of artificial intelligence. Let us review some of the key terms transhumanists use when they develop this approach in their writings:

---

[5] Hubert Dreyfus has taught for many years a university course on Martin Heidegger's *Being and Time* and published his book of commentaries on the German thinker's magnum opus: *Being-in-the-World. A Commentary on Heidegger's Being and Time, Division I*, Cambridge, MA: The MIT Press, 1991.

[6] Hubert Dreyfus, *What Computers Still Can't Do*, 1993, p. 281.

[7] An article by a senior research psychologist at the American Institute for Behavioral Research and Technology in California, Robert Epstein, called "The Empty Brain," is one of the recent publications on the subject — https://straightlinelogic.com/2016/05/25/the-empty-brain-by-robert-epstein/.

1. **"Turing Test"** — In 1950 in his paper "Computing Machinery and Intelligence" Alan Turing articulated the standard by which to decide whether the machine does possess intelligence. According to Turing, the main criterion for judgment is purely empirical. If a person cannot distinguish his IT interlocutor from a human being, then the machine is intelligent and should be treated as such.
2. **"Moore's Law"** — In 1965 a co-founder of Intel Gordon Moore observed that "transistors were shrinking so fast that every year twice as many could fit onto a chip, and in 1975 adjusted the pace to a doubling every two years."[8] The rule of exponential growth of integrated circuits proved right for the last fifty years, and on the basis of that many futurists predicted the soon-to-be-dawning era of technological singularity. It seems, however, that after half-a-century of triumph Moore's Law may be running out of steam.
3. **"Whole brain emulation"** (WBE) — or mind uploading, mind transfer, mind copying, which is an exact simulation or high-tech replica of the human brain. It is a hypothetical procedure of transferring mental content of the brain to an artificial neural network that will function in essentially the same was as the human original.
4. **"Technological singularity"** — In 1965 a British cryptologist I. J. Good formulated the idea of technological singularity, which suggested a possibility of merging human biology with computer technology. A resulting human hybrid, which is labeled "post-human" or "trans-human" being will possess a super-human intelligence and capabilities, including the capacity to live an infinitely long life, thus achieving the ultimate dream of immortality.

---

[8] Tom Simonite, "Moore's Law is Dead. Now What?" *MIT Technology Review*, https://www.technologyreview. com/s/601441/moores-law-is-dead-now-what/.

THEORIES OF HUMAN IDENTITY

The concept of singularity or the merging of human biology with computer technology applies first and foremost to the brain, which is the conduit for human mind, consciousness, and self-identity. Hence, transhumanist thought gets inevitably involved in the millennia-old polemics about the origin of life and the nature of human soul. What happens if a person's brain is irreversibly damaged and replaced by its artificial duplicate? Will it be the same human being or a different one? Where exactly the seed of human identity could be found?

According to a contemporary American inventor, transhumanist thinker, and best-selling author Ray Kurzweil (b. 1948), there are four competing theories of human selfhood. The first position, which Kurzweil, in my view, confusingly, labels the "ego theory", states that "a person's nature is her soul or nonphysical mind, and this mind or soul can survive the death of the body." The second one, called the "psychological continuity theory", argues that "you are essentially your memories and ability to reflect on yourself (Locke) and, more generally, your overall psychological configuration, what Kuzweil referred to as your 'pattern'." The third or "materialist" thesis asserts that "you are essentially the material that you are made out of — what Kurzweil referred to as 'the ordered and chaotic collection of molecules that make up my body and brain'." Finally, the fourth option or the "no self view" claims that

> there is no metaphysical category of person. The 'I' is a grammatical fiction (Nietzsche). There are bundles of impressions but no underlying self (Hume). There is no survival because there is no person (Buddha, Parfit).[9]

---

[9] Susan Schneider, "Future Minds: Transhumanism, Cognitive Enhancement and the Nature of Persons," in Vardit Ravitsky, Autumn Fiester, and Arthur L. Caplan, eds., *The Penn Center Guide to Bioethics*: New York: Springer, 2009, pp. 844–856. Quoted in James Hughes, "Transhumanism and Personal Identity," *The Transhumanist Reader: Classical and Contemporary Essays on the Science, Technology, and Philosophy of the*

Most religions, including the Bahá'í Faith, take the first position and affirm the existence of the human soul that is essentially different from the physical body. They contend that the soul is spiritual, that it survives the death of the body and that it either follows the path of reincarnation (Hinduism) or reunites with its body through resurrection (Christianity), or continues its evolution on the spiritual plane of existence (Bahá'í Faith). There are transhumanists who believe in the spiritual nature of the soul as well, especially in the Christian intellectual tradition. There exists, for example, a Mormon Transhumanist Association (MTA) that advocates "Transfigurism" as a religious brand of transhumanism. The MTA website claims that the association "is the world's largest advocacy network for ethical use of technology and religion to expand human abilities" and that they "support...members in their personal religious affiliations, Mormon or otherwise, and encourage them to adapt Transhumanism to their unique situations."[10]

A cosmologist and physicist who specializes on the general theory of relativity, Frank J. Tipler (b. 1947) is, perhaps, the most prominent among contemporary Christian transhumanists. In his 1994 book *The Physics of Immortality* he proposed his own, arguably scientific theory that links the Christian dogma of bodily resurrection with the concepts of singularity and mind uploading. According to Tipler, human drive for total knowledge will eventually lead to what he calls the Big Crunch or the Omega Point — a cosmological singularity when computational capabilities of the universe expand to infinity and transform it into a gigantic supercomputer. In such a scenario the resurrection of the dead will happen within its cyberspace where dead humans will be reconstructed as avatars inside the compuverse. The "physical mechanism of individual resurrection," Tipler ar-

---

Human Future, eds. Max Moore and Natasha Vita-More, Wiley-Blackwell, 2013, p. 230.
[10] Mormon Transhumanist Association, http://transfigurism.org/.

gues, is such that "we shall be emulated in the computers of the far future."[11]

"With few exceptions," however, as contemporary British philosopher Max Moore states, "transhumanists describe themselves as materialists, physicalists, or functionalists. As such they believe that our thinking, feeling selves are essentially physical processes."[12] One of the pioneer researchers of artificial intelligence Marvin Minsky (1927–2016) has formulated this position in a straightforward fashion:

> For ages people have wondered about the relationship between the mind and body; some philosophers became so desperate as to suggest that only the mental world is real and the real world is merely an illusion...Most thinkers have ended up with images that portray two different kinds of worlds, one of matter and one of mind...I see no merits in such ideas because as far as I am concerned, the so-called problem of body and mind does not hold any mystery: *Minds are simply what brains do*.[13]

For those secular transhumanists, like Minsky or Kurzweil, the second position of "psychological continuity" is evidently preferable to the third and fourth interpretations that eliminate the possibility for human self-identity to be relatively independent of and exist outside the human body. An ardent advocate of the second theory, Ray Kurzweil, argues that the pattern of human individuality could eventually be dissociated from its organic substratum and transferred into another, more durable technological platform. It is the first (religious) and the second (secular) approaches to the problem of human identity that we are going to compare in this essay.

---

[11] Tipler, Frank J. *The Physics of Immortality: Modern Cosmology, God and the Resurrection of the Dead*, New York: Anchor Books, Doubleday, 1994, p. 220.

[12] Max Moore, "The Philosophy of Transhumanism,' *The Transhumanist Reader*, p. 7.

[13] Marvin Minsky, *The Society of Mind*, New York: Simon & Shuster, 1986, p. 287.

KURZWEIL'S ARGUMENTS FOR SINGULARITY

In his bestselling books an American inventor and transhumanist thinker Ray Kurzweil develops a series of arguments to prove the theoretical plausibility of singularity. The most significant and philosophically far reaching, in my opinion, are those of his ideas that deal with the concepts of evolution and self-identity. In his book *The Singularity Is Near* Kurzweil defines evolution as "a process of creating patterns of increasing order,"[14] which store and transmit information. Kurzweil distinguishes "six epochs" in the process of world evolution — beginning with atomic and molecular levels studied by physics, chemistry and biology, then the appearance of neural patterns and the brain, the development of information technology, and, finally, up to the future technological singularity and the "waking up" of the universe when its "matter and energy...become saturated with intelligent processes and knowledge."[15]

One of the pressing issues in the discussion of evolution, as Kurzweil notes in another book, is whether *"an intelligence [can] create another intelligence more intelligent than itself?"*[16] His proposed solution to the problem takes the form of two mutually related arguments. In their logical reconstruction they run as follows:

First Argument:
1. The evolution is efficient but extremely slow;
2. Given the long period of time it achieved its results, evolution's IQ is only slightly greater than zero (zero would stand for truly arbitrary behavior);
3. Yet evolution created human intelligence with higher IQ;
4. Hence, evolution can create something higher than itself.

---

[14] Raymond Kurzweil, *The Singularity Is Near: When Humans Transcend Biology,* New York: Penguin Books, 2006, p. 14.
[15] Ibid, p. 15.
[16] Raymond Kurzweil, *The Age of Spiritual Machines: When Computers Exceed human Intelligence,* New York: Penguin Books, 2000, p. 40.

Second Argument:
1. Evolution has created something higher than itself;
2. Human intelligence is part of evolution;
3. Human intelligence works at a much higher pace;
4. Therefore, human intelligence can create machines that have higher intelligence than humans.[17]

Having established the theoretical possibility of the supercomputer that will exceed human intelligence, Kurzweil now turns to the problem of human identity, which may be affected by the eventual merger of human biology with superior computer technology. Here he proposes two thought experiments that in their logical formulations look as follows:

First Thought Experiment:
1. Let's assume that it is possible to scan and download a complete replica of the human brain;
2. "You-2" is behaving like you;
3. Is it really you?
4. It seems that "You-2" is another person and has a different identity.

Second Thought Experiment:
1. Your brain is replaced part by part with implants until there is nothing original in your brain;
2. Is this person still you?
3. In this case you still exist except for the fact that the conclusion of thought experiment #2 came into contradiction with the thought experiment #1.[18]

Kurzweil's answer to the paradox is simple and forthright. He believes that in both cases we are dealing with one and the same person, and that "You-2" of the first thought experiment is actually you no matter how counter-intuitive this sounds. This conclusion is based on Kurzweil's view on the nature of human

---

[17] Ibid, pp. 46–50.
[18] Kurzweil, *The Singularity Is Near*, pp. 382–87.

identity that he himself labels "patternist." As we remember, according to this position, a human being is "a pattern of matter and energy that persists over time"[19] and can be emulated on a different, non-organic platform. We will return to Kurzweil's arguments about evolution and self-identity when we compare his views with Bahá'í approaches to the issues in question.

BAHÁ'Í TEACHINGS ON HUMAN NATURE

In order to explore a Bahá'í perspective with regard to transhumanist views and doctrines, we have to revisit Bahá'í teachings on human nature first since this is the key topic in relation to both human evolution and self-identity. In his various talks the Center of the Covenant and the master interpreter of Bahá'í doctrines 'Abdu'l-Bahá addresses the issue of human nature while focusing on three central themes. First, human nature has two components — material and spiritual — or, as philosophers would say, body and soul.

"In man there are two natures," 'Abdu'l-Bahá says in *Paris Talks*,

> His spiritual or higher nature and his material or lower nature... Every good habit, every noble quality belongs to man's spiritual nature, whereas all the imperfections and sinful actions are born of his material nature.[20]

In *The Promulgation of Universal Peace* he reaffirms the same principle: "Man has two aspects: the physical which is subject to nature, and the merciful or divine, which is connected with God." 'Abdu'l-Bahá continues:

> If the physical or natural disposition in him should overcome the heavenly and merciful, he is, then, the most degraded of animal beings; and if the divine and spiri-

---

[19] Ibid, p. 383.
[20] 'Abdu'l-Bahá, *Paris Talks (PT)*, in *Writings and Utterances* of *'Abdu'l-Bahá*, New Delhi, India: Bahá'í Publishing Trust, 2000, p. 726.

tual should triumph over the human and natural, he is, verily, an angel.[21]

Second, 'Abdu'l-Bahá points out to the complexities of human character by distinguishing "the innate character, the inherited character, and the acquired character." The innate character reflects various abilities and inclinations people possess from their birth. As he says, "although the innate nature bestowed by God upon man is purely good, yet that character differs among men according to the degrees they occupy." The inherited character depends on the "strength and weakness of man's constitution" that is inborn from his parents — "if the parents are of weak constitution, then the children will be likewise, and if they are strong, then the children will also be robust." Finally, the acquired character is developed by education and the "differences of character arising from education...are great indeed, for education exerts an enormous influence."[22]

Third, 'Abdu'l-Bahá pays special attention to the interrelationship between human body, mind, and spirit. "The human spirit, which distinguishes man from the animal, is the rational soul," he says, "and these two terms — the human spirit and the rational soul — designate one and the same thing." "As for the mind," he continues,

> it is the power of the human spirit. The spirit is as the lamp, and the mind as the light that shines from it...The mind is the perfection of the spirit and a necessary attribute thereof, even as the rays of the sun are an essential requirement of the sun itself.[23]

In the "Tablet to Dr. Forel," 'Abdu'l-Bahá clarifies with more details the inter-connection between body, mind and its spirit or soul:

---

[21] 'Abdu'l-Bahá, *The Promulgation of Universal Peace (PUP)*, ibid, p. 840.
[22] 'Abdu'l-Bahá, *Some Answered Questions (SAQ)*, Bahá'í World Center, 2014, http://bahai-library.com/ abdulbaha_some_answered_questions, 57:2–8.
[23] Ibid, 55:5–6.

For the mind to manifest itself, the human body must be whole; and a sound mind cannot be but in a sound body, whereas the soul dependeth not upon the body. It is through the power of the soul that the mind comprehendeth, imagineth and exerteth its influence, whilst the soul is a power that is free. The mind comprehendeth the abstract by the aid of the concrete, but the soul hath limitless manifestations of its own...It is by the aid of the such senses as those of sight, hearing, taste, smell and touch, that the mind comprehendeth, whereas the soul is free from all agencies...[24]

BAHÁ'Í PERSPECTIVE ON EVOLUTION

Now we can return to Kurzweil's argument about evolution and analyze it from a Bahá'í perspective. His argument rests on an empirical observation that evolution works its way from simple to complex forms and produces human intelligence that is lacking in nature. Since man is a product and part of evolutionary process, it seems to follow that he himself could create an even higher intelligence and evolve into a super-being that will supersede ordinary humans in physical and intellectual abilities.

Let us discuss the initial proposition of the argument first. The observation about natural evolution is empirically correct but logically confusing. If we accept evolution on its face value, then we necessarily arrive at a conclusion that a lesser entity can produce something that is greater than itself. At the end of logical chain it means that "nothing" can evolve into "something," which from the rational standpoint is absurd. The evolutionary surplus should come from somewhere — either it potentially existed in nature and was actualized by evolution, or it was directly created by a higher power.

In Bahá'í approach Kurzweil's evolutionary paradox is resolved by a differentiation between the spiritual and material elements in human nature. The material component of humanity

---

[24] "Tablet to Dr. Forel," *Writings and Utterances* of *'Abdu'l-Bahá*, pp. 643–44.

i.e. the body is subject to evolution while the human spirit is not. Overall, as 'Abdu'l-Bahá teaches, there are five types of spirit — the vegetable, the animal, the human, the spirit of faith, and the Holy Spirit.[25] All those forms of spirit are creations of God and cannot evolve or transmute into something else, including each other. Their limits are set, and they can progress infinitely but within their own domain.

Therefore, material evolution does not "create" human intelligence but allows it to be manifested on the physical plane of existence by producing more complex bodily organisms that could accommodate it. Human spirit always existed in nature — potentially, even if undetected empirically. As 'Abdu'l-Bahá puts it,

> Just as man progresses, evolves, and is transformed from one form and appearance to another in the womb of the mother, while remaining from the beginning a human embryo, so too has man remained a distinct essence — that is, the human species — from the beginning of his formation in the matrix of the world, and has passed gradually from form to form.[26]

Furthermore, according to 'Abdu'l-Bahá, the observation that material evolution leads to the emergence of human intelligence, in fact, attests to the human spirit being not of material nature, since to think otherwise would make us stumble upon rational inconsistencies. In its logical form 'Abdu'l-Bahá's argument runs as follows:

1. What is present in parts should also exist in the whole.
2. Humans have intelligence but the natural world as a whole, lacks it.
3. Therefore, human intelligence is not part of the natural order.

Or, as he puts it himself:

---

[25] 'Abdu'l-Bahá, *SAQ*, 36:1–9.
[26] Ibid, 49:8.

> If it be claimed that the intellectual reality of man belongs to the world of nature — that it is part of the whole — we ask, is it possible for the part to contain virtues which the whole does not possess? For instance, is it possible for the drop to contain virtues of which the aggregate body of the sea is deprived? ...On the other hand, it is evident and true...that in man there is present this supernatural force or faculty which...possesses the power of idealization or intellection...Science exists in the mind of man as an ideal reality. The mind itself, reason itself, is an ideal reality and not tangible.[27]

As for the second part of Kurzweil's argument, it states that as part of the evolution man could greatly enhance his abilities and transform himself into a new immortal creature of infinitely superior intelligence. This second thesis depends on the initial assumption about evolution being able to develop something higher than itself — a premise that we have already discussed as logically questionable. But, in addition to that inconsistency, the second hypothesis involves the crucial issue of human self-identity that we must now explore further from a Bahá'í perspective.

BAHÁ'Í VIEWS ON SELF-IDENTITY

According to Bahá'í teachings, human intelligence or mind is the power of the human spirit. To use computer terminology, human mind is the interface between body and soul, between our material and spiritual natures. What are the philosophical implications of that view?

First, since the mind, as 'Abdu'l-Bahá contends, "is the power of the human spirit,"[28] it is not the seed of human identity — the spirit or soul is. Human mind is the *function* of the soul in the same way our physical abilities and powers represent the func-

---

[27] 'Abdu'l-Bahá, *PUP*, in *Writings and Utterances*, p. 1114.
[28] 'Abdu'l-Bahá, *SAQ*, 55:5–6.

tion of the human body. Second, as far as the soul is not a material but spiritual entity, the power of the mind is also essentially spiritual and is only partially reflected on the physical plane through the instrumentality of the brain. The limitations of the brain place substantial restrictions on the activity of the mind, which on the physical plane is mainly expressed through the functioning of reason and sense perception.

According to 'Abdu'l-Bahá, the potential spiritual powers of the mind are much greater than what human reason and sense perception are capable of. Those hidden abilities are only partially expressed through human intuition, visions, and dreams, which are possible due to the interconnection between material and spiritual realms. A departed soul, for instance, may communicate with a relative who is physically alive, but this would not be "as our conversation...The heart of man is open to inspiration; this is spiritual communication. As in a dream one talks with a friend while the mouth is silent, so is it in the conversation of the spirit."[29] 'Abdu'l-Bahá cautions against premature development of those spiritual powers:

> To tamper with psychic forces while in this world interferes with the condition of the soul in the world to come. These forces are real, but, normally, are not active on this plane... The whole purpose of life in the material world is the coming forth into the world of Reality, where those forces will become active. They belong to that world.[30]

In addition, Bahá'í scriptures warn about taking one's dreams and visions at their face value. In many cases those intuitions and inspirations may simply be the result of human imagination and have little if nothing to do with true spirituality. As we read in a letter written on behalf of Shoghi Effendi, the Guardian of

---

[29] 'Abdu'l-Bahá, *PT*, in *Writing and Utterances*, p. 179.
[30] Quoted in J. E. Esslemont, *Baha'u'llah and the New Era*, Wilmette: Bahá'í Publishing Trust, first published 1923, https://bahai-library.com/esslemont_bahaullah_new_era.

the Bahá'í Faith: "We should test impressions we get through dreams, visions, or inspirations, by comparing them with the revealed Word and seeing whether they are in full harmony therewith."[31]

Let us revisit in light of these Bahá'í teachings, the issue of technological singularity and its implications for the future of humankind. Would it be possible for humans to increase their intellectual capabilities by inventing a machine with intelligence that supersedes their own? Yes, in my view, it would. This would not mean, however, that humans have evolved into a different, super-anthropoid species.

In the process of evolution we have already created a great deal of machines that increase and, in fact, surpass our own powers. Cars run faster than humans, telescopes possess sharper eyesight; cranes lift heavier weights, and so on. The difference between physical and sensory abilities, on the one hand, and the power of human mind, on the other, is that we tend to associate our self-identity with the latter. If we imagine the invention of artificial intelligence that overtakes our own, we may conclude then that we are able to transform ourselves into something (or someone) else.

From a Bahá'í perspective, however, this would not be the case for a number of reasons. First and foremost, human self-identity, which is expressed on the physical plane through self-consciousness, is not a material but spiritual reality. Hence, no manipulation with or augmentation of human intellectual abilities will affect our spiritual nature. In fact, the invention of artificial intelligence that supersedes our own, which already happened in certain fields of human activity such as the game of chess or go, for instance, will prove that we are more than our capacity to reason. Otherwise, it would follow that nothing could produce something, which is logically absurd.

---

[31] *Lights of Guidance. A Bahá'í Reference File*, compiled by Helen Bassett Hornby, New Delhi, India: Bahá'í Publishing Trust, 2006, 1st ed. 1983, p. 515.

Second — and this is no less significant — as far as research into artificial intelligence remains within the limits of material reality, even the emulation of the whole human brain would imply only the capability to simulate *some* of our intellectual capacities, while the hidden psychic powers would continue to be inaccessible.

Now we can return to Kurzweil's two thought experiments and evaluate them from a Bahá'í point of view. Let us imagine that our technology is capable of scanning and downloading a complete replica of the human brain. Would such a "You-2" be really you? In my opinion, no, it would not because no material emulation of the brain will be able to capture the spiritual essence of the human being. A material replica will always remain what it is — an incomplete copy of the person that is lacking the source of that person's identity.

Then what if we are able to replace someone's brain with an artificial brain implant. Would that person retain his or her own original self-identity? The answer to this question depends on whether the implant is capable of retaining a mysterious connection between the spiritual and material parts of the human being. Regardless of technological successes in the field of artificial intelligence, however, no one will ever be able to change their own spiritual identity or to create an AI that supersedes humans on the spiritual level of existence.

REMARKS IN CONCLUSION

In the twenty-first century humanity entered the second wave of robotic evolution by having developed artificial intelligence, which is capable of learning from interaction with environment and from its own mistakes. Many thinkers and researchers of AI are now warning about the inevitable competition between humans and robots — a competition in which artificial minds will supersede the intelligence of their inventors and eventually render them — and all of us — helpless and powerless. A Swedish philosopher Nick Bostrom in his bestselling book *Superintelligence: Paths, Dangers, Strategies* addresses those challenges by discussing various AI takeover scenarios and possible human responses.[32]

Yet, in my view, this is not the only "present and clear" danger that humanity will be facing as a result of the superintelligence explosion, which is looming on the horizon. Many AI scholars and inventors such as Ray Kurzweil, dream of the era of singularity that promises not only the augmentation of human physical and mental abilities but also the prolongation of human life to the point of practical immortality.

It may as well happen that science and technology will deliver a desirable outcome and extend human life indefinitely. We may also in the future develop the abilities to rejuvenate ourselves and remain young and healthy — if not forever, then at least in the foreseeable future. However, what we won't be able to accomplish by scientific, technological or any other means, is to eliminate suffering.

Suffering and pain come to human beings on different levels and in a variety of forms. Suffering cannot be separated from life and is inevitable because it serves as an instrument of spiritual growth. Hence, the transhumanist project of achieving physical immortality would in reality mean the creation of hell on earth. How else could one describe an existential situation, which is constantly testing our endurance with no end in sight? And what is hell if not such an unending suffering with no prospect of release or light at the end of the tunnel?

References

'Abdu'l-Bahá. *Paris Talks* (PT). Wilmette: Bahá'í Publishing Trust, 1972, Bahá'í Library Online, https://bahai-library.com/abdulbaha_paris_talks.

———. *Some Answered Questions* (SAQ), Bahá'í World Center, 2014, http://bahai-library.com/ abdulbaha_ some _answered_ questions.

---

[32] Nick Bostrom. *Superintelligence. Paths, Dangers, Strategies.* Oxford, UK: Oxford University Press, 2014.

———. *Writings and Utterances of 'Abdu'l-Bahá*, New Delhi, India: Bahá'í Publishing Trust, 2000.

Bostrom, Nick. *Superintelligence. Paths, Dangers, Strategies*. Oxford, UK: Oxford University Press, 2014.

Dreyfus, Hubert L. *What Computers Still Cannot Do. A Critique of Artificial Reason*. Cambridge, MA: The MIT Press, 1993.

Dreyfus, Hubert L. *Being-in-the-World. A Commentary on Heidegger's Being and Time*, Division 1. Cambridge, MA: The MIT Press, 1991.

Epstein, Robert, "The Empty Brain," Straight Line Logic, https://straightlinelogic.com/2016/05/25/the-empty-brain-by-robert-epstein/.

Esslemont, J. E. *Baha'u'llah and the New Era*, Wilmette: Bahá'í Publishing Trust, first published 1923, https://bahai-library.com/esslemont_bahaullah_new_era.

Kurzweil, Raymond, *The Age of Spiritual Machines: When Computers Exceed Human Intelligence*, New York: Penguin Books, 2000.

———. *The Singularity Is Near: When Humans Transcend Biology*, New York: Penguin Books, 2006.

———. *How to Create a Mind: The Secret of Human Thought Revealed*, New York: Penguin Books, 2013.

Lights of Guidance. A Bahá'í Reference File, compiled by Helen Bassett Hornby, New Delhi, India: Bahá'í Publishing Trust, 2006, 1st ed. 1983.

Minsky, Marvin. *The Society of Mind*, New York: Simon & Shuster, 1986.

Mormon Transhumanist Association, http://transfigurism.org/.

"Nikolai Fyodorovich Fyodorov." Wikipedia, the Free Encyclopedia, https://en.wiki pedia.org/wiki/Nikolai_Fyodorovich_Fyodorov.

Russian Philosophy, eds. M. Edie, James P. Scanlan, Mary-Barbara Zeldin, Vol. III, Knoxville, TE: The University of Tennessee Press, 1969.

Simonite, Tom, "Moore's Law is Dead. Now What?" *MIT Technology Review*, May 13, 2016, https://www.technologyreview.com/s/601441/moores-law-is-dead-now-what/.

The Transhumanist Reader: Classical and Contemporary Essays on the Science, Technology, and Philosophy of the Human Future, eds. Max Moore and Natasha Vita-More, Wiley-Blackwell, 2013.

"Transhumanist Declaration," Wikipedia, the Free Encyclopedia, https://hpluspedia. org/wiki/Transhumanist_Declaration.

Tipler, Frank J. *The Physics of Immortality: Modern Cosmology, God and the Resurrection of the Dead*, New York: Anchor Books, Doubleday, 1994.

Ultimate Questions: An Anthology of Modern Russian Religious Thought, ed. with an Introduction by Alexander Schmemann, Crestwood, N.Y.: St. Vladimir's Seminary Press, 1977.

The Penn Center Guide to Bioethics, eds. Vardit Ravitsky, Autumn Fiester, and Arthur L. Caplan, New York: Springer, 2009.

"What is Transhumanism?" http://whatistrans humanism.org/.

CHRONOLOGIES

Articles and Books on Globalization and the Bahá'í Faith

1945

George O. Latimer, "The Lesser and the Most Great Peace." A discussion of the evolution of world peace from political to spiritual civilization. Wilmette, IL: Bahá'í Publishing Committee, 1945. 2nd edition.

1986

H. B. Danesh, *Unity: The Creative Foundation of Peace*, Bahá'í Studies Publication, Ottawa, Canada, 1986.

John T. Dale, "The Semantics of World Government," in *Dialogue magazine*, 1:3 (1986). The concept of "world federation" is tied into a variety of semantic presumptions. The term "self-government" is less authoritarian and individualistic than the term "world government." Includes response by Leonard Godwin.

1987

John Huddleston "Just System of Government: The Third Dimension to World Peace," in *The Bahá'í Faith and Marxism* (1987). Highlights a few points in the Bahá'í approach to government and collective action.

1991

George Starcher, "Toward a New Paradigm of Management," (1991). The fundamental changes taking place in management and organization in reaction to globalization and changing technology, and the new knowledge and information-based economy.

1994

Udo Schaefer, "Ethics for a Global Society," in *Bahá'í Studies Review*, 4:1 (1994). Addresses the collapse of moral order and value systems in the contemporary world, advocating in response a global ethic based on the Kitáb-i-Aqdas.

Gregory Paul P. Meyjes, "Language and Universalization: A 'Linguistic Ecology' Reading of Bahá'í Writings," in *Journal of Bahá'í Studies*, 9:1 (1994). How the promotion of linguistic minority rights may coincide with promotion of an International Auxiliary Language, opposing trends toward increased globalization and growing nationalism, and the unregulated global spread of English.

Arthur Lyon Dahl, "Social Crises and Their Connections to Global Ecological Problems," (1994). Global warming and the social roots of environmental problems.

Michael Karlberg, "Toward a New Environmental Stewardship," in *World Order*, 25:4 (1994).

1996

Keith Suter, "Economic Justice and the Creation of a New International Economic Order," in *75 Years of the Bahá'í Faith in Australasia* (1996). The "New Right," history of economic philosophy and the role of the Church in Europe, challenges of the global economy, the failure of the UN to deal with the problems of the globalized economy, and how NGOs and individuals can work for economic justice.

Fazel Naghdy, "The Future of Mankind and the Most Holy Book," in *The Kitáb-i-Aqdas: Studies from the First National Conference on the Holy Book*, vol. 1 (1996).

Noojan Kazemi, "Global Prosperity for Humankind: The Bahá'í Model," in *75 Years of the Bahá'í Faith in Australasia* (1996).

Graham Nicholson, "Towards the New World Order: A Bahá'í perspective," in *Bahá'í Studies in Australasia* vol. 3 (1996).

1997

Mary Fish, "Economic Prosperity: A Global Imperative," in *Journal of Bahá'í Studies*, 7:3 (1997). Economic growth does not necessarily enhance human welfare. The Prosperity of Humankind recognizes the role of economics in igniting the capacity of humankind. The Bahá'í concept of human nature opens a dialogue between religion and economists.

Arthur Lyon Dahl, "Sustainable Development and the Environment of the World: An Overview," (1997).

1998

Arthur Lyon Dahl, "Globalization and the Environment," (1998). Some responses to possible problems associated with globalization.

Michael Harris Bond, "Unity in Diversity: Orientations and Strategies for Building a Harmonious Multicultural Society," (1998). Insights from the discipline of psychology can be used to design societies compatible with the exigencies and opportunities provided by the twenty-first century.

1999

Graham Hassall, "Contemporary Governance and Conflict Resolution: A Bahá'í Reading," (1999).

Juan R. I. Cole. "The Universal Declaration of Human Rights and the Bahá'í Scriptures." *Occasional Papers in Shaykhi, Babi and Bahá'í Studies*, vol. 3, no. 2 (April 1999).

2000

Holly Hanson, "Global Dilemmas, Local Responses: Creating Patterns of Action that Make the World Different," (2000). Globalization through the metaphor of the world as a body: as a diseased body, as a beautiful but dead body, and of political and social institutions as a growing body.

2001

Human Rights, Faith, and Culture, Association for Bahá'í Studies Australia, (2001). The Association for Baha'i Studies Australia hosted a 50th anniversary conference on the theme of "Human Rights, Faith and Culture". It is a theme particularly pertinent to our period of history in which the inter-relationship between belief, culture and human rights is at issue in both positive and negative ways. The papers presented at the conference provide much food for thought on these questions.

Bahá'í-Inspired Perspectives on Human Rights, edited by Tahirih Tahririha-Danesh. Hong Kong: Juxta Publishing Co., 2001, http://bahai-library.com/tahririha-danesh_perspectives_human_rights.

Dan Wheatley, "International Criminal Court: A Bahá'í Perspective," in *Associate*, 33–34 (2001). Brief history of the ICC, and Bahá'í support of it.

Holly Hanson, "Living Purposefully in a Time of Violence, (2001). Contemplation of Bahá'í responses to the global issues raised by 9/11.

Ali K. Merchant, "Religious Challenges in the Twenty-First Century and the Bahá'í Faith," in *Global Religious Vision*, 1:4 (2001). Why has religion become suspect in present-day society? Do religious traditions help or hinder community? How does the Golden Rule, which exists in all religions, help build global unity?

Eamonn Moane, "Perspectives on the Global Economy at the Dawn of the 21st Century: An Irish Bahá'í View," in *Solas*, 1 (2001). The state and issues of the global economy, including Ireland, at the start of the twenty-first century. Though not intended to be a general Bahá'í critique of the world economy, the paper concludes with a Bahá'í contribution to the issues raised.

Peter Beyer, "New Religious System for Contemporary Society," in *Global Religious Vision*, 1:4 (2001). On scholarship and categories of religions in the global society, religion as a function system, and unity in differences. Contains only one passing mention of the Bahá'í Faith.

Arthur Lyon Dahl, "Sustainable Development and Prosperity," (2001).

2002

Richard Landau, "The Bahá'í Faith and the Environment," in *Encyclopedia of Global Environmental Change volume 5: Social and Economic Dimensions of Global Environmental Change,* ed. Peter Timmerman (2002). Participation of the Bahá'í International Community in UN-sponsored development and environmental initiatives for resolving the difficult challenges before humanity.

2003

Sen McGlinn, "Difficult Case, A: Beyer's Categories and the Bahá'í Faith," in *Social Compass,* 50 (2003). Beyer considers that a religious movement which seeks to have religious norms enshrined in legislation has adopted the 'conservative option' in response to globalization. Is this a useful categorization for a global stage?

2004

Christopher Buck, "Eschatology of Globalization, The: The Multiple Messiahship of Bahá'u'lláh Revisited," in *Numen Book Series: Studies in Modern Religions, Religious Movements and the Babi- Bahá'í Faiths,* ed. Moshe Sharon (2004). This paper argues that Bahá'u'lláh's signal contribution to globalization was to ethicize and sacralize it.

2005

Bahá'í and Globalization (2005). Articles from a conference held at the University of Copenhagen in 2001.

Zaid Lundberg, "Global Claims, Global Aims: An Analysis of Shoghi Effendi's *The World Order of Bahá'u'lláh*," in *Bahá'í and Globalisation* (2005). What is Shoghi Effendi's discourse on 'globalization' and 'globality', and what are the global claims and aims in *World Order*?

Todd Lawson, "Globalization and the Hidden Words," in *Bahá'í and Globalisation,* ed. Margit Warburg (2005). A philological analysis of Bahá'u'lláh's *Hidden Words*, elucidating the development of the global orientation of the Babi- Bahá'í religion in the cosmopolitan atmosphere of Baghdad.

John Thelen Steere, "Ecological Stewardship as Applied Spirituality: A Bahá'í Perspective," in *Journal of Bahá'í Studies,* 15:1–4 (2005). The significance and dimensions of environmental stewardship — the name given to the emerging practice of habitation restoration, land conservation, resource management, and parks and recreation — and its relationship to the Bahá'í teachings.

Sohrab Abizadeh, "Will Globalization Lead to a World Commonwealth?" in *Journal of Bahá'í Studies,* 15:1–4 (2005).

Stephen Lambden, "The Messianic Roots of Babi-Bahá'í Globalism," in *Bahá'í and Globalisation* (2005). Contrast of the continuity between the globalism of the Bab's Qayyum *al-asma'* and Bahá'u'lláh's globalism, verses breaks between the two, e.g. the abandoning of jihad as a means of promoting a globalization process.

2006

Michael Karlberg and Cheshmak Farhoumand-Sims, "Global Citizenship and Humanities Scholarship: Toward a Twenty-First Century Agenda," in *International Journal of the Humanities,* 2:3 (2006). In this age of global interdependence, the critique of anachronistic social constructs is necessary but insufficient. Scholars must articulate new approaches to globalization. The international Bahá'í community illustrates a constructive, humane approach.

Nalinie Mooten, "The Bahá'í Approach to Cosmopolitan Ideas in International Relations," (2006). A Bahá'í approach to the cosmopolitan tradition in International Relations theory, and what contributions the Bahá'í model can offer to this growing tradition.

Vargha Taefi, "Just War from the Bahá'í Perspective," (2006). A Bahá'í view is that the individual's will is subordinate to society's will. Comparison of this attitude with contemporary international political theory, and on justifying war as "humanitarian intervention."

2007

Michael Karlberg, "Western Liberal Democracy as a New World Order?" in *Bahá'í World*, 2005–2006 (2007).

2008

Michael Karlberg, "Discourse, Identity, and Global Citizenship," in *Peace Review: A Journal of Social Justice*, 20:3 (2008). What does it mean to be a "global citizen"? From early Greek times, the concept of citizenship expanded from "inhabitant of a city" to a democratic ideal of self-determination. It now includes global relationships, interdependence, and altruism.

Alain Locke, "Four Talks Redefining Democracy, Education, and World Citizenship," in *World Order*, 38:3 (2008). The Preservation of the Democratic Ideal; Stretching Our Social Mind; On Becoming World Citizens; Creative Democracy. Includes introduction by Buck and Fisher.

James B. Thomas, "World Peace in a Piecemeal World: An exposition on excerpts from the writings of 'Abdu'l-Bahá," (2008). World peace is a challenge facing humankind that must be clearly identified; remedies are put forth for possible solutions in vanquishing the barriers to peace; both secular and religious underpinnings are proposed to support a universal solution for peace.

Chris Jones Kavelin, "Individual Bahá'í Perspective on Spiritual Aspects of Cultural Diversity and Sustainable Development: Towards a Second Enlightenment," in *The International Journal of Diversity in Organizations, Communities, and Nations*, 8:1 (2008). This paper discusses the spiritual value of cultural diversity and explores how such reflection impacts development policy on the local, national, and international levels.

William S. Hatcher, "Achieving Planetary Consciousness: Reality, Reason, and Revelation," (2008).

2010

Michael Karlberg, "Education for Interdependence: The University and the Global Citizen," in *Global Studies Journal*, 3:1 (2010). This paper advocates the value of an outcomes-based approach to global citizenship education and suggests a framework of core learning outcomes that can guide and inform the development of global citizenship curricula in universities.

Rod Duncan, "Reflections on Climate Change: A Bahá'í Response," in *Interreligious Insight*, 8:1 (2010).

Wolfgang A. Klebel, "The Path of God," in *Lights of Irfan*, Volume 11 (2010).

2011

Julio Savi, "The Duty of Kindness and Sympathy Towards Strangers," in *Lights of Irfan*, 12 (2011). Integrating immigrants into the culture of their new country is becoming a focus in some Western states. In 2007 the Italian government issued a "Charter on the Values and Significance of Citizenship and Integration," which reflects such Bahá'í ideals.

2012

Augusto Lopez-Carlos, "Challenges of Sustainable Development," in *Journal of Bahá'í Studies*, 22 (2012). Economic growth contributes to global prosperity, but it may conflict with environmental constraints. The interactions among conservation, technology, international cooperation, and human values can prevent future crises and assist collective evolution.

Ali Nakhjavani, "Supreme Tribunal (*Mahkamiy-i-Kubra*)," in *Lights of Irfan*, 13 (2012). Meaning of " Bahá'í Court" in the writings of the Guardian and how it compares with the General Assembly of the United Nations.

Hoda Mahmoudi, "Human Knowledge and the Advancement of Society," in *Journal of Bahá'í Studies*, 22 (2012). Knowledge is the means toward realizing a global civilization. The current Five-Year Plan focuses the Bahá'í community's consultation, reflection, and global growth, and the individual's applying spiritual and secular knowledge to help this process.

Michael Karlberg, "Reframing Public Discourse for Peace and Justice," in *Forming a Culture of Peace: Reframing Narratives of Intergroup Relations, Equity, and Justice*, ed. Karina Korostelina (2012).

2013

Sovaida Ma'ani Ewing, "Collective Security: An Indispensable Requisite for a Lasting Peace," in *Lights of Irfan*, 14 (2013). The global community must come to collaborative agreements regarding policing, the military, nuclear weapons, and an international court. The Bahá'í Faith can offer much guidance for this process.

Brian D. Lepard, "A Bahá'í Perspective on International Human Rights Law," (2013). Overview of the evolution of modern "secular" systems of international human rights law and their limitations, principles in the Bahá'í Writings relevant to such laws, and implications of these principles for reform of the contemporary legal order.

2016

Rama Ayman, "Addressing the Rising Tide of Globalization and Amorality in the Present World Order and Its Implications on Extremes of Wealth and Poverty," in *Lights of Irfan*, 17 (2016). On inequality within most nations in the world at a time when wealth disparity between nations has been falling; the impact that amorality and globalization have on wealth inequality; Bahá'í teachings on alleviating extremes of wealth and poverty.

Nader Saiedi, "From Oppression to Empowerment," in *Journal of Bahá'í Studies*, 26:1–2 (2016). On four contemporary types of oppression: in the international political order, forms of the state, economic structures, and forms of cultural identity; Bahá'u'lláh's personal response to oppression; and a Bahá'í approach to empowerment and liberation.

Nazil Ghanea, "Striving for Human Rights in an Age of Religious Extremism," in *Journal of Bahá'í Studies*, 26:1–2 (2016). Bahá'í perspectives on global human rights law, community duties, religion as a pillar of justice, and the oneness of humanity.

2018

Hooshmand Badee, "Some Reflections on the Principle of Unity/Oneness," in *Lights of Irfan*, 19 (2018). Reflections on the message of Bahá'u'lláh creating the oneness of humanity and a global society that is based on unity and love rather than factors such as economic and political gains.

2022

Berger, Julia, *Rethinking Religion and Politics in a Plural World: The Bahá'í International Community and the United Nations*, Bloomsbury Academic (2022).

Sourse: Bahá'í Library Online, https://bahai-library.com/.

Articles and Books on Science and the Bahá'í Faith

1935

John B. Cornell, "Scientific Approach to Moral Conduct," in *World Order*, 12:8 (1946). Comparison of Bahá'í teachings on sexual behavior with those presented by a then-current textbook, *Personality, and the Family* (1935).

1943

Race and Man: A Compilation, by Maye Harvey Gift and Alice Simmons Cox (1943). A collection of words of scientists, sociologists, and educators, arranged to present the problem of race relations in this modern world and the solutions as great thinkers envision them, followed by Bahá'í teachings on the same topics.

1953

Glenn A. Shook, *Mysticism, Science, and Revelation* (1953). The essence of true religion is that feeling which unites man with God. Some mystics believe that man may become one with the Absolute, but this is not scientific. Differences between mystical experience and prophetic religion.

1970

Ali-Akbar Furutan, "Science and Religion," (1970). On the causes underlying the notion of a conflict between science and religion. Prophets have always stressed the need for attaining more knowledge and wisdom, so a divinely-revealed Faith bereft of superstition cannot be opposed to knowledge and reason.

1976

William S. Hatcher, "Science and the Bahá'í Faith," in *Bahá'í Studies*, 1 (1976). Seeing religion and science as in opposition derives from a conception of science as being too restrictive to apply to religion, and of religion as too subjective to be scientific.

1980

William S. Hatcher, "The Science of Religion," in *Bahá'í Studies*, 2 (1980). Contains three essays: "Science and Religion," "The Unity of Religion and Science," and "Science and the Bahá'í Faith."

1988

Brian Aull, "The Faith of Science and the Method of Religion," in *Journal of Bahá'í Studies*, 1:2 (1988).

1990

William S. Hatcher, *Logic and Logos: Essays on Science, Religion, and Philosophy* (George Ronald, 1990).

Keven Brown, "A Bahá'í Perspective on the Origin of Matter," in *Journal of Bahá'í Studies*, 2:3 (1990). The origin of matter is spiritual. Science sees that, at its most fundamental level, reality is not particular materials or structures, but probabilities and transformation. The four elements, three-fold structure of being, and balance are also examined.

Paul Hanley, "Agriculture: A Fundamental Principle," in *Journal of Bahá'í Studies*, 3:1 (1990).

Gregory C. Dahl, "Evolving toward a Bahá'í Economic System," in *Journal of Bahá'í Studies*, 4:3 (1991). Ideals are fruitless if not implemented. There needs to be a balance and an interplay between goals and actions. A "Bahá'í economic system" suggests a number of topics for further research.

Craig Loehle, "On Human Origins: A Bahá'í Perspective," in *Journal of Bahá'í Studies*, 2:4 (1990).

1993

Gary L. Matthews, *Challenge of Bahá'u'lláh, The: Proofs of the Bahá'í Revelation* (1993).

Alan Bryson, *Light after Death: The Bahá'í Faith and the Near-Death Experience,* (1993).

William S. Hatcher, "A Scientific Proof of the Existence of God," in *Journal of Bahá'í Studies*, 5:4 (1993).

1994

Arthur Lyon Dahl, "Ecological Models of Social Organization: A Bahá'í Perspective," (1994). Natural vs. human social ecosystems and the interplay of natural vs. social systems in the twenty-first century.

1995

Arthur Lyon Dahl, "The Bahá'í Approach: Moderation in Civilization," (1995). Bahá'í approach to nature and ecology.

Rick Schaut, "Toward a Bahá'í Economic Model," (1995). Summary of three positive statements which might form the basis for a Bahá'í economic model.

Robert A. White, "Spiritual Foundations for an Ecologically Sustainable Society," in *Journal of Bahá'í Studies*, 7:2 (1995).

1996

Anjam Khursheed, "The Spiritual Foundations of Science," in *Singapore Bahá'í Studies Review*, vol. 1 (1996). In contrast to modern western accounts of science, which reduce it to methods of logic and experiment, the Bahá'í reference point is the spiritual nature of man. The experience of some outstanding scientists of the past supports the Bahá'í view.

Jalil Mahmoudi, "The Institutionalization of Religion: A Sociological Analysis of Religion and Conflict," in *World Order* (1967). The life cycle of a religion can be classified into different phases or stages, such as "cult, sect, denomination, church." Does the Bahá'í Faith fit this schema?

1997

Mary Fish, "Economic Prosperity: A Global Imperative," in *Journal of Bahá'í Studies*, 7:3 (1997). Economic growth does not necessarily enhance human welfare. The Bahá'í concept of human nature opens a dialogue between religion and economists.

Keven Brown, "Are 'Abdu'l-Bahá's views on evolution original?" in *Bahá'í Studies Review*, 7 (1997).

Jack Coleman, "Common Grounds between Buddhism, Quantum Physics, and the Bahá'í Faith," (1997). Some parallels and similarities between the Bahá'í Faith, Buddhism, and physics.

Arthur Lyon Dahl, "Environmental Protection from a Bahá'í Perspective," in *Naturopa*, 83 (1997). The place of the natural world in the Bahá'í teachings.

Eberhard von Kitzing, "Is the Bahá'í view of evolution compatible with modern science?" in *Bahá'í Studies Review*, 7 (1997).

2000

Hossain Danesh, *Psychology of Spirituality, The: From Divided Self to Integrated Self*, (2000). Explores what is the nature of human reality, the purpose of human life, transcendence, and whether we have free will, using case histories, in-depth analysis, and practical examples.

Ron House, "Unhealthy Science, Religion, and Humanities: The Deep Connection and What Bahá'u'lláh Had to Say About It," (2000). How the "calamity" mentioned by Bahá'u'lláh manifests in errors in the scientific method; fundamentalism and unbelief; the philosophy of Descartes, Hume, and Kuhn; and the Big Bang.

Behrooz Sabet, "Integrative Approach to Knowledge and Action: A Bahá'í Perspective," in *Converging Realities*, 1:1 (2000). A conceptual base for the development of an integrative approach to the study of the Bahá'í Faith, based largely on the harmony of science and religion.

William G. Huitt, "The Spiritual Nature of a Human Being," in *Educational Psychology Interactive* (2000).

2001

Evolution and Bahá'í Belief: 'Abdu'l-Bahá's Response to Nineteenth-Century Darwinism, in *Studies in the Bábí and Bahá'í Religions*, Volume 12 (2001). Includes Eberhard von Kitzing's "Origin of Complex Order in Biology: 'Abdu'l-Bahá's concept of the originality of species compared to concepts in modern biology."

Keven Brown, "'Abdu'l-Bahá's Response to Darwinism: Its Historical and Philosophical Context," in *Evolution and Bahá'í Belief, Studies in the Bábí and Bahá'í Religions*, vol. 12 (2001). Editor's foreword to the collection of articles *Evolution and Bahá'í Belief.*

Farhad Rassekh, "The Bahá'í Faith and the Market Economy," in *Journal of Bahá'í Studies*, 11:3–4 (2001).

Fariborz Alan Davoodi, "Human Evolution: Directed?" (2001). Overview of contemporary biological theories of evolution and some of their failings in the face of a philosophy of evolution guided by God; includes details on photosynthesis, glycolysis, and geological time.

Keven Brown, "The Origin of the Bahá'í Principle of the Harmony between Science and Religion," (2001). On the origin of the principle of scientific/religious harmony in Islamic and Bahá'í Writings, and discussion of a letter by 'Abdu'l-Bahá on the topic.

Ali K. Merchant, "Religion and Science in the New Millennium: A Bahá'í Perspective," in *Global Religious Vision*, 1:3 (2001). An attempt to understand the essential functions of science and religion in human society, building on the work of Stanwood Cobb, William Hatcher and Anjam Khursheed, who have done pioneering research on the unity of religion and science.

2002

Vahid Brown, "The Beginning that hath no beginning: Bahá'í Cosmogony," in *Lights of Irfan*, Book 3 (2002).

Bryan Graham, "Bahá'í Faith and economics: a review and synthesis," in *Reason and Revelation: Studies in the Babi and Bahá'í Religions*, volume 13 (2002). Review of the secondary literature on the subject and some issues of methodology.

Robin Mihrshahi, "Ether, Quantum Physics and the Bahá'í Writings," in *Australian Bahá'í Studies*, vol. 4 (2002). Analysis of

'Abdu'l-Bahá's use of the term "ether", correlated to His definition of this term as a medium not only for the propagation of electromagnetic radiation, but also for the communication of spiritual impulses to the physical world.

Justin Scoggin, "Forging the Divine Economy," (2002). Advancing the establishment of Bahá'u'lláh's divine economy through the operation of community currency.

Robert Sarracino, "The Seven Valleys and the Scientific Method," in *Lights of Irfan*, Book 3 (2002).

Keven Brown, "A Reflection on the Theory of Alchemy as Explained in the Bahá'í Writings," (2002).

2003

Courosh Mehanian and Stephen R. Friberg, "Religion and Evolution Reconciled: 'Abdu'l-Bahá's Comments on Evolution," in *Journal of Bahá'í Studies*, 13:1–4 (2003).

2004

Evolution and Bahá'í Belief, by Keven Brown and Eberhard von Kitzing: Review and Commentary, by Eamonn Moane, in *Solas*, 4 (2004). Lengthy overview of the Bahá'í response to Darwinism and the concepts of parallel evolution and species change.

Bahman Nadimi, "Do the Bahá'í Writings on evolution allow for mutation of species within kingdoms but not across kingdoms?" This paper explores the possibility that Baha'i writings on evolution allows for mutation of species within each of the kingdoms (such as vegetable or animal) but not across these kingdoms.

Gearóid Carey, "Towards a Complete and Fully Integrated Model of the Human Species," in *Solas*, 4 (2004). An adequate model of human evolution must integrate current scientific information as well as metaphysical insights from divine revelation. The human species model before and after the Neolithic revolution must include both.

2005

Giuseppe Robiati, *Economy for a New World Order*, (2005). A new vision of economics inspired by unity in diversity, respect of nature and other humans, and thermodynamic principles like conversion-of-energy to describe economical processes. Includes foreword by Ervin Lazlo.

John Fitzgerald Medina, *Faith, Physics, and Psychology: Rethinking Society and the Human Spirit*, (Bahá'í Publishing, 2006).

John S. Hatcher, *The Purpose of Physical Reality*, (Bahá'í Publishing, 2005).

2007

Necati Alkan, "Dreams and their Interpretation in the Bahá'í Religion: Some Preliminary Remarks," in *Online Journal of Bahá'í Studies*, 1 (2007). Outline of the importance of dreams and their interpretation in the Bahá'í Religion; dream interpretation in Islam; statements on dreams by Bahá'u'lláh and 'Abdu'l-Bahá; a dream interpretation by 'Abdu'l-Bahá in Ottoman Turkish.

Jack McLean, "Erich Fromm and the Bahá'í Faith," (2007). Brief examination of psychologist Fromm's exposure to and influence by Bahá'í teachings.

2008

Wolfgang A. Klebel, "Emergence, Enchantment, Entanglement and Excellence of the Cosmos," in *Lights of Irfan*, Volume 9 (2008).

2009

Rafie Mavaddat, *Evolutionary Pathways in an Unfolding Universe*, (2009). History of events that have transformed primordial matter into present-day complex systems and the emergence of life, consciousness, and societies. Includes many passing mentions of the Faith, esp. pages 155–156.

Jena Khadem Khodadad, "The Bahá'í Worldview on Unity of Religions: Progressive Revelation: Principles and Insights from the History of Science," in *Lights of Irfan*, Volume 10 (2009).

Ramin Neshati, "Man Is Man: 'Abdu'l-Bahá on Human Evolution," in Lights of Irfan, Volume 10 (2009).

Wolfgang A. Klebel, "In the H*eart of All Tha*t Is: 'Heart' in Bahá'í Writings and Science," in *Lights of Irfan*, Volume 10 (2009).

2010

Michael Karlberg, "A Post-Competitive Human Image," in *Beyond One* (2010). Science is now challenging old simplistic models of human nature. Attitudes, behaviors, and institutional structures must shift to translate holistic self-understanding into new, interdependent social modes in family, education, and government.

2011

Eliane Lacroix-Hopson, Creation, Evolution and Eternity: A Bahá'í Perspective on *Religion and Science*, (YACHAY WASI, 2001).

2014

Bernardo Bortolin Kerr, "The Death of Death: A Study of Self-Annihilation and Suicide in the Light of Sufi Thought and Bahá'u'lláh's Early Texts, (2014). On theories of suicide in the field of conventional psychology and the writings of Bahá'u'lláh.

2015

Wolfgang A. Klebel, "Freud's Transference and the Four States of Bahá'u'lláh," in *Lights of Irfa*n, 16 (2015). On the tetrarchic structure of Bahá'u'lláh's "Firstness and lastness, outwardness and inwardness" and Freud's concept of transferences, which are impulses from the past that the patient experiences as present and mistakenly relates back to the therapist.

Michael L. Penn, "Human Nature and Mental Health: A Bahá'í-Inspired Perspective," in *Journal of Bahá'í Studies*, 25:1-2 (2015). Overview of one research-practitioner's understanding of the nature of mind from the perspective of the Bahá'í teachings, and implications of this view for understanding mental health and mental illness.

2016

Rhett Diessner, "The Beauty of the Human Psyche: The Patterns of the Virtues," in *Journal of Bahá'í Studies*, 26:4 (2016). Insights from science and the Bahá'í Writings combine to show how the human soul is a shining of divine attributes reflected into our mind, where they manifest as virtuous thoughts and spiritual emotions.

Paul Lample, "In Pursuit of Harmony between Science and Religion," in *Journal of Bahá'í Studies*, 26:4 (2016). The capacity to unite in the investigation of truth for the advancement of civilization requires the harmony of science and religion, in which science is freed from materialism and religion from superstition.

Wolfgang A. Klebel, "The Language of the Heart: From Dream Language towards Understanding the Language of the Heart," in *Lights of Irfan*, 17 (2016). On the form and style of the language of the heart; ways this language differs from our normal language and thinking as it is developed in the human brain; the language and logic of dreams; effects of heart transplants.

Vahid Houston Ranjbar:
"Plato, Modern Physics and Bahá'u'lláh," https://medium.com/hackernoon/plato-modern-physics-and-bahau-llah-ee3f8740fddc.

"The Known and Unknown: Physics and the Revelation of Bahá'u'lláh," https://vahidhoustonranjbar.medium.com/the-known-and-unknown-physics-and-the-revelation-of-bahau-llah-35ad4e026a78.

"Does the singularity of God require singularity of religion?" https://vahidhoustonranjbar.medium.com/does-the-singularity-of-god-require-singularity-of-religion-29ca96535851.

"One Physicist's First Look at 'Abdu'l-Bahá's Tablet of the Universe," https://vahidhoustonranjbar.medium.com/one-physicists-first-look-at-abdu-l-baha-s-tablet-of-the-universe-db541a951348#.hrwqiaxx2.

2017

Matthew Hughey, "Race and Racism: Perspectives from Bahá'í Theology and Critical Sociology," in *Journal of Bahá'í Studies,* 27:3 (2017). Review of the concepts of race and racism based on social scientific understanding, in order to better understand their definition and to delineate their relation to one another and correlate them with the Bahá'í Writings.

Hooshmand Badee, "An Inquiry on the Role of Religion in Wealth and Poverty," in *Lights of Irfan,* 18 (2017). There are areas where religion has contributed to the debate on wealth creation and poverty eradication. Partnership of two disciplines — religion as a spiritual realm and economics as a social science — fosters human well-being.

2019

Todd Smith, "Science and Religion in Dynamic Interplay," *Journal of Bahá'í Studies,* 29:4 (2019), https://bahai-studies.ca/wp-content/uploads/2020/03/29.4-Smith.pdf.

2020

Augusto Lopez-Claros, Arthur Dahl and Maja Groff, *Global Governance and the Emergence of Global Institutions for the 21st Century* (Cambridge: Cambridge University Press, 2020).

2021

Klebel, Wolfgang A, *The Human Heart One and Undivided,* George Ronald, Oxford (2021).

Mustakova, Elena, *Global Unitive Healing: Integral Skills for Personal and Collective Transformation,* Light on Light Press, Fort Lauderdale, FL (2021).

Sourse: Bahá'í Library Online, https://bahai-library.com/.

About the Authors

HOOSHMAND BADEE is an academic economist, writer, and researcher with more than thirty year of teaching experience at several colleges and universities. He is an advocate of ethical and spiritual economics. His Doctorate research title was "Bahá'í writings on economics and their implications for the Bahá'í community and wider society." His two recent books are *Economics and the Bahá'í Faith*; and *Principles of Spiritual Economics — A Compilation of the Bahá'í Writings*. Hooshmand has delivered talks and presented numerous papers on economics and related subjects at various international academic conferences. He is currently a faculty member at the Wilmette Institute and the Bahá'í Institute for Higher Education (BIHE) in Iran. He is the founder of 'Inspired', an enterprise training program for refugees coming to Scotland voluntarily.

Inspired by the message of the Universal House of Justice in 1983, he got involved in Bahá'í social and economic development projects in Bangladesh and later in St. Vincent and the Grenadines. He was instrumental in establishing tutorial schools by putting the grass root population at the center of economic activities.

Hooshmand is a Canadian citizen born in Iran. He married and left Iran in 1975. He and his family have lived in both developed and developing countries, in Bangladesh, Canada and the Island of St. Vincent and the Grenadines before moving to the United Kingdom in 2001 in a professional capacity and to serve. Currently, he lives in Glasgow, Scotland.

ANDRES ELVIRA ESPINOZA is a freelance writer, independent scholar, and second-generation Bahá'í who was born and raised in California. He received his undergraduate degree in philosophy — with a minor in anthropology — at Cal

Poly Pomona, and a Master's degree in bioethics at Loyola Marymount University. His first publication was "The Excellence of h+: Virtue, Utility, and Human Enhancement" in *The Rutgers Journal of Bioethics*. He currently writes and researches freelance, has served as a volunteer Teaching Assistant for two courses at the Wilmette Institute, and intends to return to graduate school to receive further degrees in the next few years. His interests span the sciences and humanities, including the philosophy of science, biomimetics, and literature of all genres.

SOVAIDA MA'ANI EWING is a prolific author, speaker, and international lawyer with twenty years of experience in public and private legal practice. She is the founding director of The Center for Peace and Global Governance (cpgg.org), a virtual think tank and online forum that pools and proposes principled solutions to pressing global challenges. She has published five books in the area of peace and global governance including *Building a World Federation: The Key to Resolving our Global Crises*. Her latest book, available on Amazon, is *The Alchemy of Peace: 6 Essential Shifts in Mindsets and Habits to Achieve World Peace*. She also hosts a vlogcast "Re-Imagining Our World" on the CPGG YouTube channel — https://www.youtube.com/c/center forpeaceandglobalgovernancecpgg — that is dedicated to creating a vision of the world we want and infusing hope that we can make the choices necessary to attain it.

PAUL HANLEY has published six books and 1600 articles on the environment, sustainable development, agriculture, and other topics. He is editor and co-author of *Earthcare: Ecological Agriculture in Saskatchewan* (1980) and *The Spirit of Agriculture* (2005). His book *ELEVEN* (2014) received the 2015 University of Saskatchewan President's Award for Non-fiction and the 2015 ABS North America Award for Distinguished Scholarship. Paul's biography *Man of the Trees:*

About the Authors

Richard St. Barbe Baker, the First Global Conservationist, features a foreword by HRH Prince Charles and introduction by Jane Goodall. Paul is a recipient of the Food System 2050 Vision Prize from the Rockefeller Foundation for kwayēskastasowin wâhkôhtowin, a food system vision for the Canadian Prairies.

GRAHAM HASSALL, B. Ed (Art), B.A.(Hons), Ph D., has taught at universities in Australia, Switzerland, Papua New Guinea, Fiji, and New Zealand. He is a life-member of the United Nations Association of New Zealand and was a founding Board member of the New Zealand Centre for Global Studies. His research interests include government and public policy in the Pacific Islands; global studies including United Nations studies; and Bahá'í history and biography. Recent publications include *Government and Public Policy in the Pacific Islands* (2021); *New Zealand and the UN Security Council 2015–16* (2020), and *Social Policy and Processes in Aotearoa New Zealand* (2021). His monograph *The United Nations and the Pacific Islands* will shortly be published by Springer.

HARRY P. MASSOTH has worked as a musician, human relations director, and plant scientist. After obtaining a B.A. in music he worked as a professional trombonist with celebrity orchestras in Reno, Nevada. He served three years as the director for the National Conference of Christians and Jews in Northern Nevada where he became interested in teaching courses on comparative religion. He also served on the Governor's Commission on the Future of Nevada in the late 1970s. After completing a M.S. in plant sciences, he went on to work for a major seed company in Idaho developing improved varieties of peas, beans, and corn. While working as a support breeder/pathologist Harry contributed to the development of the sugar-snap pea, the brain child of the pioneer botanist Calvin Lamborn and his colleagues Ors. M. C. Parker and Paul Moser. A member of the Baha'i Faith since 1966, Harry, a father of three and grandfather of five, now lives with his wife on a small farm in Caldwell, Idaho.

VAHID RANJBAR is a research physicist working at Brookhaven National Laboratory. His field of research is spin and beam dynamics for which he has published extensively and has served as a reviewer for the American Physical Society's Physical Review Journals. He is currently leading the development of the electron injector complex for the future Electron Ion Collider. He received his Ph.D. in Physics from Indiana University and did his post-doctoral work at Fermilab working on collective effects in the Tevatron. He grew up living in Tanzania, India, Pakistan and in the US and spent three years studying physics in Novosibirsk Russia. He is an occasional contributor to bahaiteachings.com magazine writing on subjects related to science and religion.

HAROLD ROSEN is a Bahá'í and a Community Interfaith Educator living in Ladysmith, BC, Canada. He has been teaching community courses fostering interfaith understanding and cooperation for over twenty years. Earlier (1976 to 2000) he served as a Unitarian Universalist parish minister and religious educator. He has three master's degrees — in Religion, Education and Philosophy — and is the author of *Founders of Faith: The Parallel Lives of God's Messengers*. He attempts full-time dedication to a community-building process toward a unified and dynamic global civilization.

MIKHAIL SERGEEV (Ph.D. in religious studies from Temple University, 1997) is a religion, philosophy, and modern art historian. He has served as an editor of the book series Contemporary Russian Philosophy at Brill Publishers in the Netherlands (2016–2019) and as Chair of the Department of Religion, Philosophy, and Theology at the Wilmette Institute (2017–21). Sergeev teaches courses in humanities at the University of the Arts, Philadelphia, and the Graduate

Theological Union (Berkeley, California). He is also an Affiliate Professor at the United Theological Seminary of the Twin Cities in New Brighton, Minnesota. Sergeev has published more than two hundred scholarly, literary, and journalistic articles in the United States, Canada, Great Britain, the Netherlands, Poland, Czech Republic, Greece, Slovakia, Russia, Japan, Kyrgyzstan, Uzbekistan, and Azerbaijan. He is the author and contributing editor of fourteen books, including *Russian Philosophy in the Twenty-First Century: An Anthology* (Brill, 2020). Web site: http://uarts.digication.com/msergeev/.

PETER SMITH — Ph.D. in the Sociology of Religion from the University of Lancaster in England, Associate Professor. He helped establish what is now Mahidol University International College in Thailand, and later served as the first Chair of the College's Social Science Division as well as its Deputy-Director responsible for Academic Affairs. He is now retired. His publications in Bahá'í Studies include *The Babi and Bahá'í Religions* (Cambridge, 1987), *A Concise Encyclopedia of the Bahá'í Faith* (Oneworld, 1999), and *An Introduction to the Bahá'í Faith* (Cambridge, 2008).